THE GODDESS

Temple of Hera at Olympia

THE GODDESS

*Mythological Images
of the Feminine*

CHRISTINE DOWNING

CROSSROAD · NEW YORK

1987
The Crossroad Publishing Company
370 Lexington Avenue, New York, NY 10017

Library of Congress Cataloging in Publication Data

Downing, Christine, 1931–
The goddess: mythological images of the feminine.
Includes index.
1. Goddesses. 2. Mythology, Greek. I. Title.
BL785.D66   292'.211   81-7851
ISBN 0-8245-0091-1   AACR2
ISBN 0-8245-0624-3 (pbk.)

For my mother and my daughter

To us who have spoken thus concerning myths
May the gods themselves
And the spirits of those who wrote the myths
Be kind.

Saloustios

Contents

Illustrations

Acknowledgments

So many more have contributed to giving this book its present shape than I can possibly name. Without the many figures in my life who appear anonymously in these pages as among those who have made the goddesses real to me this book is unimaginable. Without the students and friends and colleagues who have blessed my beginnings, shared my enthusiasm, encouraged my continuing, and known when to disagree or to question, it would never have been brought to completion. From among the many there are, however, some I must name. Among these are some women: Karen Brown, Carol Christ, Jan Clanton, Linda Dutton, Adria Evans, Pat Finley, Joan Mallonee, Herta Rosenblatt, Toby Sitnick, Kay Turner; and also some men: Allan Anderson, David Cohen, William Doty, George Downing, Dennis Dutton, Richard Underwood, Martin Worman. My most especial thanks are owed to Peter Wayson, whose sensitive ear for language, scrupulous scholarship, at-home-ness in the world of classical mythology, and regard for me and my work transformed what could have been the tedious task of a final reworking into a joyful consummation; and to my caring, careful editor at Crossroad, George Lawler.

I am grateful also to those who have typed the manuscript at various stages: Eric Downing, Elaine Estwick, Ruth Ferm, Ramah Fitzgerald, Beda Johnson, Carol Pederson, Joan Petrina, Peter Wayson; and to Carol Marcy for preparing the index.

Earlier versions of some of the chapters have appeared in *Anima, Arché, Facing the Gods, Lady Unique, Quadrant, Southern Humanities Review*. My research was supported in part by a grant from the San Diego State University Foundation.

Christine Downing
Del Mar, California

Preface

Strange that the self's continuum should outlast
The Virgin, Aphrodite, and the Mourning Mother,
All loves and griefs, successive deities
That hold their kingdom in the human breast.

Abandoned by the gods, woman with an aging body
That half remembers the Annunciation
The passion and the travail and the grief
That were the mask of my humanity,

I marvel at the soul's indifference.
For in her theatre the play is done,
The tears are shed; the actors, the immortals
In their ceaseless manifestation, elsewhere gone,

And I who have been Virgin and Aphrodite,
The mourning Isis and the queen of corn
Wait for the last mummer, dread Persephone
To dance my dust at last into the tomb.

Kathleen Raine [1]

I have learned about myth from myth—from the discovery
of what it means to live a myth. I have learned my way of
attending to myth as I went along. Sometime along the way
I realized that what I was writing was a kind of autobiography. These chapters interweave childhood memories, dreams
from many different periods, and a complex history of identifications. Yet they are clearly written from the perspective of the

middle, not the end, of life; what appear are disordered and sometimes contradictory fragments, not a chronologically shaped, unbroken narrative.[2] I have learned that recognition of the archetypal and universal dimensions of one's experiences can help free one from a purely personal relation to them. I also believe that one can celebrate the mythic patternings without losing an appreciation of the concrete and unique moments that constitute one's existence. This is what Freud meant by transference—knowing that one is Sigmund Freud *and* Oedipus, that I am Christine Downing *and* Persephone. Either description alone is insufficient. Recognition of the many goddesses that inform one's life also helps protect one against inflationary identifications and against the sense of being swallowed up by some fatally determining mythic pattern. The goddesses also seem to find ways of reminding us that they are indeed numinous forces, never reducible to our attempts at psychological interpretation.

Through attending to them I have begun to understand what Thomas Mann means by the mythical point of view becoming subjective, by the ego's becoming conscious "proudly and darkly yet joyously, of its recurrence and typicality." I agree with him that "the myth is the legitimization of life; only through and in it does life find self-awareness, sanction and consecration." [3]

We need images and myths through which we can see who we are and what we might become. As our dreams make evident, the psyche's own language is that of image, and not idea. The psyche needs images to nurture its own growth; for images provide a knowledge that we can interiorize rather than "apply," can take to that place in ourselves where there is water and where reeds and grasses grow. Irene Claremont de Castillejo speaks of discovering the inadequacy of all *theories* about the female psyche, including the Jungian framework into which she had for so long tried to fit her own experience and that of her female patients. For now, she suggests, we need simply to attend lovingly and precisely to the images spontaneously brought forward in our dreams and fantasies.[4]

For me the quest for the goddess began with a dream:

In the dream I find myself in a state of confusion and despair. I decide to drive into the desert alone, hoping there to rediscover the still center I have lost. I drive far into the night on unfamiliar and seemingly rarely traveled byways. Then, in what feels like the middle of nowhere, a tire goes flat and I remember I have no spare. It seems unlikely that anyone would come by soon to offer help, but far in the distance I see a light which might mean someone available to assist me or at least a telephone. I set out toward it and walk and walk. It is some time before I realize the light is no closer and that I am no longer sure it is there at all. I turn around, thinking it might be better after all to wait by my car; but it has disappeared, as has the road.

At that point a figure appears from behind a sagebrush in the strangely moonlit desert night, the figure of a wizened but kindly appearing old man. "Can I help?" he asks. "No," I say. "You and I have been through this before. This time I need to go in search of Her."

So I set out across the desert, seeming now to know in what direction to proceed, though there are no marked ways and I know I had never been there before. Hours later I find myself at the foot of some steeply rising sandstone cliffs. I make my way up the cliffs, heading straight for a deep small cave just large enough for me to lie down. Still seeming to know exactly what I must do, I prepare myself to sleep there, as though to fall asleep were part of my way toward Her.

While I sleep there in the cave I dream that within the cave I find a narrow hole leading into an underground passage. I make my way through that channel deep, deep into another cave well beneath the earth's surface. I sit down on the rough uneven floor, knowing myself to be in her presence. Yet, though She is palpably there, I cannot discern her shape. Though I wait and wait, expecting to be able to see Her once my eyes grow accustomed to the darkness, that does not happen.

I returned to waking consciousness, aware that, though I did not know who *She* was, it was indeed time for me to go in search of Her.

I sensed that the pull to Her was a pull to an ancient source. "In the beginning, people prayed to the Creatress of Life, the Mistress of Heaven. At the very dawn of religion, God was a woman. Do you remember?" [5] To remember is to be remembered, to have our own lives made whole and our connections with others healed. My dream expressed the same homesickness for myself, for Her, so powerfully communicated in Adrienne Rich's "Transcendental Etude":

> *But there come times—perhaps this is one of them—*
> *when we have to take ourselves more seriously or die;*
> *when we have to pull back from the incantations,*
> *rhythms we've moved to thoughtlessly,*
> *and disenthrall ourselves, bestow*
> *ourselves to silence, or a severer listening, cleansed*
> *of oratory, formulas, choruses, laments, static*
> *crowding the wires. . . .*
>
> *But in fact we were always like this,*
> *rootless, dismembered: knowing it makes the difference.*
> *Birth stripped our birthright from us,*
> *tore us from a woman, from women, from ourselves*
> *so early on*
> *and the whole chorus throbbing at our ears*
> *like midges, told us nothing, nothing*
> *of origins, nothing we needed*
> *to know, nothing that could re-member us. . . .*
>
> *Homesick for myself, for her. . . .* [6]

I soon discovered that my search was not mine alone, that in recent years many women have rediscovered how much we need the goddess in a culture that tears us from woman, from women, and from ourselves. [7] To be fed only male images of the divine is to be badly malnourished. We are starved for images which recognize the sacredness of the feminine and the complexity, richness, and nurturing power of female energy. We hunger for images of human creativity and love inspired by the capacity of female bodies to give birth and nourish, for images of how humankind participates in the natural world suggested by reflection on the correspondences between menstrual rhythms and the moon's waking and waning. We seek images that affirm that the love women receive from women, from mother, sister, daughter, lover, friend, reaches as deep and is as trustworthy, necessary, and sustaining as is the love symbolized by father, brother, son, or husband. We long for images which name as authentically feminine courage, creativity, loyalty, and self-confidence, resilience and steadfastness, capacity for clear insight, inclination for solitude, and the intensity of passion. We need images; we also need myths—for myths make concrete and particularize; they give us situations, plots, relationships. We need the goddess and we need the goddesses.

In a book written almost fifty years ago, Esther Harding suggested that our appreciation of contemporary dream images could be deepened and enriched by relating them to the age-old representations of the feminine contained in ancient myths and rituals. Her book presents the goddesses not as objects of worship but as figures through whom we might discover the various forms of the archetypal feminine—that is, of the eternal and therefore divine aspects of the feminine. She called her book Woman's Mysteries, in part to draw the attention of modern women to the mysteriousness, the unknown-ness, of their own femininity, and also because the book is largely devoted to the esoteric mystery rites which, until the Hellenistic period, were female cults. The book initiates us into the secret of these mysteries, the knowledge that "the 'gods' are not beings external to man but rather psychological forces or principles which have been projected and personified in 'the gods'." [8]

Harding and de Castillejo initiated a process in which many others now participate whereby women seek to nourish one another by sharing images and stories discovered through their researches in "herstory" and through attention to their dreams and other numinous experience. The search for Her leads us to ourselves, to the women we know and love, the women we learn from and learn with, and to the ancient prepatriarchal traditions about the sacred power and varied shapes of feminine energy. [9]

As we seek to re-imagine ourselves, we naturally return to the beginnings, to the archaic traditions about the Great Mother, a mother whom we already know, at least in our unconscious.[10] Finding is here, most certainly, remembering. For in the beginning, in our infantile beginnings, god, the immediately present divine power, for all of us was a woman: our mother. The search for our origins inevitably returns us to her. Freud discovered this in his later years as he became increasingly aware of the importance of the pre-Oedipal phase. According to him, this period is particularly important in the lives of women for whom, more than is true of men, it is radically differentiated from the later Oedipal phase during which the girl is expected to focus her libido onto her father. Freud explicitly recognizes this "matriarchal" phase as analogous to the pre-Homeric Minoan-Mycenean period in Greek religion when mother-goddesses dominated.[11] Knowing ourselves means becoming conscious of those beginnings, reawakening our phylogenetic memory and thus recovering the key to the storehouse of racial memories.

Jung, too, encourages our reengagement with such ancient images, although unlike Freud he does not see them as a seemingly dead deposit inherited from the archaic past. Rather, he believes that there exists is us the capacity (too often ignored, disvalued, or uncultivated) for spontaneously making the same kind of symbolic associations so conspicuous in myth. Recognition that the ancient mother-goddesses and the powerful female figures who appear in our own dreams are expressions of the same mother archetype may open us to dimensions of our experience and being to which we would otherwise be closed. Exposure to the inherited traditions may bring us in touch with what Jung calls the "collective unconscious" and help us to know that there is more to us than the personal and historical. What we are hungry for, from Jung's perspective, is an immanent *She,* transcendent to the ego but discovered within— initially perhaps more easily recognized in outward projections like those of ancient cult and myth.

In response to my dream of Her in the cave, I was pulled to myths and goddesses I had not known beforehand really applied to me. Like Jung I had needed to learn which myth was living me, and learned there were many. I learned that the myths about the goddesses and my own dreams and fantasies and events in my waking life were mutually illuminating. I cannot even say which is the goal and which is the way. Therefore, in seeking to communicate what I have learned of these goddesses in a way that leads to a discovery of their pertinence to self-understanding, I have had to include the references to that personal material which has been intrinsic to my searching and finding. As Freud said was true of himself: I have been my most important patient. This seems inevitable in part because I have come to believe that each of these goddesses relates to the whole of our lives, not just to a dream, a relationship, a particular phase, and the only whole life I have any access to is necessarily my own. It has also been important to me to take into account other women's experiences of these goddesses, especially as such experiences have been given shape in contemporary poetry. I have found my own understanding significantly enriched through my participation in that sharing of images with others to which I referred earlier—and especially by the responses to my initial drafts of those who were deeply implicated in my involvement with a particular goddess. Thus my daughter's response to what I initially wrote of Persephone, my mother's and husband's to the first draft of Hera, what Ariadne evoked in my lover—all these in turn led me to revision once again.

My search for Her led me to the goddesses of ancient Greece, but the original *She* is the one we discover by returning to more archaic mother-goddess traditions. To appreciate the significance of the more highly differentiated images of feminine divinity represented by the Greek goddesses we must first understand the richness of the primitive (primary) background out of which they emerge.

NOTES

1. Kathleen Raine, *Collected Poems* (New York: Random House, 1956), p. 83.

2. See Christine Downing, "Revisioning Autobiography," *Soundings,* Summer 1977, pp. 210–28.

3. Thomas Mann, "Freud and the Future," in *Essays* (New York: Vintage Books, 1957), p. 317.

4. Irene Claremont de Castillejo, *Knowing Woman* (New York: Harper & Row, 1974), pp. 165ff.

5. Merlin Stone, *When God Was a Woman* (New York: Dial Press, 1976), p. 1.

6. Adrienne Rich, *The Dream of a Common Language* (New York: W. W. Norton, 1978), pp. 74, 75, 76.

7. See especially Carol Christ, "Why Women Need the Goddess," in *Woman Spirit Rising,* ed. Carol Christ and Judith Plaskow (New York: Harper & Row, 1979).

8. Esther Harding, *Woman's Mysteries* (New York: Bantam Books, 1973), p. 162.

9. This search for Her is not only pertinent to women nor are only women engaged in it. Nevertheless, it is important, I believe, for us to be engaged in it ourselves and for ourselves as women. We should not be drawn into doing it *for* men, to be pulled again to responding to the plea: be our souls, our mothers, our muses; comfort us, nurture us, inspire us; teach us how to feel, to relate, to listen to our intuitions. If what we learn also feeds men, fine; but that cannot be our primary purpose. I happen also to believe that images of the ancient male gods are also pertinent to the self-understanding of contemporary women, but that is not the point here. Until we have fully appropriated how the goddesses inform our being as women we cannot possibly move toward a postpatriarchal appreciation of the male gods.

10. Some of the earliest research on the ancient mother-goddess traditions was done by men: Bachofen (whose first important essay on mother-right appeared in 1859, the year of Darwin's *The Origin of Species*), Jung (the first version of whose *Symbols of Transformation* was published in 1912), Briffault (who published his prodigious *The Mothers* in 1927), Erich Neumann (whose *The Great Mother* appeared in 1955). There is, of course, much useful information in these works; nevertheless, their helpfulness to contemporary feminists interested in goddess traditions is limited by their so clearly being written from the perspective of the son's image of the mother. Thus they are most directly pertinent to an understanding of male psychology and the male's initiation into "matriarchal consciousness."

11. Sigmund Freud, "Female Sexuality," in *Sexuality and the Psychology of Love* (New York: Collier Books, 1963), p. 195.

·I·

TO START US IMAGINING
The Goddess

*Myths do not tell us how, they
simply give us the invisible
background which starts us
imagining, questioning,
going deeper.*

James Hillman [1]

It seems established that the earliest object of religious
worship was the Great Mother who from the beginning
was associated with nurturing, with the provision of food.
All her other functions and attributes seem to be dependent on this one, just as in individual history (at least according
to Freud) even sexual desire is anaclitic on infantile hunger.
What first inspires worship is that there is food; the first focus of
worship is the source of food. All else follows from that; but
there is much that follows.

In the oldest artifacts yet excavated we discover the female as
primal power. She is at the very center of what is sacred and
necessary. Although there is still disagreement among ar-
cheologists as to whether the female clay figurines of the
Paleolithic period are to be regarded as evidence of goddess
worship, the coincidence of the development of conscious agriculture in the Proto-Neolithic period (c. 9000–7000 B.C.) and
attested worship of feminine divinities is generally accepted.
Myths corroborate this. Demeter and Ceres, Ninlu and Isis, are
represented as having taught humans to grow grain. Interpretations which see them as dramatically exaggerated retellings of
historical events would read these myths to mean that human

Stone Idol from Sparta
National Archaeological Museum, Athens

women were responsible for the discovery of food cultivation.
And, indeed, this may well be so. As food gatherers in tribes
where the men went off to hunt, women may have been the first
to recognize that grain grew from seed and could be deliberately planted and harvested. Although we should not be moved
by this possible correlation between history and mythology to
interpret all myth so literally, correspondences between the
goddesses and their human counterparts tend to be more direct
than is true of the male divinities of patriarchal religions. Unlike
so many of the gods, the goddesses were never transcendent to
earth and were never conceived in the abstract terms favored by
philosophers and theologians.

The well-fed voluptuous shape of so many of the ancient
figurines (think, for instance, of the Venus of Willendorf) illustrated how for the myth-making imagination being and function
are always closely intertwined: what a goddess does she also is.
So the giver of food is herself food. The sculptural stress on the
goddess's fleshy breasts and generous hips was intended to
suggest not so much sexual attractiveness as the prodigality of
the milk-giving mother and her procreative potency. That goddesses identified with vegetal fertility should also be associated
with human fertility seems inevitable. Women were linked with
food not only because they cultivated and prepared it but also
because their own bodies were a source of food and life. They
not only tilled the earth but in their reproductive aspect were
like the earth. Ancient agricultural rituals were shaped by an
intuition of the analogies between planting and sexual intercourse, between harvesting and childbirth.

What provoked goddess veneration was recognition of
feminine energy as transformative energy. The food associated
with the feminine is food as mystery, food as a transformed
substance. Through cultivation and cooking, grass becomes
bread. Women perform this transformation and incarnate this
transformative power in their capacity to make milk out of
blood and to give birth out of their own bodies to an utterly
other creature: a male, a son. Yet these transformations are
never absolute spiritualizations; the corporeal realm is never
wholly abandoned. The various extensions of the goddess's

province always retain a connection to her essential identification with physical sustenance, with the material realm. From the goddess-worshiping perspective, the necessarily more alienated and intellectualized creative capacity of men is but a pallid imitation of women's natural procreative capacity.

We are so accustomed to equating civilization and the masculine that we may be surprised to discover how obvious it seemed at one time that the goddesses responsible for the beginnings of agriculture were also involved with the beginning of all cultural activity. Historically, we know that the development of metallurgy, pottery, weaving, and writing are closely connected to the changes in living made possible by the establishment of settled planting communities. Mythologically, this conjunction was expressed by affirming that the goddess involved with the introduction of grain cultivation also taught humankind these other skills.

It is not much of a jump to recognize the goddess also as creatrix—mother of all that is—and thus to view the universe as a woman giving birth to all forms of life. Not only does the goddess create the world; her body is the world. As not only the giver of grain but as herself the grain, the goddess naturally participates in the cyclical pattern of vegetal life: Demeter mourns for months while her daughter is in the underworld and nothing on earth grows. The goddess's cyclic disappearances and reappearances are closely connected to her association with increase and decrease, protection and desertion, vision and lunacy, creation and destruction, life and death, feast and famine. What she gives, she also takes away.

To see the goddesses only as fertility goddesses is to see them as they were viewed in a later period. Recovery of the full scope of the goddesses' power during the period in which their worship predominated reveals that, like any primordial archetype, the Great Mother provokes profound ambivalence: her cruelty is no less salient than her benevolence. The nurturing goddess is also the devouring one. In the world of the goddesses, creation-and-destruction and feast-and-famine were seen as two phases of the one ever-recurring inescapable pattern, not as irreconcilable opposites. Perhaps it is the greatest gift of the goddess to teach us that good and evil, life and death, are inextricably intertwined.

The fertility goddesses are thus always also goddesses of the underworld, the realm of death. To die is to return to the receptive, generative mother. The earth is womb; burial is in the fetal position. When the world is conceived in cyclical terms, death is the prelude to rebirth. The goddesses of the underworld are the goddesses of the realm of the soul. Underworld and unconscious are analogues. The goddess nurtures not only physical life but the life of the soul. Rebirth is not understood as the return of the same but as metamorphosis, transformed consciousness. Death and new vision are closely intertwined. The goddess is the giver of dreams and omens, of the understanding of the hidden. She is the source of vision—and of lunacy, which is altered vision. She is the poppy as well as the grain, the giver of intoxicants (and poisons) as well as of food.

The being of the goddess is related to her having a feminine body but is not delimited by that. Indeed, the earliest traditions seem to have imagined her as parthogenetic and thus androgynous. She is feminine—and masculine. She represents a unity that encompasses this duality as it encompasses kindness and cruelty, life and death. Once upon a time the goddess was thus the most potent exemplification of divine power.

That goddess religion answers to a perennial human need is suggested by how strongly it persists even in cultures where it is officially excluded. Most of us tend to forget, for instance, how much the day-to-day religion of the ancient Hebrews differed from the faith promulgated by the prophets and thus fail to recognize the importance that goddesses had in the life of Israel during the whole period from the arrival of the Hebrews in Canaan until the destruction of the first temple. The scriptures show the continued importance of the ancient Canaanite goddesses, Asherah, Astarte, and Anath, among Israelites who acknowledged their devotion to Yahweh. Indeed, the scriptures portray those goddesses as a source of temptation throughout the biblical period. A central theme in the prophetic literature is protest against the way the people continually turned from

Yahweh back to the Baals and the Asteroth. The biblical tradition itself shows that for most of the people, most of the time, worship of the goddess and worship of Yahweh were not felt to be contradictory. It is likely that for many of his worshipers, Yahweh was viewed as the victorious rival of Baal, a more recently arrived consort of the goddess. During the time of the monarchy, strict Yahwism was probably only a prophetic ideal, shared by a few kings, but not really the religion of the court or the temple, much less of the people.[2]

As we try to understand the attempt to suppress goddess worship, we discover that the focus on Yahweh as the only god is related to the desire to validate a new social order and a new psychology in mythic terms. The attempt to establish the monotheistic cult paralleled the attempt to establish a society in which father-right predominated and in which fealty to the central monarchy took precedence over tribal loyalty. Yahwism is part of the endeavor to break the importance of matrilineal bonds and to break the allegiance to the clan. Yahwism thus represents a national political cult in conflict with what are primarily local fertility cults. Yahweh is presented as a god who claims to be the only god but who is always defending himself against other gods (whom the prophets deem demons or idols). During the time when there were kings in Israel, the attempts to overcome the other gods, and particularly the attempts to eradicate worship of the goddess, were infrequent and ineffectual. It was only in the later postexilic period that the suppression became effective: when that happened, patriarchal monotheism was read backward into the earlier period.

My belief is that all of us are likely to embrace the later official view more than we realize. We tend, for instance, to accept uncritically the retrospective evaluation of the kings of Israel on the basis of one criterion, a religious one: the good kings were those who gave all their religious devotions to Yahweh. We also may too easily adopt the rabbinic reduction of goddess cults to fertility cults, ignoring the fact that the most frequent title given to the Canaanite goddess was not that of earth mother but rather of queen of heaven. The goddess was not associated only with fertility, whether agricultural or human, but was also viewed as creatress of all; she was spoken of as prophetess, as inventor, healer, and warrior.

Worship of the goddess persisted among the early Hebrews, for men as well as women, because there were essential needs for which Yahweh did not provide. The prophetic emphasis on the moral and intellectual side of religion implies a relative neglect of the emotional and ritual side. To understand the role and meaning of the goddess in ancient Israel, we should remember that the arrival of Yahweh in Canaan was that of an invader who brough havoc and destruction. Throughout the early period, Yahweh was seen as the god to invoke in times of national political crisis. In times of peace, when most of the people's energies were given to life sustenance activities, to hoping that crops would grow, that there would be children and that they would survive—in such times worship was directed to the ancient goddesses who, from time immemorial, had been associated with these aspects of human life.

The austere aniconic worship that Yahweh seemed to demand ("Thou shalt make no graven images") left frustrated the yearning for an imaged faith, for divine beings whose presence could be made visible. The goddess cults did not denigrate the desire for an experience of religious enthusiasm, for being overwhelmed by the immanent presence of the divine. The ascetic denial of any kind of individual immortality that characterizes ancient Yahwistic faith may well have been too demanding for most of the people; Yahweh was the god of the living, whereas the goddesses were connected also to death and to the affirmation of some kind of continued life for the dead. The goddesses seem also to have been responsive to the perennial longing to know the future; they were associated with prophetic dreams, with oracles, and particularly with consultation of the dead. Thus Saul, at the most desperate moment of his life, believing himself utterly deserted by Yahweh, went to the witch of Endor to consult her clairvoyant powers.

Worship of the goddesses also implied the recognition that the divine did not appear only in the realm of history. Nature itself was experienced as sacred; it had intrinsic meaning and importance, was not there simply as material for human projects. The acknowledgement of the divine in the natural world made permissible the recognition of the sacred dimension of such biologically rooted experiences as childbirth and sexual intercourse. Nor did the goddess cult explain all of the evil in the world by referring it to human sin and guilt. The stubborn reality of pain and suffering was a difficult problem in a monotheism which stressed the goodness of the divine and which then tended to lay the responsibility for all suffering and evil on human sinfulness. The goddess cults may also have spoken to a sense that there was something inadequate in a purely linear conception of time and in the correlative notion that all meaning, all fulfillment comes in the future, comes at the end of time. The goddess cults were connected with the more cyclical notion of time that characterizes mythological consciousness, with a valuing of the alternating rhythms of waxing and waning, growth and decay, waking and sleeping, activity and receptivity, extroversion and introversion.

There was a long period in Jewish history during which the goddess seemed to disappear, yet her subliminal presence remained in mystical Judaism and in the wisdom traditions, and as the Shekinah she reemerged in the Kaballah. In Christianity, though the goddess was officially suppressed, her irrepressibility is evidenced in the devotion directed to female saints and the Virgin Mother,[3] in medieval witch cults, and in the matriarchal bias of many folk tales.

The search for *Her* which has animated so many women in recent years has thus led to discovering goddesses as the most revered divinities in the earliest religious traditions of humankind and to uncovering their vital importance even in cultures from which they were officially excluded.

The same search has taken me in a somewhat different direction. My dream of the unseen She in the cave led me to return to the goddesses of Greek mythology to whom my mother had introduced me as a child but to whom I had paid little conscious attention in the intervening years. I discovered that they had nevertheless been actively present in my life all along and that attending to their presence yielded a hitherto unknown depth to my own experiences, particularly some that had earlier seemed meaningless, trivial, or unredeemably negative.

The gods and goddesses of ancient Greece were recognized presences in my childhood home. My mother was (and is) a storyteller; the stories she knew and loved best were the household tales of the German peasantry as collected by the brothers Grimm and the myths of the Greeks. My father, like Freud, was a scientist educated in a classically oriented *Gymnasium* where he learned the love of Greek literature and philosophy, which he communicated to me. My parents in no way thought of themselves as pagans or polytheists; there was nothing self-consciously reverential in their respect for the Olympian divinities. What they communicated to me was an understanding very like that expressed by Walter Otto: "This religion is so natural that holiness seems to have no place in it." [4]

I realize in retrospect that I have never doubted the reality or power of the Greek divinities. Perhaps because they were self-evident presences long before I came up against Yahweh's (or Jesus') call for exclusive devotion, I could never quite believe in the claim of this late-arriving intruder to be the only true god. I have always loved Nietzsche's account of how the old gods laughed themselves to death at this uproarious proposition:

> For the old gods, after all, things came to an end long ago; and verily, they had a good gay godlike end. They did not end in a "twilight," though this lie is told. Instead: one day they *laughed* themselves to death. That happened when the most godless word issued from one of the gods themselves—the word: "There is one god. Thou shalt have no other god before me!" An old grimbeard of a god, a jealous one, thus forgot himself. And then all the gods laughed and rocked on their chairs and cried, "Is not just this godlike that there are gods but no God?"
> He that has ears to hear, let him hear! [5]

Nietzsche knew, of course, and Freud discovered that gods and goddesses never really die, they just go underground. "Mythology, like the severed head of Orpheus, goes on singing even in death and from afar." [6] (Thus Zeus does not eliminate the Titans, although he confines them to Hades; Athene cannot do away with the Furies, although she can persuade them to redirect their power.)

That the Greek gods are self-evident realities—as alive today as in the ancient world—is beautifully expressed by Walter Otto:

> In ancient Greek worship is revealed to us one of humanity's greatest religious ideas. . . . The faculty which in other religions is constantly being thwarted and inhibited here flowers forth with the admirable assurance of genius—the faculty of seeing the world in the light of the divine, not a world yearned for, aspired to, or mystically present in rare ecstatic experiences, but the world into which we were born, part of which we are, interwoven with it through our senses and, through our minds, obligated to it for all its abundance and vitality. And the figures in which this world was divinely revealed to the Greeks—do they not demonstrate their truth by the fact they they are still alive today, that we still encounter them when we raise ourselves out of petty constraints to an enlarged vision?
>
> They saw the divine as the fundamental basis of all being and happening.[7]

Auden, too, sees that for the Greek, for the pagan, the sacred is self-evident (though he believes that for the Christian "the Incarnation puts an end to all claims of the imagination to be the faculty which decides what is truly sacred"):

> To the imagination, the sacred is self-evident. It is as meaningless to ask whether one believes or disbelieves in Aphrodite or Ares as to ask whether one believes in a character in a novel; one can only say that one finds them true or untrue to life. To believe in Aphrodite and Ares merely means that one believes that the poetic myths about them do justice to the forces of sex and aggression as human beings experience them in nature and their own lives.[8]

In Auden's sense I think I have always believed in the Greek gods and goddesses. Nevertheless, I had largely ignored their presence for years before the night of the dream in the cave and, certainly, had never before focused on the goddesses as particularly calling for my attention, nor sought to make conscious the relation between my life and these ancient deities.

Because my turning to the goddesses in my middle years was experienced as a return, it is inevitably somewhat different from that of women who discover them for the first time as adults. In a sense, I may take the goddesses for granted more than some others do. I may also respond to them less "religiously" in our everyday sense of that word. My *religio* consists not of worship at an altar but simply of trying to attend to their presence as it is evident in my dreams, as it shapes how I relate to both men and women, to parents and siblings, husband and children, lovers and friends, as it informs my sense of self and of feminine possibility. I do not mean that the goddesses are "nothing but" projections of human psychology (as Harding on occasion seems to suggest) for I believe them to represent transhuman forces (as is implied by their having animal byforms and by their original connections with aspects of the natural world). Yet the sharply delineated personal character of the Homeric goddesses does make them more directly illuminative of personal psychology than is true of the more ancient mother-goddess.

I understand that some women regard the goddesses I know and love as too contaminated by the patriarchal biases of classical Greece to be much help to those of us looking to goddesses to help us free ourselves from patriarchally inspired stereotypes of the feminine. Perhaps it helps that I knew them first as a daughter learns of them from her mother. For as presented to us by Homer, Hesiod, and the tragedians (the most highly elaborated classical representations and the sources likely to be most familiar to us), the Greek goddesses are not very attractive creatures. These texts all evidence a deep suspicion of feminine power; they all seem concerned to validate the priority of the social over the natural order and to record the establishment of a "rationally based" polity in which rulership was no longer to be determined matrilineally. One no longer became king by being a mother's favorite (and probably youngest) son or by winning a regnant king's daughter as one's bride or by killing him and marrying his wife. (Oedipus's murder of Laius and marriage to the king's widow echoes the ancient pattern.) The classical literature is explicitly patriarchal, though it is imbued with a profound sense of continued threat from the older order.

In Homer and subsequent retellings, the original ties of the goddesses to the natural world have been rationalized, reduced to metaphor or to habitat or attendant creature. "The Olympian religion countenances only the human form in deity." [9] The goddesses no longer appear as bird or animal, though the owl is still Athene's, the dove Aphrodite's, and the peacock Hera's, though the deer is still associated with Artemis and the goat with Aphrodite. Athene is no longer the Acropolis rock and Artemis no longer the Arcadian wilderness. Aphrodite is no longer the mist rising from sea to sky or the rain falling from sky to earth, although she may still envelop a favorite hero in a cloud to hide him from an enemy's fatal attack. Some once potent goddesses (Ariadne and Helen, for example) are reduced to purely human status in the classical literature. The *Odyssey* shows Artemis, the only goddess still more bound to the natural than to the interhuman world, as a clumsy child, out of her climate, when she leaves her forest haunts.

That the establishment of the Olympian order was a revolution is made plain in the *Theogony;* there Hesiod recounts Zeus's battle against all the generations of divine beings who had preceded him (including eventually even the mother who had at first encouraged him against his father). Within the hierarchy thereafter ruled by Zeus (especially in Homer's accounts), the goddesses clearly become subordinate divinities. Aphrodite, described by Hesiod as generations older than Zeus, is in the *Odyssey* the daughter of Zeus and Diane. Hera, known to be a more ancient divinity than Zeus and so represented by Hesiod as his elder sister, becomes in Homer not only a needy, dependent spouse but a younger sibling. Even Athene, whose stature is less diminished, is made into a goddess entirely dependent on male power, proud to be motherless, Zeus's parthenogenetic creation.

The goddesses are not only subordinated to the god, they are defined as being in their very essence related to men, each in a very particular way: Hera *is* wife, Athene *is* father's daughter, Aphrodite *is* the responsive beloved, Artemis *is* she who shuns men. When thus represented from the perspective of male psychology, they are both sentimentalized and denigrated.

The dominion and powers of each goddess are considerably more narrowly delimited within Homer's Olympian world than was true earlier. Aphrodite is now only the goddess of physical beauty and human sexual love; Artemis is primarily the goddess of the hunt; Athene is the protectress of cities and patron of the arts. This delimitation may reflect a male longing to be able to deal with each aspect of feminine power separately, as though to have the full range embodied in one being would be too overpowering. Not only is each given a distinct sphere of power but the worst fantasies about how patriarchy leads women to distrust and betray one another are realized in Homer's representation of the implacable hostilities among the goddesses. A rather backhanded tribute to the continued potency of the goddesses is evident in his attributing the rise of the Trojan War to the unmitigated rivalry among Athene, Hera, and Aphrodite. Athene's denial of any mother-bond provokes Jane Ellen Harrison to announce: "We cannot love a goddess who on principle forgets the earth from which she sprang." [10] But Athene is not the only one whom it is hard to love as this literature presents her to us. (Nor is she the only one separated from a contact with the earth and the realm of the dead that is spoken of as the underworld. The goddesses' chthonic aspect, their relation to death and transformation, like their relation to the natural world and to vegetal fertility, is emphatically ignored except in the case of Demeter, the goddess of the grain, and Persephone, the goddess of the underworld—and neither of them is given an active role in the Homeric epics.) I believe we should acknowledge our disappointment in these goddesses and any anger we may feel at their seeming cooption by the Zeus-ruled hierarchy. Yet it is my conviction that the disappointment and anger should lead us not to abjure these divinities but rather to learn "to recognize the untruths Homer told and why," [11] and to discover the truths he sought to suppress. For it is possible to recover much of how these goddesses were seen in the pre-Olympian world and much of how they were known and worshiped by women.

I believe we must inevitably and necessarily begin with the familiar classical presentations, the later versions of the myth, versions which Otto suggests are really already postmythological. It is only gradually, as we keep working with the myth, that we discover earlier versions, buried strata, different layers. The process is very much like that of interpreting a dream, where we start with the manifest version and discover as we keep working that it is a cover for a much more complex, unfamiliar, and strange story—one that is, therefore, more informative and potentially more transformative. We do not need to invent, though we may need to use our intuition to make connections, fill in gaps, develop possible interpretations. It is important to try to discover as much as we can about how the goddesses were imagined by the Greeks and not to confuse those discoveries with our own wish-fulfilling imaginings about what the consummate goddess would be like. For it is their dark sides, aspects of them we initially resist, that so often end up being most transformative and illuminating. We only recover the fullness of the archetype as we know both its light and dark sides: goddesses have to do not only with our joys and accomplishments but with our wounds and failures. We will need to keep imagining after we have learned all we can, but our imaginings will be richer and more nourishing the more they are rooted in what can be learned.

I believe we need to start with the familiar Homeric version of the goddesses precisely because they are *there*—not just in the texts but also in ourselves, even in those of us who were not explicitly introduced to them in early childhood. They are present in our language and in our literature; the sense of feminine possibility and delimitation they represent is active in our institutions and in our own unconscious presuppositions. Our culture's and our own attitudes toward marriage are still connected to Hera far more than we probably recognize, as our sense of intellectually competent women is still shaped by the classical descriptions of Athene. Patriarchy is active not just in the external social world but also in our unconscious—even among those of us who have tried to free ourselves from patriarchy's values and assumptions. Freud and Jung have taught us how deeply our thoughts, feelings, and modes of response are informed by mythic prototypes of which we may have no conscious cognizance. To know who we are means knowing who they are. If we ignore them, they act on us and in us in ways we fail to recognize. They act as delimiting stereotypes. It is only as we recognize their presence and seek to know them as fully as possible, to reimagine them, that their power to open up new dimensions of feminine life is released. Only then can they become life-giving archetypes.

The very differentiation we may at first experience as diminution may help us sort through the various aspects of our femaleness in a way that the undifferentiated wholeness of the archaic mother-goddess cannot do. (We miss much if we interpret this differentiation only as a patriarchal power play. In the Olympic world the male gods too were clearly distinguished from one another and assigned distinct dominions. Artemis and Aphrodite, Hera and Athene, were already recognizably different from one another in the pre-Homeric traditions; Homer exaggerates these differences in ways that distort and delimit—but which also illuminate.) The differentiation helps us to comprehend ways in which each of us differs from other women and to celebrate our variety. It may help us to understand (and perhaps overcome) differences with other women that are experienced as difficulties. The differentiation also provides us with a language for understanding some of the stages in our own lives and some of the particular inner conflicts we feel at a given stage. Thus, for instance, whereas at one time I lived a struggle between Hera and Aphrodite, I now find myself pulled between Aphrodite and Artemis. I am persuaded that some of the tension between the goddesses is implicit in who each is, that the conflict between them is not all Homer's invention. It is important to me not to imagine that all human difficulties can be laid at the door of patriarchy.

The Olympian goddesses are involved with men in a more complex variety of ways than is true of the mother-goddess, for whom there is only an anonymous male figure who plays in turn the roles of son, lover, and victim, and is then replaced by an equally anonymous successor. Though we may justifiably resent the male domination so often present in the encounters between the goddesses and the gods, we must surely value the recognition of the many distinctive ways in which men enter our lives: as grandfathers, fathers, uncles, stepfathers, brothers, lovers, husbands, sons, nephews, stepsons, grandsons, companions, rivals, teachers, students. The myths also show that the domination-submission grid is too simplistic to do justice to the multiple forms relationships between the goddesses and gods may take—including even the resolute avoidance of contact with men represented by Artemis. Explorations of the relation between a goddess and the males in her life may also reveal how she represents a particular way in which a woman may relate to the so-called masculine within.

Attention to the uniqueness of each of these goddesses and how differently each has informed my life has opened me to an appreciation of its multidimensionality which I might otherwise have missed. Each suggests an entirely new way to imagine the whole. That there are many goddesses rather than a goddess seems self-evident to me—perhaps because I knew the goddesses long before I heard of the goddess. But the plurality, the polytheism, seems true to the concrete richness and complexity of my experience. To speak of *the* goddess is to me an abstraction. I sometimes wonder if doing so arises from a longing for a feminine divinity equal in power and significance to the god of patriarchal monotheism.

Yet I, too, know how in the moment of revelation there is only *the* one who appears, and I respect the pull to unify our experiences which I see motivating the search for *the* goddess. Still, my own pull is more toward honoring the polymorphousness of experience and I see the goddesses as supporting the valuing of the concrete and the many as over against the abstract and singular. I am also convinced that thinking of *the* goddess as the *mother*-goddess can delimit our imagining. Perhaps that is why I value the particularity of the mythological representations of the feminine over the purely archetypal. The archetype is represented simply as an image: the mother, the maiden, the wise old woman. The myth gives us a goddess who *is* the plots in which she figures and the relationships she has with others. *Mythos* means plot, action, motive, narrative; a myth is a story. Hera *is* her relation to her husband and children, her fits of jealousy and unquenchable longing for deep mutuality. The language of myth is powerful just because of its precision—and suggestiveness.

As we seek to discover more about these goddesses than Homer reveals, we quickly discover that there are many variants of every myth and no true version; each offers another relevant view of the goddess and her powers. Studying these mythological figures means attending to all the variations and also to the details in each telling that may at first seem trivial or accidental. We come to recognize how necessary each detail is or, rather, we learn to our surprise that a particular detail, hitherto unobserved, is essential to the whole; and we begin to believe that this is true of all the others we still do not understand or still may not consciously even notice.

Our knowledge of the prepatriarchal traditions is deeply indebted to the work of the classicists and anthropologists of the last century or so who have devoted themselves to searching out the traces of the Minoan-Mycenean religion and to studying the survival and transformation of these traces in the classical world. It is now recognized that the sculpture and other monuments, vases, coins, and inscriptions often tell us more about popular belief and cult than do literary texts; we can understand much of the ancient conception of a divinity by recognizing why a specific site was felt to be hers, why it was just *there* that a temple to a particular goddess should be built.

The sense that each divine being represents a world of her own, a peculiar illumination of the whole compass of human existence, is shown especially clearly by Walter Otto and Carl Kerenyi in their writings on the Greek divinities. Each has written more on gods than goddesses, and each naturally communicates a man's experience of the goddesses when he writes of them. Nevertheless, their bringing together of scholarship, intuition, and a willingness to be moved by what they encounter can serve as a model. The living significance of the goddesses has been made visible even more powerfully in the writings of the classicist Jane Ellen Harrison and the Jungian psychologist Esther Harding, two women who combine deep learning, a gift for perceptive interpretation, and openness to the emotional power of the ancient traditions.

I agree with Ezra Pound:

> Certain it is that these myths are only intelligible in a vivid and glittering sense to those people to whom they occur. I know, I mean, one man who understands Persephone and Demeter, and one who understands the Laurel, and another who has, I should say, met Artemis. These things are for them *real*.[12]

Truly to know these myths means recognizing ourselves within them. One learns about myth from myth—from the discovery of what it means to live a myth.

The discovery of a mythical pattern that in some way one feels is connected to one's own life deepens one's self-understanding. At the same time, the discovery of the personal significance of a mythic pattern enhances our understanding of the myth and its variations. Appreciation of the connection between a myth and my life seems simultaneously to make me more attuned to the myth's unity and to help me understand how moments in my life which otherwise might seem accidental or fragmentary belong to the whole. Indeed, we may thus come to recognize the *mythos,* the plot, the connecting thread, the *story* of our life. As we come to appreciate the way in which all the variations, transformations, and elements that go to make up a myth are integral, necessary parts of it, we uncover its psycho-logic. Such attending to the psycho-logic of myth and the mytho-logic of the psyche's processes might be described as an exploration in *mythopoeisis,* in soul making, for it gives us some sense of how the soul, our soul, is given its shape through poetry, through images.

We come then to recognize our involvement in a number of different mythic patterns. One of Jung's primary accusations against Freud was that Freud seemed to be aware of only one archetype informing his life pattern and, by extension, the life pattern of all of us—the Oedipus myth. It was Jung's conviction that a psychology really attuned to the soul's processes admits our implication in a variety of myths. Similarly, James Hillman states that archetypal psychology is polytheistic, is aware of the activity of many divinities in our soul.[13] Thus we are speaking of living *mythoi,* of being involved in several life stories, not just one.

We become more aware of the archetypal dimensions of our own experience by going deeper and deeper into a myth and, indeed, into several myths. It is my experience that the myths we enter most deeply are not ones that we choose out of some book of myths. Rather, in some profound way, these myths choose us.

When I first went in search of Her after that dream vision in the cave, I began "in all innocence," which is perhaps why I had to begin with Persephone, the innocent goddess of spring. This was a goddess to whom I had felt close since I was a very young child when my mother introduced me, born on the vernal equinox, to the Greek goddess of spring. Thus, as long as I can remember I had associated the deep bond that exists between daughters and mothers with Persephone and her passionately devoted mother, Demeter—and had known, if only tacitly, that there was something divine in this bond. I understood this more fully when I in turn became a mother with a daughter of my own. Being a daughter, having a daughter; being a mother, having a mother—these were mysteries which the goddesses had helped me enter more deeply than I might have without their aid.

Yet the dream vision pointed to a darker mystery and suggested that I had come to a point in my life where a deeper knowledge of whatever I might mean by *Her* had become imperative. The place to begin was still with Persephone—but not now with just the Persephone who is Demeter's daughter and who experiences the separation from her mother as abduction, as separation from self, but more importantly with the Persephone who comes to love the underworld god, Hades, and who becomes herself the silent goddess of death. The pull to Her was somehow connected with my being at a time in my life when I was done with literal mothering and with putting most of my psychic energy into personal relationships, when I was ready to devote myself to the underworld, the realm of soul, the imaginal. Having explored my relation to the dark side of Persephone, I thought I had come to terms with the darkness in the cave. I was no longer consciously in search of Her. It did not occur to me that I had only begun.

Then unexpectedly I found myself having to attend to Ariadne, a goddess who had initially come into my life much later than Persephone and more casually, when a young lover experienced me as the one who had made it possible for him to enter his own labyrinth without fear of being lost there. Since then Ariadne had dropped out of consciousness. Because I believed I had long since gotten past the temptation, so powerful when I was younger, to live the life of an anima woman, I could not understand what present pertinence Ariadne might have. Yet I felt compelled to learn as much about her as I could and thus discovered that she is not just the young maiden holding the spool of thread at the entrance to the labyrinth, but that she occupies its center. To attend to this Ariadne was to attend to my own soul, not to serve as anima for another. It was to confront again the goddess of my cave vision.

The truth both goddesses communicate is a truth that emerges out of darkness. Though there is much in me that yearns for the depths that Hades represents, being taken there is always an abduction. One never feels quite whole or courageous enough to go there on one's own. Though in my dreams I can respond so confidently to the call to solitude and soul, in waking life I must be abandoned before I'm willing to be alone.

The next goddess to appear on this serpentine path was Hera. Again, a goddess with whom I thought I had long since done, who belonged to my past, to the early years of my marriage, was suddenly imperiously present. As I had had to penetrate more deeply than before into the mysteries of the relationship between mother and daughter, between lover and beloved, so now it was time to confront more directly the dark and transformative aspects of the relationship between wife and husband. During the confrontation with Hera I began to see that each of these goddesses met me as yet another psychotherapist might. By each I was being taught a new mode of attending to soul; each made possible a new and more imaginal reconnection with a disclaimed or neglected aspect of my past.

I have learned that when we have, at least for the moment, done with one goddess, another appears. I have also learned how each goddess plays a role within a pantheon of gods and goddesses. I am many; I am one.

NOTES

1. James Hillman, *Re-Visioning Psychology* (New York: Harper & Row, 1975), p. 158.

2. Much of this is based on Raphael Patai, *The Hebrew Goddess* (New York: Ktav, 1967).

3. See Carl Jung's discussion of the psychological significance of the promulgation of the dogma of Mary's assumption at the end of "Answer to Job," *Collected Works* 11 (Princeton, N.J.: Princeton University Press, 1969).

4. Walter F. Otto, *The Homeric Gods* (Boston: Beacon Press, 1964), p. 3.

5. Friedrich Nietzsche, *Thus Spoke Zarathustra,* in *The Portable Nietzsche,* ed. and trans. Walter Kaufmann (New York: Viking Press, 1954), p. 294.

6. C. G. Jung and C. Kerenyi, *Essays on a Science of Mythology* (Princeton, N.J.: Princeton University Press, 1969), p. 4.

7. Otto, *Homeric Gods,* p. 11.

8. W. H. Auden, *The Dyer's Hand* (New York: Random House, 1962), pp. 456f.

9. Otto, *Homeric Gods,* p. 29.

10. Jane Ellen Harrison, *Prolegomena to the Study of Greek Religion* (New York: Meridian Books, 1957), p. 306.

11. E. A. S. Butterworth, *Some Traces of the Pre-Olympian World in Greek Literature and Myth* (Berlin: DeGruyter, 1966), p. 14.

12. Ezra Pound, *The Quest* 4, no. 1 (October 1912): 44, cited in Lillian Feder, *Ancient Myth in Modern Poetry* (Princeton, N.J.: Princeton University Press, 1977), p. 92.

13. James Hillman, "Psychology: Monotheistic or Polytheistic," *Spring,* 1971.

·II·

PERSEPHONE IN HADES

Sleep on the stones of Delphi—
dare the ledges of Pallas
but keep me foremost,
keep me before you, after you, with you,
never forget when you start
for the Delphic precipice,
never forget when you seek Pallas
and meet in thought
yourself drawn out of yourself
like the holy serpent,
never forget
in thought or mysterious trance,
I am greatest and least.

H.D.[1]

As far back as I can remember there have been several mythic patterns with which I have felt myself to be closely identified. These have not always been myths in which a female played the central role nor only the classical myths of Greek antiquity. American Indian legends, the Grimms' fairy tales, and some of the books I read and reread as a child and early adolescent have impressed me just as deeply.

Even when very young I recognized myself in the stepmother who peers anxiously into her looking glass as well as in Snow White, knew that I was more like the spoiled, idle, and irredeemably selfish second daughter in "Mother Holle" than like her admirably selfless sister. As an oldest child, I felt myself more Hansel than Gretel. Later, but still long before college, I

Persephone and Hades
Trustees of the British Museum, London

knew I was the Joseph K. of Kafka's *The Trial* whose early morning arrest propels him into a strange world of undefined accusation and ineluctable guilt, and the Ivan Karamazov who is overwhelmed by the nihilist conclusions of his own relentless reasoning. I longed for the kind of education Hans Castorp received on the magic mountain.

The power some of these figures hold for me has deepened through the years; others (like Jo of *Little Women*) I have long ago left behind, though I can still recognize why they seemed so important "once upon a time." Sometimes it happens that a god or goddess, a hero or a heroine, with whom one has never felt any particular connection suddenly asserts his or her claim upon us. That happened for me most recently with Artemis as an unexpected consequence of my turning to this apparent stranger among the goddesses while composing this book.

Sometimes, too, it has been others who have recognized that for them I incarnate a mythic fiture. They suggest an identification I later come to admit as integral to my own self-understanding. I can remember—as I mentioned above and as I will relate in more detail in the next chapter—being told that I was another's Ariadne, that I had held the thread which gave him the courage to dare exploration of his own inner labyrinth. But because I knew that Ariadne later is left on Naxos, I resisted seeing myself in this role. It has been only gradually and reluctantly that I have come to appreciate that all of Ariadne's story is indeed connected to my own.

So there are the jealous stepmother and Jo March, Aphrodite and Ariadne, and many others. Nevertheless, Persephone has a special place. From her I learned a relation to myth different from that which all these other identifications, and all my familiarity with many mythological traditions and with much of the scholarly writing about mythology, had taught me. From my lifelong involvement with this particular myth I discovered how the apprehension of a mythic pattern teaches one that there may be symbolically meaningful connections between events which otherwise might seem isolated moments or stages. There is an inner bond between what one does and what apparently happens to one.

Often, in ways that continue to surprise, I have found that there are correlates in hitherto unnoticed parts of the Persephone myth to apparently isolated fragments or accidents of my life—and then I am less sure those personal experiences are adventitious after all.

I have come to understand, also, through my involvement with this myth, the difference between relating to a myth and relating to a mythological figure. It seems vitally important no longer to identify with only one character in the myth, Persephone, nor to focus on one episode within the story, Persephone's forced abduction by Hades. This transformation was not something at which I deliberately aimed. There was rather a gradual and seemingly inevitable discovery of how all the elements of the myth necessarily belong together, so that I now see that the myth is the *mythos,* the plot, the action, not the figure abstracted from it. Persephone *is* the one about whom this story, with all its ramifications, is told.

In ways that I am still discovering, her story is my story. "Always," as far back as I can remember, I have been Persephone. I am spring's child, born on the first day of spring; Persephone is the goddess of spring. My mother loves myths and fairy tales and loves to tell them. Her own children and now grandchildren, too, have outgrown having such stories told to them, and so she tells them instead to the children of strangers in parks and libraries. Probably it was from her that I first learned I was Persephone. I do not know. I cannot remember a time when it was not so.

Yet in many ways it seemed that it was only because of having been born on a particular day that I happened to be *this* maiden among the many other possibilities. As a child and young girl, I felt almost as closely identified with several others of the maiden goddesses: with Athene, bright and tomboyish; with Artemis, shy and often solitary. I felt related also to other maidens who like Persephone are carried off or abandoned: to Ariadne as I have already noted and to Psyche, who must struggle so long to attain reunion with Eros. I am struck, since I have begun to examine the myths associated with these figures more consciously, by how the ancient hymns and epics confirm my

intuitive sense of the intimate connections among these goddesses. It is precisely Artemis and Athene who are at play with
Persephone before her abduction—as though to say that it is
only the abduction that marks her differentiation from them,
only through it that she becomes *Persephone*.

The connections among Ariadne, Psyche, and Persephone
are more intricate and more intriguing. Theseus, as a young
hero, carries Ariadne away from her Cretan homeland and then
abandons her on Naxos. On a subsequent adventure he seeks to
help his close friend, Perithous, kidnap Persephone and bring
her up out of Hades to be Perithous's bride. They mistakenly sit
on the seats of Lethe (forgetfulness) and find themselves stuck
fast forever. (Though some accounts say Herakles eventually
comes to at least Theseus's rescue.) Ariadne, as the Cretan
Mistress of the Labyrinth, is like Persephone a goddess of the
realm of the dead. Theseus tries to leave the goddess of death
behind him on Naxos and tries to separate her from the realm
of death in the later adventure, but then finds he himself cannot leave. Once he could enter the labyrinth and safely
reemerge, but the entry into Hades proves more dangerous. Persephone seems to be a deeper, darker version of
Ariadne.

The last task Aphrodite imposes on Psyche as she works to
recreate her union with Eros is to journey to Hades to obtain
Persephone's beauty box. Thus the always physically beautiful
maiden acquires the psychic beauty whereby she truly becomes
herself: *Psyche*. Perhaps Psyche is that aspect of Persephone that
cannot stay in the underworld, the human soul that knows it is
not the goddess.

That there are, indeed, significant ways in which these goddesses are like one another I did not know consciously when I
first became aware that I felt more closely connected to Persephone than to the others. I only knew how very little sense I
had of who she was herself, of what it is to be Persephone.
Persephone is at first simply one among many maidens with no
clear differentiation from the others; this is indicated in the
Homeric hymn "To Demeter," the most richly detailed ancient
account of her abduction, by presenting her playing

With those big-breasted
daughters of oceanos,
picking flowers,
roses
and crocus
and beautiful violets,
in lush meadow,
and iris,
and hyacinth,
narcissus even.[2]

This scene calls vividly to mind a dream I had some twenty years ago:

> In this dream I am one among a group of young women of the tribe, hardly conscious of myself as more than just one of them, until the handsome young chief of our people calls me to dance with him and thus signals his choice of me as his bride. Though this choice, through his recognition of me, I become aware of myself and through the warmth of his love and its sensitivity, I become more and more some-one worthy of it, someone able to receive and in time to return. Then there is a drought and our people must go elsewhere in search of water. I am left behind alone, with the unborn son, their future leader, in my womb as token of their hope to return. I have become one who can wait alone and in peace for the birth of this son who now repre-sents the future of my people.

At that time I was indeed a young woman of the tribe, hardly conscious of myself as more than just one of them. Hardly conscious, either, as I have said, of Persephone as more than just one of the many maiden goddesses, though I did feel an identification with the rhythms of her life: the summers of ripe-ness and the winters of separation and loss, and the always unexpected (though always dreamt-of) rescue by the messenger god. There were many parts of the myth which seemed less relevant, like the parts of a dream which one is not yet prepared to understand.

In the years of my own budding womanhood, just before my marriage, Persephone was preeminently spring and the beauty of spring. This aspect is represented toward the beginning of Nathaniel Tarn's *The Persephones* (p. 3):

> *She is the most beautiful among the flowers of the field*
> *she is among the greenest of the grasses*
> *she is the essence of grass she is the most beautiful*
> *and among the flower-carriers she carries the finest flowers*
> *in the finest arrangements and her hair smells of praise.*
>
> *She is covered with butterfly wings as they hatch*
> *she is covered with turquoise, blue, sulphur and scarlet*
> *brown and orange of admiral, mosaic of tortoiseshell*
> *and she gives out in her body thru all these wings*
> *that same lost purpose men love in butterflies.*
> *She is clothed in feathers of goldfinch and warbler*
> *her feathers are full-colored, half-colored, stripe-colored*
> *of the finest sheens and satins and the airiest.*
>
> *She moults in our sight, you can see the dull feathers of winter*
> *turn gradually to the colors of her preferred season*
> *the colors steal over her day by day until she stands*
> *in all the radiance we call her the most beautiful for*
> *the one the dark hand most wants to pick as it reaches up.*
> *He has no time for the dark roots in his fingers*
> *the buds on the roots their promise he has no time for*
> *it is the most beautiful flower of the field he wants*

I was only very subliminally aware of that dark hand reaching up. Tarn's poem goes on to suggest that in some sense Persephone recognized Hades when he appeared:

> *By his cunning, by his agreement, our father's*
> *there'd grown, in the middle field, to which she came*
> *out of her innocence with the big-breasted daughters*
> *of ocean, in her flower-days,*
> *that vast plant with its flowers piercing the sky*

making gods and men to wonder and she reached
                              out to pluck the fragrance
which owed something to sky and something to honey and something to
the gifts of she who gives the seasons, and some to her own thighs
          but as she plucked delicately the fragrant head
a column of horses gushed from the ground
                    untiring
                              horned
                                        unfrightened horses
with black mist in their eyes
and the smokes of death's kingdom.

          His own eyes black
among the marigolds, hands black, among the poppies,
arms black with the soot of untold cremations
among anemones
                    and she recognized the bridegroom
to whom she had been condemned though she did not want him
the loss which had been prophecied
                              though he had emerged
as an earthquake among the horses unannounced
and it wd. have fitted the legend perfectly also
          as they told it in later times
if she had not known.[3]

But before I could appreciate the Hades part of the story, I needed first to understand more clearly what the Homeric hymn assumes to be the starting-point of the Persephone story: "Demeter, that awesome goddess, with her beautiful hair."

In my early twenties I began to discover my relation to her, to Persephone's mother, and to apprehend why this myth is the basis for the "cult of the two goddesses," the Eleusinian mysteries. It is the relation to Demeter which makes Persephone different from the other maidens, the other anima figures, whose mother is an insignificant and often wholly disregarded aspect of their lives. (Indeed, it is an important part of the traditions associated with Athene that she has no mother but sprang forth from Zeus's split-open head; and according to Hesiod, Aphrodite, too, is motherless, born in the foam that gathers about the severed genitals of Ouranos.)

Persephone is the maiden who has a mother. Indeed, as the title of the Homeric hymn "To Demeter" indicates, our most important source for the Persephone myth is one that views it from Demeter's perspective. That perspective was one I began to understand some time during the years when I was literally becoming a mother myself. In losing my own maidenhood, I experienced what it is to lose one's dearly loved maiden daughter. I had indeed lost her, my own maidenness—not just in losing my biological virginity but also in losing that in-one-selfness which Esther Harding has helped us to recognize is the essence of virginity. There was part of me that mourned the end of the period of introspective self-enclosure that had characterized the earlier years, as another part of me rejoiced in motherhood and an existence primarily given over to relationships, to giving birth and nurturing.

Were it not for my dreams, I might not know how deeply being mother enters into my ways of being in the world. The dreams reveal the centrality of mother/child imagery to my way of perceiving even situations which have little to do with biological relationships. The most often recurring dream motif in my adult life is that of having a child.

> I have several times dreamt of having a beautiful baby daughter who lives in a room in my house which I rarely enter. Whenever I want to see her she is bubbling, alive and happy; she has a way of smiling at me that shows she knows as well as I that it is really she who takes care of me. Once I had a very scary dream in which, as I went into the room to see my lovely daughter, the crib, as I approached it, seemed to be empty. When I drew closer, I saw that in the furthest corner was a shriveled and shrunken little thing, about the size of a thumb. With fear and trembling and utter gentleness, I picked it up and bathed it in lukewarm water. I prayed with an intensity I had never before experienced, awake or in dreams, that the child might live.

Here the dream broke off. It was years before I saw that beautiful smiling baby again—and when she does appear, as now occasionally she does, it is always cause for wonder. She awakens in me as nothing else does a trust in my own capacity to grow, to feel wonder, to experience metamorphosis. The many times I appear in my dreams as a mother have served to make me realize that I am as much mother as daughter, as much Demeter as Persephone.

As Persephone is not just any maiden, so Demeter is not just any mother. There are many incarnations of the Great Mother who gives and devours—and most of them represent the mother as the hero-son relates to her. Demeter, on the other hand, exemplifies the mother's own experience of motherhood. How different that perspective is. From the maternal side we are brought in touch with how much of motherhood is loss. Demeter, as this myth shows her to us, is the grieving mother. She experiences the loss of the other, the loss of her child, as the loss of self (which as Freud taught us is what deep mourning always feels like). All of us who are mothers know the truth of this, know how intimately the cutting fear of loss, the searing pain of loss, are interwoven with our mothering. To let go of a child—to death, to another, to madness, to simply going its own way—is more than we can bear and yet we must. The extravagance of Demeter's grief is something we can well understand. I feel in it her suspicion that in some way the loss is due to her own neglect (wholly irrespective of whether that is objectively so or not). Though my own expressions of mourning are muted and muffled in comparison with hers, I can nevertheless identify with how entirely she allows herself to be taken over by her anger and sorrow, how ready she is to let everything else fall apart and simply *be* grief. Only a goddess could mourn so extravagantly:

> *And she made this*
> *the most terrible year*
> *on this earth*
> *that feeds so many,*
> *and the most cruel.*

The earth
did not take seed
that year,
for Demeter
in her beautiful crown
concealed it.
And the cattle
many times
pulled
their bent ploughs
in vain
over the land,
and many times
the white barley
fell
uselessly
upon the earth.
And in fact
she would have wiped out
the whole race
of talking men
with a painful famine,
and deprived
those who live on Olympos
of the glorious honor
of offerings and sacrifices
if Zeus
hadn't noticed it,[4]

I am struck, too, by how Demeter in the course of her dis-consolate wandering ended up mothering again after all, serving as nurse to another woman's child—intent, this time, on raising a child who would escape death and the fates. This hope, too, had to be surrendered.

Carl Kerenyi has understood well what it is to enter into the figure of Demeter: it "means to be pursued, to be robbed, raped, to fail to understand, to rage and grieve, but then to get everything back and be born again."[5] The hymn to Demeter is *her* hymn, as the open part of the Eleusinian rites seems to have been devoted to her. As long as the focus is on the mother/daughter aspect of the Persephone mythologem, the mother does have the more important role. As long as the focus is here, the Persephone mythologem is clearly more directly pertinent to women than to men. In classical Athens, the most important Demetrian cultic event was the Thesamorphia, a woman's ritual which took the shape of an imitation of Demeter's grief. This representation of the basic emotions of woman's life as divine provided solace and encouragement.

Demeter's story ends in a reunion with her daughter, a reunion beautifully described in the hymn: "Their hearts had relief from their griefs while each took and gave back joyousness." [6] Kerenyi's reading of this reunion rings true. It shows, he suggests, that the two, mother and maiden, are one. (This is represented in the mythological traditions about Persephone and Demeter by "doubling"—Demeter, too, is raped; Persephone, too, becomes a mother.) Motherhood and maidenhood are two phases of a woman's life, endlessly repeating: the maiden becomes mother, the mother gives birth to the maiden, who becomes mother, who. . . . To recognize one's participation in this ongoing pattern is to be given access to a kind of immortality, an immortality very different from the hero's self-perpetuation. It seems also to mean that being mother does not, after all, have to mean *not* being the maiden. One can be experienced *and* innocent, turned toward others *and* in-oneself. Demeter and Persephone are distinguished in the myth and rite, but precisely in order to insist on their unity. They are the two goddesses who share one cult. Of the two, Demeter is the more accessible, the more human and kindly, the one more concerned with the practical needs of human life. (Within the Olympian pantheon, Demeter's sphere is not as all-embracing as that of the ancient mother-goddess; she is goddess of the grain, of that which grows to human benefit, not goddess of all that grows.) Most importantly, nothing connected with Demeter is secret.

However, there is another part to the myth which we have thus far neglected: Persephone's experience in Hades and her relation to its dark god. For a long while when I attended to this part of the story, I did so from the perspective of the upper world, understood it as Demeter does and as does that part of Persephone that longs to return. I knew that her joy in the reunion was as great as Demeter's for I know how deep in me is the longing to be mothered—and I do not expect there will ever be a time when my mother-longing will be entirely assuaged. I am the abandoned child in my dreams as well as the neglecting and grieving mother.

I felt I knew all too well what it is to be pulled into the underworld. I related time spent in the underworld to times of depression and separation, times when I felt I had lost my ego independence, times when I felt taken over by something outside myself. During such times, I wanted only and desperately to "get back"—and knew only a messenger from the gods could make that happen. I could not bring it about myself. Being back meant health and innocence, wholeness and happiness.

I could understand Persephone's abduction in another sense as well, as initiation into sexual experience (and beyond that into motherhood). The sexual symbolism is obvious—the radiantly awesome flower which Persephone reaches out to pluck as the earth opens up and Hades appears is clearly a phallus; the red-juice-dripping, seed-filled pomegranate she eats in Hades clearly suggests the womb. (Ovid, who often retells these myths in less subtle ways than do more ancient writers, reports that Aphrodite induced Eros to inflame Hades with love because she was jealous of Persephone's seeming determination to remain a virgin. Ovid also has Persephone eat of the pomegranate out of her own careless innocence rather than at Hades' deceitful urging.) The Oedipal element is also apparent—Hades, who is sometimes spoken of as the chthonic Zeus, is here brother to Zeus and has Zeus's paternal permission to seize Persephone. Indeed, the sun, only witness to the abduction, tells Demeter, "There is no other god responsible but Zeus." And in the Orphic tradition it is Zeus himself, in the form of a serpent, who seduces Persephone. (As Tarn's poem puts this dark truth, there is a sense in which Persephone *recognizes* Hades when he appears.)

The myth captures the ambivalence of the maiden's relation to sexuality as I myself remember it—she reaches out *and* is taken, the lover is deeply familiar *and* a stranger, she is still the person she was (Demeter's daughter) *and* so changed that she will never be the same again. This "being taken" is in part being taken over by one's own capacity for passion; it is sexual ecstasy. The male as rapist, the male as chance agent of self-discovery—both are true. Thus for a long while Hades meant two quite different things between which I perceived no connection: he took me from myself (by pulling me into times of depression and inertia); he gave me to myself (through a sexual initiation experienced as a self-discovery in which the male's participation was almost incidental). My sense of this is that I still understood Hades in terms of his influence on Persephone's relation to Demeter. I did not discern that Persephone's relation to Hades had an integral meaning of its own. Hades was what or, more appropriately, *who* (for the personification of these energies is integral to mythology's value to a deep psychological understanding) separated Persephone from Demeter, an experience which was at the same time loss of mother and gain of self.

Only recently have I come to see that the relation to Hades is just as central a part of Persephone as her relation to Demeter. In the National Museum at Athens there is an important relief depicting two scenes: in one Demeter and Persephone are seated at a banquet, in the other Persephone is seated with Hades. The two parts of the story are equally important and belong together. This is further confirmed by there being a temple dedicated to Hades at Eleusis (set, most appropriately, in a natural cave within the rocky side of the hill—the *temenos,* the threshold, of the world). Only as we understand Hades' role in the myth and what it means that Persephone should stay with him as goddess of the underworld can we appreciate how the Eleusinian cult could become the most important mystery in late classical and Hellenistic times for men as well as women. It then becomes evident why Persephone is the focus of the secret part of the cult, as Demeter is the focus of its exoteric side—and why it is that the secret cult, the mystery, is the one that matters in the Hellenistic period, as Demeter's cult may have dominated in an earlier agricultural period. Later, Demeter is important not so much because of her relation to grain but because she is the first initiate, the first to understand what has happened to her daughter. Persephone is regarded as the secret, hidden, ineffable goddess, related to things beyond, not even to be named except as *Thea*. She is, as Freud called her, the silent goddess of death.

I have had an entirely different relationship to this long-familiar myth since I have begun to see Persephone in Hades as its center. When one begins there and sees that the whole story is told about a figure who first and foremost is goddess of the underworld, one understands very differently what it means to say that she is also goddess of spring and renewal. To start with death, with the underworld, as a given is to see life in an entirely different way.

To be Persephone, to be *this* goddess, Persephone *must* be raped. Nor can the rape any longer be understood as necessary only as prelude to the joy-filled reunion with Demeter. That reunion is part of the public happenings—it is not the secret. The secret has to do with Persephone's relation to the secret world, the hidden world, the underworld. Persephone gives herself to Hades; she becomes his consort. All the stories that are told about her (other than Demeter's hymn) refer to her in this role. There are no myths which tell of someone arriving in Hades and finding her absent. As goddess of the underworld she is always there. It seems important that she does not bear Hades any children (though in some traditions she and Zeus are the parents of Dionysos). The queen of the underworld is not the Great Mother. She is not the source of literal, physical life.

For a long while I understood Persephone as the innocent victim of Hades' rape, just as Freud allowed his early patients to convince him they all had been infantile victims of parental seduction. I laid all the blame for Persephone's being in Hades on the apparent abductor—and saw it as a bad experience, saw it as meaning bad experiences, from which one could of course learn and from which one would, one hoped, eventually recover. Then I began to see Hades as meaning not "bad" but "deep"—and to recognize how much in me, although not quite consciously, yearned for the depths that Hades represents. I also see now why being taken to those depths is always an abduction. For we—or, at least, I—never feel quite whole enough, quite courageous enough, quite mature enough to go *there* on our own. We are always still virginal before the really transformative (killing) experiences.

I now understand Hades' realm, the underworld, the depths, to mean the realm of souls rather than of egos, the realm where experience is perceived symbolically. In the *Odyssey,* Hades is next to the house of dreams. The Greek underworld is not terrible and horrifying, full of punishments and tortures, but simply: beyond life. Hades is not only the god of the underworld but the god of wealth, hidden wealth. I now see Hades very differently than I had previously. Earlier I had welcomed Hermes as the guide *out* of the underworld; now I have come to welcome Hades as the guide *into* it. I feel I understand now how Persephone moves from defense against Hades to love for him. When Orpheus comes to beg for Eurydice's release, he appeals to Hades and Persephone, "If there is any truth in the story of long ago, then you yourselves were brought together by love." [7] James Hillman helps me say it: "Life becomes relieved of having to be a vast defensive arrangement against psychic realities." [8] I now understand those times of confusion and hopelessness, which once were so self-evidently "away from myself" experiences, as times of being pulled *to* myself. I had been accustomed to look at Hades from the perspective of everyday life, from the perspective of Demeter when she resents Hades, rejects Olympus and lives in "the cities of men." I can still remember a period about ten years ago during which I felt propelled, as though by outward circumstances, into a kind of death.

It was a time during which there was no hoping or dreaming left in me at all. I knew a despair utterly different from any confusion or depression I had ever experienced earlier. I discovered that I could not extricate myself. There did not seem to be any way out of having to be in this

apart-from-myself kind of place. There was no way of forc-
ing my way out and no way of cheating my way out, or
pretending that things were different than they were. One
of the things that was most difficult about this time for me
was that it was a time when I really could not imagine that
things would ever be different, because I could not even
imagine what being different might be like. Among the
most painful aspects of this experience was that during this
time I did not seem to be dreaming at all. I was not in touch
with the part of me that dreams. That was difficult because
dreams would have given me a sense that, somewhere,
there was something that was still alive in me, but I had no
contact with that vital core at all. I knew there was no
choice: this had to be lived. That is all there was to it. In a
literal, outward, practical way I functioned well through all
this, but none of that functioning seemed to have anything
to do with me in ways that mattered at all. I thought that to
be alive again would be to be back in the daylight world
feeling it to be real, to love another again, to be involved
with others and with my work. But I knew that for the time
being at least, all I could do was simply stay with how
things were. Eventually I discovered that there is indeed a
natural healing process. There is an end to an experience
like this that we do not make happen, but that comes. In
my particular situation this came when I finally had a
dream. It was a frightening dream in which I died. But that
dying was the first sign of life I had had; that dying was the
beginning of a gradual emergence back to health.

That experience taught me some important things. I learned
that things can be *that* bad, which I had not known before, and
that one is a different person after having lived through something so powerful. I learned that one recovers, and that being
here in this world of others in an ordinary, simple kind of way is
a gift. But I was still very much caught (as I look at it from
where I am now) in an ego relationship to the experience. I
looked on it from the perspective of the consciousness of the
daylight world, in relation to the image of heroic endurance. I
was aware of having come through something and now, thank
God, being on the other side of it. I believed that having had

such an experience was something important, something to be grateful for, but I was also very grateful to have it behind me. At this time I felt most closely connected to that moment in Persephone's myth when Persephone is reunited with her mother. I felt the joy of being back from the underworld, of the reconnection between those two halves of myself, the abducted half and the grieving half. That there *is* joy in such returns I would not even now deny. But I do now understand the time *in* the underworld differently.

This changed understanding of Hades came not from meditating on the myth but from a personal experience which I only afterward saw as connected to the Persephone mythologem.

> A few years ago, I participated in a visionary experience in which I felt myself pulled to my own dissolution. I felt myself being pulled toward death or to a state that was indistinguishably death or madness and I felt very powerfully my fear of that—and particularly my fear of my fear. I discovered that night how afraid I was (and have always been) of being anxious, fearful, weak, helpless. But somehow I let myself fear and I let myself go mad and I let myself die—because I realized that not to let myself die would be a much worse death. I felt, and I think this is part of what provoked the fear, that this dying that I felt happening to me was a kind of unending fall into nothingness, nothingness, nothingness. But I discovered that the more I allowed myself to fall, the less it felt like that. I discovered that I had never really believed that there is a center at the center. And that there is. It was not at all a case of overcoming my fear, of overcoming my fragmentation or my hurts—but precisely a discovery that such overcoming is beside the point. The fear, the pain, the incompleteness, the woundedness, the dying were there. They were my pain and my fear and my fragmentation, but I had come to a kind of objective relation to them. The fear was no longer fearsome; I could just let it be, rather than trying to run away from it. I saw then that wholeness did not mean not being in parts, that health did not mean not hurting.

During that night I relinquished my negative view of illness, suffering, and mourning. I no longer saw these as things to get over, to put behind or deny. I now see that night as a night spent in Hades.

The Persephone of the Eleusinian rites, the Persephone who is Hades' bride, enables us to confront the most formidable moments of our lives as integral to them, as occasions for a deep see-ing. The mysteries were show-ings and see-ings. Some scholars believe that the climax of the rite was an announcement of the birth of a divine child, Brimos, and that this might be an alternative name for Dionysos, who in the Orphic tradition is indeed held to be the son of Zeus and Persephone. The significance of this association between Dionysos, the god of ecstasy, and that revaluation of the dark effected by the rites underlies H.D.'s poem, "At Eleusis":

> *What they did,*
> *they did for Dionysos,*
> *for ecstasy's sake:*
>
> *now take the basket,*
> *think;*
> *think of the moment you count*
> *most foul in your life;*
> *conjure it,*
> *supplicate,*
> *pray to it;*
> *your face is bleak, you retract,*
> *you dare not remember it. . . .*
>
> *What they did,*
> *they did for Dionysos,*
> *for ecstasy's sake:*
>
> *Now take the basket—* [9]

The secret of the Eleusinian rites seems to be that they give one a happy arrival in the underworld. "Thrice happy are those of mortals, who having seen these rites depart for Hades; for to them alone is it granted to have found life there; to the rest all there is evil," cries Sophocles, and Pindar tells us: "Happy is he who having seen these rites goes below the hollow earth; for he knows the end of life and he knows its god-sent beginnings." [10] The Eleusinian initiation provides an entrance now (not just after death) to this realm where the perspective is in a sense *post mortem:* transpersonal and imaginal. But time spent in Hades that is not spent trying desperately to get out also leads to the discovery of the power and beauty of the dark moments in our life, the real confusions and desolations. Fear is so different when one does not have to fear fear but can simply *fear;* incompleteness and hurt are also different when one sees them not as something to get beyond but as something to live. I think again of the beauty box that Psyche had to obtain from Persephone—clearly the beauty it provides is very different from any Aphrodite might have power to bestow. I think also of Sophocles' *Oedipus at Colonus.* Because Oedipus had so fully lived his years of harried exile and blind wandering, his death on the outskirts of Eleusis is itself a mystery, a nonritualistic but nevertheless blessed initiation into Persephone's realm:

> *the underworld*
> *Opened in love the unlit door of earth.*
> *For he was taken without lamentation,*
> *Illness or suffering; indeed his end*
> *was wonderful if mortal's ever was.* [11]

As I try to consider again the whole mythologem and what I have thus far discovered in it and through it, I realize how important it is that Persephone does and does not return from Hades. Though from the point of view of the cult, Persephone is always there, she does not belong only with Hades but also with Demeter, not only in the underworld but also here on earth. I understand too that I am and am not Persephone. Even today it is the maiden Persephone with whom I identify; the goddess of the underworld is still a deep mystery to me. I am pulled to the underworld and return. She remains.

The goddess who rules in Hades represents the mystery of the unknown, its fearfulness and its unforgivingness. She is the unseen goddess of my cave vision. I am struck that she was, indeed, known as *She,* the dread name of the underworld goddess not to be spoken. She is not called, as is Hades, "the unseen" but in *Oedipus at Colonus* only the aged blind king can "see" to follow "veiled Persephone's" lead.

Many have voiced their amazement that Persephone's secret, the secret of the Eleusinian mysteries, was so faithfully kept not only in antiquity but even in the Hellenistic world. That seems self-evident to me. For this is the mystery about mystery.

NOTES

1. H.D., "Demeter," in *Collected Poems* (New York: Liveright, 1925), p. 163.

2. *The Homeric Hymns,* trans. Charles Boer (Chicago: Swallow Press, 1970), p. 91.

3. Nathaniel Tarn, *The Persephones* (Santa Barbara, Calif.: Christopher's Books, 1974), unpaginated.

4. *Homeric Hymns,* p. 118.

5. C. G. Jung and C. Kerenyi, *Essays on a Science of Mythology* (Princeton, N.J.: Princeton University Press, 1969), p. 123.

6. "To Demeter," in *Hesiod, The Homeric Hymns and Homerica,* trans. Hugh G. Evelyn-White (Cambridge, Mass.: Harvard University Press, 1974).

7. Ovid, *The Metamorphoses,* trans. Mary M. Innes (London: Penguin Books, 1955), pp. 225f.

8. James Hillman, *Re-Visioning Psychology* (New York: Harper & Row, 1975), p. 208.

9. H.D., *Collected Poems,* pp. 265f.

10. Both cited in George E. Mylonas, *Eleusis: The Eleusinian Mysteries* (Princeton, N.J.: Princeton University Press, 1974), pp. 284, 285.

11. Sophocles, *Oedipus at Colonus* 1662–1665, trans. Robert Fitzgerald, in *The Complete Greek Tragedies,* vol. 2, *Sophocles,* ed. David Grene and Richmond Lattimore (Chicago: University of Chicago Press, 1959), p. 150.

·III·

ARIADNE
Mistress of the Labyrinth

Back to the labyrinth where either
we are found or lose ourselves for ever.
                    W. H. Auden [1]

My way to the center of the labyrinth has been a serpentine one. When I had finished exploring the changing shapes of my lifelong relation to Persephone, I believed I had fulfilled the claim on me imposed by my dream vision. But soon thereafter another mythical figure, Ariadne, came forward to announce that it was time for a reckoning between us.

Though Ariadne had once been a conscious presence in my life, for a long while, perhaps twenty years, that relationship had been dormant. Only recently have I become aware of my slowly dawning, almost invisibly dawning, appreciation of the full significance of this goddess.

Several nearly simultaneous events conspired to help me recognize that the time had come to return to Ariadne to discover who she might be for me now. First, I found several passages which referred to Ariadne as a Persephone figure. Never having thought of the two together, I began wondering whether attending to one might demand a look at the other as well. Then I taught a course on mythology in which just by chance, as I thought, I included both Dionysos and Theseus. Only well into that course did I start wondering, "Why did I choose just these two figures out of the whole range of Greek heroes and Greek

Sleeping Ariadne

gods? Why *the* hero and *the* god who figure so importantly in
the Ariadne mythologem? It must be because some part of me
is ready to confront Ariadne again." Then I bought a house
which, I discovered after I had already recognized it as mine,
stands at the intersection of Avenida Primavera (suggesting
Persephone) and Serpentine Drive, the labyrinthine way.
Clearly it was time to ask again: Who is Ariadne?

As I began to do that, I learned that my involvement with
Ariadne is just as important for me as the connection with
Persephone. Living more than one myth does not mean that
one is schizophrenic; rather it is what keeps mythic identification from stultification or inflation. What makes my relation to
Ariadne very different from the one to Persephone is that it
began as another's projection on me, not as a self-identification.
Return to this myth meant exploring the pertinence of
another's view of who I am. In ways which we may not at first
fully understand but should not ignore, what another sees in us
that may be invisible to ourselves can be a clue to who we really
are. Heeding the other's view may elicit a hitherto not understood connection between what Sartre would call the *en soi* and
the *pour soi,* the "for others" and the "for ourselves."

This turning to Ariadne felt like a return or like being returned to a "big dream" that I might have had fifteen or twenty
years earlier—a dream that I had now redreamt or that in some
way was itself insisting on being looked at anew. Suddenly it
was there. This time new things would be discovered in it.
Otherwise, why would it need to appear again?

As I have said, a dear friend told me years ago that I was his
Ariadne. By this he meant that my being toward him as I was
had given him the strength, the courage, the insight, the readi-
ness to risk the exploration of his own labyrinth, his own soul,
in a way that he felt would otherwise have been impossible. To
say "Ariadne" was to say this more precisely and more fully than
any other language available to him. It was also to suggest that
the relationship between Theseus and Ariadne might be a
paradigm for our relationship in ways not yet fully discernible
to either of us. Now that is not at all the way that I, from my
side, would have described what was happening between us at

that point. I, of course, understood what was happening between us in terms of *my* myth: at that time I saw him as a
Hermes who would appear whenever really needed to rescue
Persephone from the depths. Strange . . . each saw the other as
psychopomp; but he saw me as someone who would guide him
into the depths and I saw him as one who would help me back
out. (Only now can I see how Hades and the labyrinth represent
two rather different imaginings about the realm of soul and how
the differences in our fantasies correspond to the two different
conceptions of the underworld or afterworld.)

I was moved, flattered, perhaps a little inflated, by what my
lover had to say about my meaning for him. I was also scared.
For, though I did not know very much about Ariadne, I did
know that the story does not end with Theseus's safe return and
then some variant of "They lived happily ever after." Myths do
not end like that. As Geza Roheim once remarked, though Eros
may triumph in fairy tales, Thanatos does in myths. I knew that
Theseus had come from Athens to Crete as part of the Athenian
tribute, and that for him and his companions to be free to sail
back home he needed to penetrate the labyrinth and slay the
Minotaur. Ariadne's holding the thread enabled him not only to
make his way into the labyrinth but also to make his way safely
out. She was thus essential to the adventure's success. I knew
that and I knew one other thing about Ariadne and Theseus—
the part that frightened me: I knew that Theseus, out of
gratitude to Ariadne, agreed to take her with him from Crete.
On the very first night of their journey, they stopped on the
island of Naxos; early the next morning Theseus set sail, leaving
Ariadne behind. I feared that if my lover and I were indeed
living the myth about Ariadne and Theseus, then desertion was
a part of our story that was still to be lived.

And it happened: a separation that felt like a desertion even
though at some rational level it was right and necessary. When
we reflect on Theseus and Ariadne, it is important to remember
that integral to their story is that moment when Ariadne knows
herself to be deserted. In Richard Strauss's opera, *Ariadne Auf
Naxos,* she first appears at that moment, the moment when she
wakes up to find that Theseus is gone. The music renders her

sense of abandonment and gives unforgettable expression to her feeling: "I will never love again, and therefore in some sense, I will never live again." So in our story, there was that separation; it felt like betrayal, and like death.

Two years later in a way that seemed a gift, my lover returned. The relationship between us seemed immeasurably different. Literally, it was a connection with the same person; at some more real level, it was with another. Our interaction was no longer colored with the confusions, the possessiveness, the betrayals that are part of the love that we think of as mortal love. The only way I know to speak of it is as a kind of immortal love, though that suggests just the romanticism that had been left behind. It seemed clear that the renewed connection would be lived in an eternal kind of way, even though our literal times together would henceforward be few. That seemed to be beside the point. What mattered was the feeling that our love no longer carried with it the danger of interfering with or disrupting our everyday lives.

Even more important was the sense that each of us now had our center in ourselves. We were no longer dependent on each other for our connection to soul. I was aware of the power of being with a man so in touch with the feminine in himself that he did not need to look to me to supply it for him. Only much later did I learn that something very similar happens to Ariadne in the myth. After Theseus deserts her, a god appears and makes Ariadne his bride. This god is Dionysos. When I learned that, I thought, "Yes, that's what happened." But at the time that analogue seemed interesting rather than important. When it was introduced, I was not paying attention to the parallels between the Ariadne myth and what was happening in my own life, and so I saw no current pertinence to my expanded knowledge of the myth. I understood what had happened between my lover and myself as just good luck, as a blessing, not as mythologically inevitable. (I am still not sure how often the inner bond between Theseus and Dionysos is expressed through the same man playing both roles. But I do know that it is often difficult to distinguish between Theseus and Dionysos in ancient vase paintings and that there is often confusion between them in the mythological tradition: it is not quite clear who fathered Ariadne's children, for instance, or to whom the crown properly belongs that now adorns the heavens as *corona borealis*.)

I have come to understand that Theseus's abandonment of Ariadne is the necessary prelude to her relationship with Dionysos. If Ariadne helps Theseus, then Ariadne must be left behind. That may sound a little odd at first hearing, but it is absolutely essential to the understanding of this myth. It relates of course to the fact that in the Ariadne/Theseus part of the story Ariadne is another anima figure, though different from Persephone. Because Ariadne takes more initiative, she has to be deserted rather than raped. The story suggests that anima dependence must be overcome. Theseus cannot stay with Ariadne; he has to be able to leave her behind. It is just as important for Ariadne that she be left behind, so that she might leave behind her dependence on playing the role of anima. Only after a Theseus has left and after an Ariadne has been left, only after both of them have really integrated that separation, is there the possibility of either having his or her own connection to soul. Here Dionysos appears. The relationship with a man who has his own soul is inevitably that with one who is psychologically androgynous, as is Dionysos. Just as one needs to wrest Persephone free from her ties to Demeter in order really to see her, so, too, one needs to separate Ariadne from Theseus. Ariadne must be abandoned just as Persephone must be abducted. Only then are we able to appreciate fully the significance of Hades or of Dionysos.

Yet, during the years following my lover's departure, I was not understanding my life in terms of the myth. Only recently did those events occur which suggested that there was more to all of this than I had realized thus far, that it was time *now* to discover my own relationship to Ariadne, not the other's relationship to Ariadne through me. That led me to understand much better than I had before why I had instinctively shrugged off the Ariadne identification when the Theseus figure had first proposed it. Something about that had not quite rung true to my sense of who I am, because the version of the myth that I had known then—the version which I suppose is most familiar—is the man's version. Only as I came to penetrate to some of the myth's earlier strata, to some of its buried aspects, could I come to my own connection to it.

The familiar version, just because it is the man's version, has some truth for us women so long as, and to the degree that, we are defined by our relationships with men and by their relationships to us. Because the masculine perspective is in a significant sense an ego perspective, it may also help us women to discriminate between those aspects of Ariadne which are human—and which we may incarnate—and those other divine aspects from which we also must learn to differentiate ourselves. It is not only men who are in danger of being swallowed by a goddess.

It is important to see how this way of telling the myth grows out of the heroic, the Olympian, the male- and ego-dominated world. Indeed Theseus—perhaps especially in Mary Renault's retellings of the legends associated with his name, *The King Must Die* and *The Bull From the Sea*—really represents the emergence of the patriarchal perspective. In all the different stories that have been attached to the figure of Theseus, one theme keeps recurring: Theseus is the male hero who continually finds himself in conflict with the matrilineal world, the "king must die" world. As the hero most deeply aware of the danger and the appeal of the feminine, he spends his life battling against being overtaken by it. Not only Theseus but the heroes of many of the Greek myths that we know best—Orestes and Oedipus, for example—seem to represent precisely the moment of transition in Greek cultural history from the matrilineal to the patrilineal. In the earlier period the sacred was experienced most powerfully as feminine; political power, if not directly in the hands of women, was defined by one's relation to them: one married the king's daughter or stole his wife from him. This is still dimly evident in the received versions of the ancient tales, but the Greek myths as we get them from Homer and Hesiod, from Aeschylus and Sophocles, are written from the perspective of the patriarchal period, a perspective that issues in the reduction of ancient goddesses into figures with whom men can safely deal.[2]

So it is that the major Olympian goddesses, Hera and

Athene, Artemis and Aphrodite, are each identified with one aspect of the feminine. This perspective which seeks to validate and buttress male power differentiates the feminine. Each goddess is assigned a role; she is wife or comrade, the elusive or the generously available lover. One can deal with each isolated aspect safely, whereas dealing with the whole panorama of femininity, all at once, is much too fearful. It is safer if one can differentiate, as it is also safer if one can humanize. Thus in the Homeric world there are female figures—not just Ariadne but also Helen of Troy, for instance—who were clearly once goddesses but who have now been divested of their overwhelming magic by being made human. Over and over again, even in Homer, there are clues that these women once had much more power, scope, significance than they do on the surface in the accepted versions.

There are clues in the *Odyssey* that Ariadne was once something much more than the helpful but clinging mortal girl whom Theseus took away from Crete.[3] His desertion of a simple maiden would not have been celebrated as something brought about by Athene to save Athens from contamination by overwhelming feminine power. Homer's telling of the story even excuses Theseus of any conscious cruelty. He wakes up in the morning; he has somehow quite forgotten he had Ariadne with him and thus in all innocence sets sail back to Athens. When he remembers her, he is so grief stricken that he forgets to change the sails which would have assured his father of his safe return. Homer implies that Theseus unconsciously left Ariadne because she has to be left. He has to leave her, not just before he gets to Athens but immediately, before there is any opportunity for the consummation of their love—for afterwards, he might not be able to leave.

Events in myth are often overdetermined; Theseus's departure is associated not only with Athene but also with Artemis who intervenes at Dionysos's instigation. Dionysos orders Artemis to make sure that Ariadne is left behind—which suggests that the connection with Dionysos, not with Theseus, is the really central one, the one that gives Ariadne's story its shape. Ariadne belongs to Dionysos in her essence (not just because of chance cult associations at a later period, as some scholars have suggested). Artemis's intervention reveals that Dionysos already has a claim, for Artemis assails only the faithless.

All the variations and transformations of a myth are meaningful. Thus, although one version asserts that Dionysos only appears in Ariadne's life after she has been deserted by Theseus, another suggests that she already belonged to Dionysos before Theseus ever came into the story. Both are true. It is as though Ariadne only recognized Dionysos's prior claim in her life after she had betrayed it. There is evidently a tradition that already on Crete, before she ever became involved with Theseus, Ariadne had been the betrothed of Dionysos. According to one version, the crown she gave Theseus to light his way through the labyrinth had earlier been given her by Dionysos. (This makes sense at the personal level; perhaps we can serve another as anima only because of our prior experience of the sacred. Clearly, even as mortal maiden, Ariadne knows much more than Theseus about encounters with the divine in its fearful aspects.) She is killed as punishment for having turned from the immortal god to a mortal lover. There are other stories in Greek mythology—the story about Koronis is the one that immediately comes to mind—of a similar pattern where a woman betrays a god—in this instance, Apollo who has been her lover—for the sake of a mortal. In that story, too, it is Artemis who brings death.

It is not difficult to have some understanding of what such a betrayal means and why one would commit it. There are clearly times when we are pulled to an involvement with a human other as an escape from a connection with the transcendent that really has a kind of prior claim on us—a connection that is somehow too much for us. We flee to the heroic mortal lover to escape from the deeper experience. Kerenyi says that in all of us there lurks an enemy of Dionysos as well as a devotee.[4] There are moments for all of us when the ec-stasy Dionysos represents is more than we feel we can handle or sustain; and so we turn our backs on it.

In the Homeric version of the myth, Ariadne is killed by

Dionysos or at his suggestion. In Hesiod, Dionysos appears to rescue and make her his bride, and then Zeus grants her immortality. Another tradition has Dionysos put Ariadne so soundly asleep on Naxos that Theseus cannot awaken her and so reluctantly leaves her behind. There is even a version in which Dionysos kidnaps Ariadne, forcefully taking her from Theseus. She is both married to Dionysos and dies because of her connection with him. There is more buried here than the mythological version of an original conflict between two cults and its resolution through the absorption of the Ariadne cult by the one dedicated to Dionysos.[5] The relation between Dionysos and Ariadne cannot be reduced to historical accident. It communicates an intuition about the relation between love and death: Ariadne is a bride of death. The Ariadne cult in southern Italy seems to have consisted primarily of rituals intended as preparations for death. To go to death as bride is to go to death as enhanced life.

As we begin to explore what it means that Ariadne is primarily connected to Dionysos, we get closer, I believe, to what Ariadne means as women know her. When we start with the connection to Dionysos, Ariadne assumes an entirely new power and significance. If her relation to Dionysos is not just compensation for her abandonment by Theseus, then perhaps the clue to Ariadne's essence is to be found through trying to understand this primary other in her life. Who is this god for whom she is the female other? I find it intriguing that Ariadne is *the* counterpart of Dionysos, *the* wife, *the* chosen one. In her book *Goddesses, Whores, Wives, and Slaves,*[6] Sarah Pomeroy says that in all of Greek mythology Dionysos is the only god who does not exploit females, the only faithful husband. Ariadne is the woman to whom he is faithful.

The version of the story that focuses on Ariadne and Dionysos shows Ariadne made immortal, made a goddess, through her connection to him (as is also true of his mortal mother, Semele). To know who she truly is thus depends on learning who he is. Though Dionysos is a complex god, we can begin to describe him by saying he is the god of women. Dionysos is unique in Greek mythology in that his most frequent and characteristic worshipers were humans of the *other* sex; his primary attendants were always women, the maenads; and men were excluded from their rituals. That Dionysos is the god of women means that he is masculinity, male sexuality, as women experience it. Because he is a phallus at the disposal of women, he can be represented either as disembodied phallus or as emasculated god. Dionysos is also the god of madness and ecstasy, the god of vitality, the god in whose realm everything is turned upside down. He means madness and mystery— "Madness not as sickness . . . but a companion to life at its healthiest." [7]

This god who comes to women in their most impassioned moments is a god connected with visionary eroticism, as imaginal sexuality. We should not reduce these sexual experiences to narcissistic or masturbatory fantasies; they are lived as intercourse with another, a divine other. This is the sexuality of what Esther Harding calls the virgin, the woman who has her center in herself, the woman who is able to indulge in her passion without thereby becoming dependent on relationships with others. For women to be thus in touch with their own life-giving energy inevitably provokes the opposition of Hera (the archetypal wife) and of husbands. Dionysos is the lover of women who have their center in themselves, who are not defined by their relationships with literal men. The image of women yielding themselves to their own passion strikes fear in men, and even women know how close such ecstasy is to annihilation. (Ariadne comes from a family of women susceptible to being overwhelmed by their own passion: her mother Pasiphae's infatuation with a bull issues in the birth of the death-dealing Minotaur; her sister, Phaedra, is destroyed by her incestuous lust for Hippolytus.) The bride of Dionysos is the bride of death.

Dionysos is often called the womanly one. That Dionysos is an androgynous god is suggested in many parts of his story. He is so able to bring men in touch with their femininity that he can even make Zeus into a woman: after Hera had caused the death of Dionysos's mother, Zeus makes his thigh into a womb which contains Dionysos for the last three months before his birth. To protect him from Hera's still unappeased wrath, Dionysos is raised as a girl. Later, he goes to the underworld in search of his mother whom he wants to take to Olympus and make into a goddess. On his way he is helped by a man who shows him the gate by which he enters the underworld. In recompense he promises to serve this man as a woman on his return journey. (As it happens, by then the man is dead, so Dionysos has intercourse with an enormous wooden phallus instead.)

The emphasis on Dionysos's bisexuality suggests that there must be a comparable element in Ariadne as well. As the fully appropriate consort of the androgynous god, she must herself be androgynous. Indeed, she has a brother called Androgeos whose death lay behind the Athenian obligation to pay the tribute to Crete. Another brother is the Minotaur. We have already noted that she is a very assertive young woman even in the episodes that link her to Theseus. Like Dionysos, Ariadne was sometimes given the power to bring men into touch with female experience; in the Cypriot rituals dedicated to her men simulate the pain of childbirth. One of her sons is Thoas, king of Lemnos, the island which is taken over by women after they kill all their husbands and sons.

Studying the mythological traditions associated with Ariadne introduced me to hitherto unguessed-at aspects of this goddess, and these new aspects clarified why Ariadne had reappeared as presently pertinent. For the hidden Ariadne means woman in relation to her own powers, not as defined by relationship with others. She is woman unafraid of her own sensuality or of her own capacity for ecstasy. She epitomizes what Esther Harding meant by "in-herself-ness." Having seen that, I began to glimpse the earliest Ariadne of all, the Ariadne who on Crete is identified as the Mistress of the Labyrinth. This Ariadne belongs to an ancient matrilineal period of mother-goddess worship. She is not just a mortal girl who is Theseus's beloved, nor is she just someone made a goddess through her connection to the god Dionysos. She is immortal in her own being. She is not a mortal who becomes immortal, but an immortal the later traditions have transformed into a mortal. Ariadne is one of the prepatriarchal goddesses who blend in and out of each other in confusing ways because they are women in their woman-ness. From that perspective the nice, neat, clear-cut differentiations do not quite work; we know we are each all of those possibilities, at least potentially.

Ariadne is one of the Great Mothers, a great goddess of Crete. As such she is titled the Potent One, the Mistress of the Labyrinth, the Untouched One.[8] To ask who Ariadne is, to follow the thread all the way to the end, leads us to the center of a labyrinth and at that center we find Ariadne herself. In the beginning there is Ariadne, a goddess complete in herself, androgynous and self-perpetuating, creating out of her own being with no need of another. This earliest tradition is obscured by the more familiar later ones. The original self-sufficient Ariadne is superseded by another who is related to the masculine as something outside herself which is nevertheless her creation and entirely at her disposal. At this stage, Ariadne is represented as accompanied by a clearly subordinate male figure, the dying-rising male who is son and lover and, eventually, victim. As we pursue this story it is clear that originally Ariadne was the important figure and Dionysos the necessary other. Because Dionysos began as a dying and rising god, he is still the appearing and disappearing deity, even in the classical period. Even on Olympus, Dionysos serves to remind us of the time when gods were sons and then lovers, who died and then reappeared as newborn sons, became lovers again and died, again and again.

As one of the ancient mother-goddesses, Ariadne is more than just a vegetal goddess.[9] The vision is much more profound and comprehensive than that. She is connected not just to animation, to natural life, but to anima, to the soul.

An all-important aspect of Ariadne is her relationship to the realm of death. Death in Ariadne's world is significantly different from death in Persephone's. (The Persephone/Ariadne parallels, particularly the way in which each is related to both Theseus and Dionysos, must be fully admitted before we can appreciate the more subtle significance of the differences.) That in Crete the afterworld is associated with water (unlike in Greece where afterworld is underworld) suggests it is more like

Jung's unconscious than like Freud's—a source of continual renewal rather than a depository for what has been banished from
the world of the living. Ariadne seems always to be linked to
islands; death in her world takes one to the islands of the
blessed, to the Elysian realm. In classical Greek mythology this
becomes a privileged area within Hades ruled by Ariadne's
father, Minos, where the specially favored do not truly die but
are allowed to live in death. The Cretans' vision of the life
process as moving from life to death to life is utterly different
from the radical distinction the Greeks made between life and
death. For the Greeks (although this changes when the mystery
cults become important) life is life and death is death. Mortals
die and the gods do not; their immortality constitutes their
theos. On Crete there is not that clear-cut differentiation between the divine and the human, nor such an abrupt and final
demarcation between life and death.

Ariadne's special connection with death is preeminently represented by the labyrinth from which most never return; the
few who do, however, return transformed. In Argos, appropriately for a goddess of death, Ariadne's tomb serves as an altar.
But the most intriguing thing about Ariadne and death is that
she herself suffers death in so many ways. Among these death
stories is the one we have already considered according to
which she is killed by Artemis. Another story relates that
she simply dies of grief, and a third tells us that she commits
suicide by hanging herself from a tree in despair at Theseus's
departure.

Most interesting of all is the tradition according to which
Ariadne dies just prior to giving birth. This myth asserts that
Theseus reluctantly left Ariadne in the care of midwives on
Naxos (or Dia, another island that is often named in the
Ariadne traditions) because her time had come. Artemis is reported to have killed her with the child still in her womb, an
account which recalls the deaths of Koronis and Semele. But
whereas Asklepios and Dionysos are rescued from their dying
mothers' wombs just in time, Ariadne enters the realm of death
with the unborn child still within her and gives birth in the
underworld. This is the only account in Greek mythology of a

birth in the world of the dead, a clue that something profound and fascinating is present here.

What does it mean for a child to be born in the afterworld, for birth to take place in the realm of death? Again, as so often in connection with Ariadne, there is a suggestion that somehow birth and death are not mutually exclusive but rather are intimately intertwined. The child, like the thread Ariadne holds for Theseus, unites this world and the other, the outer and the inner, life and death. Birth is not opposed to death; they are not even to be understood as following one another sequentially. That this birth is only possible in death marks it off as a birth entirely different from that of the other sons attributed to Ariadne (who are all related to Dionysos's more worldly side, to grape and vine and wine).

We need to attend to what the myth has to say about the identities of the father of this child and of the child itself. It is clear that the father is Dionysos; after all, Ariadne is killed because of her unfaithfulness to him. Kerenyi believes that the child who is born must also be Dionysos.[10] (There is confirmation for his suggestion in the many parallels between Ariadne and the other goddesses named as mothers to Dionysos: Semele and Persephone.) This fits in with the ancient son and lover motif, but there is more here than is usual in the archaic pattern—the more suggested by the unique locus of the birth. This birth does not occur in the "real" world; it is not a literal birth. It represents the fullness of what birth means when we understand it not literally but symbolically. To recognize birth as a mystery is to see it in relation to the afterworld. Intercourse with Dionysos when he is fully present and not only as god of wine and physical fertility issues in a birth into death, into the imaginal, a birth in the soul, a birth of soul. Ariadne is the one through whom such birth is possible.

That returns us to where we began. Kerenyi says that Ariadne represents "the archetypal reality of the bestower of soul, of what makes a living creature an individual."[11] Thus at the center of the labyrinth we come to the point where one returns to the beginning. The serpentine way, to recall Eliot's words, returns us to the place where we started; returned, we *know* it for the first time. So we find ourselves now where we began, with Ariadne as anima, Ariadne as soul.

But this is so in a much, much deeper way. Ariadne is no longer the anima who waits outside the labyrinth while another enters. She means soul in the sense of what is at the center of the labyrinth, what is at the center of the self. Ariadne means soul, center, the goddess, what I call *She*. As James Hillman has shown, at its most important levels, anima has nothing to do with contrasexuality.[12] The anima is not the magically attractive, seductive, bewitching woman; the anima is not most adequately described as a man's feminine side. Rather the anima is soul, to which we women need to relate just as truly as do men. The anima is "what gives events the dimension of soul," what attunes us to the imaginal significance of the experiences in which we participate.

When I come to know Ariadne as Mistress of the Labyrinth, I reject the identification with Ariadne not any longer because I do not want to be left behind, but because she is a goddess and because I, as surely as any man, know that at the center of the labyrinth I find not myself but *Her*. I begin to understand that at this point in my life I am pulled back to Ariadne because it is time to give my devotion to her and to the child born in the realm of death, the child born in the realm of soul.

NOTES

1. W. H. Auden, "The Dark Years," in *Collected Poems* (New York: Random House, 1976), p. 223.

2. See E. A. S. Butterworth, *Some Traces of the Pre-Olympian World in Greek Literature and Myth* (Berlin: DeGruyter, 1966).

3. See Homer *Odyssey* 11.321–25.

4. Carl Kerenyi, *Dionysos: Archetypal Image of Indestructible Life* (Princeton, N.J.: Princeton University Press, 1976), p. 241.

5. See Martin P. Nilsson, *The Mycenean Origin of Greek Mythology* (Berkeley: University of California Press, 1972), p. 172.

6. Sarah B. Pomeroy, *Goddesses, Whores, Wives, and Slaves* (New York: Schocken Books, 1975), p. 12.

7. Walter F. Otto, *Dionysus: Myth and Cult* (Bloomington: Indiana University Press, 1965), p. 143.

8. Charles F. Herberger, *The Thread of Ariadne* (New York: Philosophical Library, 1972), p. 90; T. B. L. Webster, *From Mycenae to Homer* (New York: Barnes & Noble, 1960), p. 50.

9. See Nilsson, *Mycenean Origin,* p. 175.

10. Kerenyi, *Dionysos,* pp. 108, 277.

11. Kerenyi, *Dionysos,* p. 124.

12. James Hillman, "Anima," *Spring,* 1974, 1975.

·IV·

COMING TO TERMS
WITH HERA

I have been taught by dreams and
fantasies
Learned from the friendly and the
darker phantoms
And got great knowledge and courtesy
from the dead. . . .
            Edwin Muir[1]

In her essay "The Older Woman," Irene Claremont de Castillejo says, "I believe one has to return to one's past, not once, but many times, in order to pick up all the threads one has let fall through carelessness or unobservance. I believe above all one has to return again and again to weep the tears which are still unshed."[2] Each such return involves for me the discovery of the importance in my life of yet another goddess—a goddess who has perhaps been present all along but who only now becomes observable or just now needs to be newly observed.

Soon after the revisioning of Ariadne I realized that the goddess before whom I needed to bring myself was Hera. After having been married for more than twenty-five years, I was about to be divorced. My husband and I had been separated for several years; the divorce felt right to each of us but I knew that for me some ritual observance of the ending was essential. The intuition led me to recognize that what I wanted to do was to come to terms as wholly as I could with what "wifeness" had meant to me. My way of doing that was to turn

Head of Hera (from Temple of Hera at Selinus)
Hirmer Verlag, Munich

to the Greek mythological representation of wifeness, the figure of Hera, and ask what role she had played in my life.

As wife to Zeus, king of the gods, and as the only goddess centrally defined by her marital role, Hera is *the* wife of the Olympian pantheon. The most accessible classical accounts of her tension-filled relationship with Zeus suggest that being wife is singularly unfulfilling. This coming to terms seemed to provide me with a way of understanding myself more fully, more consciously, and more symbolically than I had before—at a point in my life where in an outward literal sense I was no longer to be defined by my relation to her. I hoped that in this way I might now become more aware of the life I had lived and what it meant, not to wish it away nor to get free of it through understanding it. It was not that I felt my life should have been different, but that I wished to know it better.

I spent most of a winter weekend lying on my bed, propped up by pillows, surrounded by books and half-emptied coffee cups, writing about Hera, about me, about our connection. I had imagined this as a kind of ritual farewell to Hera—and so it was—but it became a kind of greeting as well. I had thought of it as something I was doing only for myself, but found when I finished that I wanted to share what I had written with my husband three thousand miles away, though I had no sense at all of what he might be able to make of it. For him, too, it turned out to be an important way of naming where we had been and where we now were. "I have just been reading Philip Zabriskie's 'Goddesses in Our Midst,' " he wrote back, "and realized that, like it or not, Hera is the goddess who has been most actively present in my life."

A few months later my mother was to celebrate her seventy-fifth birthday. As I considered what might serve as a gift which could adequately articulate all that she had been in my life, all that she had given me, consciously and unconsciously, I remembered what I had written that earlier weekend of how Hera had first been present in my life through my mother's ambivalent allegiance to her. Since it was from her that I had first learned of the living power of Greek mythology, I knew that if I sent her the pages she would understand the medium, though I was not at all sure how ready she would be to receive what I was communicating through it. Yet her response indicated that again my reflections on Hera worked as a way of naming experience more true to its complexity and depth than could have been possible in less symbolic language. She said she had been led by what I had written to imagine a scene in which we two would approach this goddess together and then each in turn step forward to voice our thanks and our complaint.

Their response, my husband's and my mother's, and that of a few others, led me to recognize that the predominantly negative image of Hera with which I began was not peculiar to me but rather had been conveyed to me not only by my family's but also by my culture's messages about what "wife" means. The negative view had been reinforced by my own discovery early in my marriage that I could never be comfortably contained within that role. This contemporary depreciative image of wife is congruent with the one that emerges from the most familiar classical mythic accounts of Hera which present her as unhappy, jealous, possessive, and vindictive.

The Hera of the Homeric and post-Homeric world is, of course, Hera as viewed by men. Because she is seen from the perspective of a patriarchal culture, she might seem irrelevant to those of us who want to move beyond the limitations and distortions of that perspective. Yet this *is* the Hera with whom we necessarily begin, the Hera alive to some degree in the unconscious of each of us, and deeply embedded in our language, literature, and social institutions. I believe we must begin with her and then go in search of an earlier Hera belonging to the period dominated by female divinities. The more archaic Hera thus discovered still lives in us, simultaneously with the later one. Speaking of the Hera of Homer as "the powerless half of a whole needed by her and not by Zeus," Carl Kerenyi says: "Hera cannot originally have been like this! A figure as dependent as this could not have been the object of a cult." [3] Jane Ellen Harrison agrees:

> The figure of Hera remains. At first sight she seems all wife, not maiden; ... but a moment's reflection on the

facts of local cultus and myth shows that this marriage was not there from the beginning. . . . In fact Zeus is practically non-existent. In Olympia, where Zeus in historical days ruled if anywhere supreme, the ancient Heraion where Hera was worshiped alone long predates the temple of Zeus. At Argos the early votive terra-cottas are of a woman goddess, and the very name of the sanctuary, the Heraion, marks her supremacy. . . . At Stymphalus, in remote Arcadia, Pausanias says that Hera had three sanctuaries and three surnames: while yet a girl she was called Child, married to Zeus she was called Complete or Full-Grown (Teleia), separated from Zeus and returned to Stymphalus she was called Chera (Widow). Long before her connection with Zeus, the matriarchal goddess may well have reflected the three stages of a woman's life; Teleia, full-grown, does not necessarily imply patriarchal marriage.[4]

Even in classical Greece Hera was seen as Hera Teleia, Hera Fulfilled. I felt a need to recover that Hera, to understand her pathos and power as well as her lack of fulfillment, her pathology. This Hera is visible in the sculptural representations which show her as serene and poised, as vibrant with a youthful maturity. Hera Teleia is associated with the moment of the emergence of the female into her womanhood, her full essence—a moment recognized as the mystery underlying the *hieros gamos,* the sacred wedding. Hera's daughter, Hebe, the goddess of youth and her double (as same-sex offspring so often are in Greek mythology) represents precisely this moment of transition from maiden to woman. Kerenyi, speaking of Hera's (and Hebe's) Roman counterpart, Juno, says that every woman possesses a young feminine nature comparable to the "genius" of a man: this is her Juno, her individuality, an eternally self-renewing youthful femininity.[5] The statues and bas-reliefs surprise: I had imagined Hera differently, as more matronly, harsher, somewhat heavy in a coarsened way, somehow both smug and discontent. I had forgotten the mythological accounts of the pride Hera takes in her beauty: how she had expected Paris to judge her to be more beautiful than Athene or Aphrodite, how she had sent Orion's wife, Side, to Hades for claiming to be more beautiful than she. The Hera of cult, the Hera celebrated by women, is viewed in terms of this beauty, envisioned as quietly content, filled with a secret smiling knowledge. The Orphic hymn to Hera invokes her thus:

> *You are ensconced in darksome hollows, and airy is*
> *your form,*
> *O Hera, queen of all the blessed consort of Zeus.*
> *You send soft breezes to mortals, such as nourish*
> *the soul,*
> *and, O mother of rains, you nurture the winds and*
> *give birth to all.*
> *Without you there is neither life nor growth:*
> *and, mixed as you are in the air we venerate, you*
> *partake of all,*
> *and of all you are queen and mistress.*
> *You toss and turn with the rushing wind.*
> *May you, O blessed goddess and many-named queen of*
> *all,*
> *come with kindness and joy on your lovely face.*[6]

The Hera of cult was worshiped by all women and was pertinent to every stage of a woman's life. She was Hera Parthenos, Hera Teleia, Hera Chera: maiden, wife, and also woman on the other side of marriage, woman separated from her spouse, woman as widow or divorcée. As M. I. Finley puts it, Hera was "complete female whom the Greeks feared a little and did not like at all." [7] I wanted to recover this complete Hera, to discover those positive aspects of which I knew almost nothing. To start there, with the dark, would be an appropriate approach to this goddess who is associated with the dark time of the new moon, with the month following the winter solstice, with childbirths that take place in caves, and with light issuing forth from darkness. With Persephone it happened the other way around—I began with the maiden goddess of spring and only later discovered the integral importance of her underworld role. That discovery had taught me how the dark side of the goddesses is most intimately connected to their association with transformation. To resist turning from this side of them may lead toward a new relation to our own woundedness and woundingness, to what Jungians would call our shadow. One learns: stories about goddesses, and true stories about ourselves, are not pretty. Orual, Psyche's sister, in C. S. Lewis's *Till We Have Faces,* begins her review of her relationship to the gods with the question: "Why must holy places be dark places?"

> I say the gods deal very unrightly with us. For they will neither (which would be best of all) go away and leave us to live our own short days to ourselves, nor will they show themselves openly and tell us what they would have us do. For that too would be endurable. But to hint and hover, to draw near us in dreams and oracles, or in a waking vision that vanishes as soon as seen, to be dead silent when we question them and then glide back and whisper (words we cannot understand) in our ears when we most wish to be free of them, and to show to one what they hide from another; what is all this but cat-and-mouse play, blindman's buff, and mere jugglery? Why must holy places be dark places?

Yet she finds herself changed by the very careful articulation of her complaint:

> Since I cannot mend the book, I must add to it. To leave it as it was would be to die perjured; I know so much more than I did about the woman who wrote it. What began the change was the very writing itself. Let no one set lightly about such a work. Memory, once waked, will play the tyrant. I found I must set down (for I was speaking as before judges and must not lie) passions and thoughts of my own which I had clean forgotten. The past which I wrote down was not the past I thought I had (all these years) been remembering. I did not, even when I had finished the book, see clearly many things that I see now. The change which the writing wrought in me (and of which I did not write) was only a beginning—only to prepare me for the gods' surgery. They used my own pen to probe my wounds.[8]

As we turn to Hera, we begin where we must, with Hera as wife, yet also with Hera as maiden and widow, for it is an essential part of her relation to wifeness that marriage never quite contains her. Indeed, the very ambivalence toward wifeness suggested by her triple status may lead toward an appreciation that marriage is in its very essence something to which women are both pulled and resistant.

This central ambivalence, the double message associated with Hera, was, I have come to realize, clearly present in the image of Hera first conveyed to be by my mother. "I have chosen Hera as my goddess," she seemed to be saying all through my childhood, "but she asks too much; I will protect you from her. This goddess demands total allegiance. If one is wife, that is all one gets to be." (Even as a child I was aware, though only subliminally, how those aspects of my mother's psychic energy which could not be expressed within the role of wife had only indirect outlets: how they went into migraines and menstrual cramps, into dreams for her daughters, and somewhat sentimental poetry, into a slightly hysterical preference for her own playfulness and spontaneity, and into her sensitivity to feeling and intuition.)

In his essay on the mother archetype, C. G. Jung says daughters must come to recognize "the human being who is our mother" as the "accidental carrier" of the archetype.[9] Yet, as Greek mythology suggests, the Great Mother has many guises; each of the goddesses gives a different archetypal perspective to motherhood. All of them may enter into our relation to the archetype, but probably each of us bears the mark all of our life long of the particular goddess who first initiated us into the realm of the mothers. (Though it is too simple to understand our mother "imago" as direct transmission of what was objectively the case in our childhood history.) Neither Hera nor either of her Olympian sisters represent the full scope of mothering encompassed by the earlier mother-goddesses. In Rome, Hera's spinster sister, Hestia (as Vesta), became the symbol of idealized maternity. Mothering in Hestia's realm is radically differentiated from biological procreation; it is a warm and protective but essentially impersonal and impartial nurturing love. Demeter, on the other hand, represents an intensely partial devotion to her child. To be introduced first to the mother archetype as embodied by Demeter is very different indeed from knowing mother first in her Hera aspect. For Demeter's existence is defined by her relation to her daughter; the relationship to the child's father is really incidental. So basic is the antagonism between Hera and Demeter that in Athens the temple of one goddess would be closed whenever that of the other was open. (My own mother's delight in having her first daughter born on the first day of spring expressed in part, I imagine, her fantasy that if I were Persephone, then she might be Demeter and not only Hera.)

Yet it is as Hera that I most often experienced her. For Hera the relation to husband takes precedence over all other relationships. At least on Olympus, whatever she may have been earlier, Hera was not the Great Mother but rather the spouse. That Hera is preeminently wife means that although she is a mother she is not mother as mother but mother as wife. The pervasive influence of this aspect of the mother on our entire lives is a central theme in Sigmund Freud's psychological vision. This is the mother whom we discover as already somebody's wife, the mother of the Oedipus triangle whose exclusive love we covet but will never receive.

In Hera's sphere wifehood and motherhood belong together. Sexuality is not primarily directed to ecstasy but to procreation; children are seen as the cocreation of wife and husband, as living embodiments of their bond. Thus, although Hera is a goddess of childbirth, she extends her aid only to mothers giving birth to legitimate children. She prohibited her daughter, Eileithyia, the divine midwife, from attending Alcemene when in labor with Herakles, and tried to keep her from assisting Leto when "for nine days and nine nights she was subjected to unimaginable pain," [10] struggling to give birth to Apollo. How different this is from Artemis's relation to childbirth which expresses her attachment to all that is young, wild, and vulnerable, and from Athene's which is directed toward insuring generational continuity, the future of the polis.

It follows that, unlike Demeter, Hera is in the classical period not a fertility goddess, though there are reminiscences of the cosmogonic holy marriage between earth goddess and sky king in Homer's description of Zeus's and Hera's lovemaking:

> So speaking, the son of Kronos caught his wife in his arms.
> There underneath them the divine earth broke into young,
> fresh grass, and into dewy clover, crocus and hyacinth so
> thick and soft it held the hard ground deep away from
> them. There they lay down together and drew about them
> a golden wonderful cloud, and from it the glimmering dew
> descended.[11]

Archaeological excavations have discovered a marriage bed in central place in Hera's temples, which suggests that ritual enactment of the sexual consummation of the marital bond played an important part in her cult. Nevertheless, the evocation of a passionate connection between Zeus and Hera as in the above passage from the *Iliad* is rare in the mythic and epic accounts. Indeed, the Hera of the myths seems so fearful of all that challenges the contained love of husband and wife that she often appears obsessively antisexual. Her opposition to Dionysos and his women devotees, the maenads, stems from her recognition that sexual ecstasy pulls women away from their husbands. Perhaps the fear is really directed toward her own repressed sexuality. There is a tale to the effect that at one time Zeus and Hera were debating whether men or women had greater pleasure from sexual intercourse. They called upon Tiresias, the only being who had lived as both male and female, to arbitrate their dispute. When he confirmed that women experience nine times more satisfaction, Hera was so infuriated that she blinded the seer on the spot.

Hera's absolute commitment and fidelity is at the very heart of her self-image. In the myths this is represented by the violence with which she rejects those men who dare to try to seduce her: Endymion is condemned to sleep eternally; Ixion to be chained forever to a revolving fiery wheel. Ephialtes is bound with snakes to a pillar, back to back with his twin brother Otus (one had dared to woo Artemis while the other pursued

Hera). Ceyx was turned into a bird for bragging that his wife was Hera. Hera's very faithfulness seems to provoke Zeus to test it. He filled the giant Porphyrion with lust for Hera and then killed him with a thunderbolt when he tried to rape her. He will not believe in Hera's report of Ixion's desire for her and her resistance, until he tricks the mortal into making love to a cloud shaped in the goddess's likeness.

Her faithfulness is a provocation to Zeus because it encompasses the demand that she should be loved for what she has sacrificed. In return for her renunciation, she expects absolute fidelity and is inevitably jealous of any other who receives his attention. Hera, as so many of the myths represent her, is a wife who always expects as her due a more total commitment from her husband than she will ever get. Her jealousy is most virulently evoked by Zeus's sexual involvements with other females, but Hera-women may be just as jealous of their spouse's devotion to parents or children, job or hobby. Truly to understand the Olympian Hera is to realize that Zeus's promiscuity is not her bad luck, not something that could have been different. That she experiences him as betraying her is the inevitable correlate of her own obsessive fidelity; it is a necessary part of being Hera so long as we see Hera, or she sees herself, only as woman defined by being wife. She projects onto her husband not only the sexuality but also the libido in the more extended Jungian sense that she has repressed in herself. We might note that actually Zeus's other involvements are all ephemeral dalliances; her primacy is never really threatened. Indeed, as Philip Slater suggests, perhaps Zeus's promiscuity, his flagrant display of sexual potency, can best be understood as an expression of his own insecurity.

Thus, although Zeus and Hera are supposed to represent the ideal patriarchal family, they seem to represent instead the tensions which undermine its stability. That there is something radically amiss here is also reflected in the remarkable lack of lawful offspring, particularly the lack of the lawful male heir so important to the perpetuation of patriarchy. Zeus and Hera are sister and brother before they are wife and husband; some of the strife between them has the flavor of unmitigated sibling rivalry. She is the elder, at least in Hesiod's account (in Homer's more patriarchal version, Zeus is the oldest of all Rhea's and Kronos's children). Sometimes Zeus turns to her as to a mother, as in Pausanias's account of their wooing which describes Zeus coming to Hera as a half-frozen cuckoo in search of shelter from the rain. Yet in a strange way Zeus plays a kind of mother or at least midwife role in Hera's life too. He is responsible for Kronos's vomiting up the five children he had swallowed in fear that one of them would overthrow him as Kronos had overthrown his own father, Ouranos. Thus it is through Zeus's intervention that she reenters the world.

Such overdetermination of relationships is obviously present, confusingly, in marriages in our world as well. Much of what happens within the Hera-Zeus marriage is contaminated by their prior histories. The myths emphasize that this divine couple is not the primordial couple, that they enter their marriage as persons already involved in a complex interpersonal system. Both Hera and Zeus are much more "human" than the previous generation of gods, the Titans; this may both facilitate our recognition of their pertinence to our own lives and betray us into seeing the connections too literally, too personally. Certainly it is easy for me to recognize aspects of my mother's marriage and of my own in this carry-over of childhood experience into the unconscious expectations and patterns of response that shape how Hera lives out wifeness.

Since Zeus began as his mother's pawn in her struggle against her husband, he not surprisingly inherits his father's anxiety that he, too, might someday be overthrown by one of his children. He enters marriage with Hera imbued by a distrust of matriarchal ambition, a fear of spouses who are mothers first and foremost. In none of the traditions is Hera his first consort. The goddesses with whom he is earlier involved more closely incarnate the Great Mother paradigm. The first two were his mother's sisters: Metis, the goddess of wisdom, who, according to prophecy, was destined to give birth to a son stronger than his father; and Themis, the goddess associated with the very existence of natural order. His union with Demeter was one in which he was used, as the earth mother has primordially used her male consorts. Dia (or Dione) whose name is simply the feminine form of Zeus's own suggests an almost opposite conception: a consort who has no individuality of her own, who exists only as Zeus's counterpart. Hera is the first (and only) *wife*. She is of the same generation as he and thus a putative equal. That she is somewhat older reflects the priority of the matriarchal order. It may also be a way of compensating (mythically) for the inferiority within a patriarchal order of female to male and thus of emphasizing the mutuality and equality toward which this marriage is ideally directed. Zeus turns to Hera as spouse—but perhaps he never quite trusts her not to be the Great Mother after all.

Zeus may have been contaminated by a childhood spent too exclusively in the female realm, with his mother and grandmother and their nymphs, and thus have grown up with the typical mother's son's anxieties about his ability to ever fulfill her expectations or to be more than her phallus, the instrument of her power. Similarly, Hera may have spent too much of her early life swallowed up by her father. Losing her mother too soon may have provoked in her (as perhaps it did in Athene, as well) what Jung calls a negative mother complex, an overidentification with her own masculine, aggressive side. Those years spent in Kronos's stomach may also be connected to her oral conception of love as meaning swallowing or being swallowed, containing or being contained. Hera grows up expecting from men the nurturing and confirmation for which many women turn to other females. Perhaps those years in Kronos's womb are analogous to the experience all of us have of growing up in a male-ordered world—though obviously our responses to that may vary as much as do Hera's and Demeter's. Initially Hera seems to have turned to Zeus for the sake of her own self-completion. Here she expresses a primary narcissism that involves the longing for a return to the *father's* womb. Her possessiveness and jealousy represent her resentment that he is not entirely hers. The early loss of her mother shows in the power of her fear of abandonment—clearly an extrarational fear since, despite his many affairs, there is never any real danger of Zeus leaving her. This fear is evident on the part of her sisters as well, though expressed differently—in Hestia's refusal to make the kind of personal commitment that would expose her to abandonment, in Demeter's convulsive reaction to Persephone's abduction.

Both Zeus and Hera were brought up with a heavy emphasis on the contrasexual, perhaps responsible for the strong pull each feels toward psychological androgyny, toward an in-one-self-ness that encompasses their feminine and masculine potentialities. Each, for example, is represented as tempted to parthenogenetic creation of offspring. The sons Hera has without the aid of any father are, as we shall see, clearly expressions of her own unconscious masculinity, of her "animus." These sons seem to merit some of the denigration so often associated with that Jungian term. Zeus's children, Dionysos and Athene may be more successful creations—but then they were originally conceived in female wombs before being transplanted for a final period of incubation in his. Claims to parthenogenetic capability are not entirely foreign to our experience either. It is not only Zeus or Hera who wish to see "our" children as just "my" children.

As I look back on my own childhood, I remember not only how my mother encouraged my identification with Persephone (and thus indirectly suggested that my sexuality, my pull toward men, represented an abduction from my true being) but also how my father inspired me to imagine myself as an Athene—another sexless virgin but one wholly and proudly identified with the world of men, a brave and victorious warrior, clear-eyed, rational, practically creative, never possessed by emotion or passion. Each liked to imagine me as being really only *their* child. Both seemed to wish to protect me from Hera. Though they could not succeed, perhaps because the one thing forbidden is always the one thing we must have, they may have had much to do with Hera's never having been my only goddess. I am well aware of the same pull in myself. I remember how important it was to have as my own secret for a time the conception of our first child, and how equally important it was to give birth to our last without my husband's participation. And, of course, the pull to have our children be mine was there in other than these literal ways.

In mythology another typical symbol of androgynous yearning is brother-sister incest. This, too, is present in the Hera-Zeus traditions. When they have intercourse together, they do so without their parents' knowledge. The secrecy may represent something unconscious in their connection, and the unconsciousness may signify a regressive return to a lost undifferentiated wholeness. To believe that we have long ago transcended the longing for fusion may for any of us always be, in part, illusion. Become conscious, incest longing symbolizes what Jung calls the *mysterium coniunctionis*—the goal of the individuation process.

The relation between Hera and Zeus has in it elements that express the pull in any marriage to escape differentiation and also elements that pertain to the longing for participation in a match between two self-fulfilled persons—but primarily it reflects the struggle that ensues when both partners are confusedly and contradictorily trying to realize both aims. Their relationship also illustrates how this struggle is exacerbated in a patriarchally determined marriage where the wife will almost inevitably become pathologically possessive and jealous.

There is no doubt about it—Hera's jealousy *is* pathological. Indeed, in some sense Hera *is* this jealousy. As Jung said, the gods (and goddesses) have become diseases. Hera's jealousy is a goddess's jealousy; it is divine jealousy, eternal, a mystery. In fact, it may be precisely in her jealousy that the Olympian Hera is divine, as Demeter is divine in her grief, Persephone in her rapedness, Ariadne in her desertion. To understand Hera means going into this dark side, not to cure but to interpret. This means recognizing that Hera's jealousy is a particular mode of jealousy, intertwined with all that she is, not an isolated symptom. Hera's spousal jealousy is different, indeed, from Artemis's jealous regard for her own purity and that of her nymphs, different from the jealousy Aphrodite directs toward females who threaten to rival her beauty, and also different from Demeter's jealousy of anyone who might separate her daughter from her.

Though provoked by Zeus, Hera's jealousy is most actively directed into persecution of his mistresses and their children: Semele and Dionysos, Alcmene and Herakles, Io and Epaphus. She seems not to discriminate between those who knowingly welcome Zeus into their arms and those who like Io energetically resist his advances or who like Callisto and Alcemene were deceived by the god's coming to them disguised. That her anger is played out against women suggests that much of it may still be directed against her own (and Zeus's) mother—and against her own feminine identity. The Hera of Olympus does not like women—or being a woman—at all. She is singularly without any positive relation to other females—except for the two daughters whom she completely dominates. They are perfect examples of that form of the mother complex which Jung describes as leading into identification with the mother and to paralysis of the daughter's feminine initiative: "A complete projection of her personality then takes place, owing to the fact that she is unconscious both of her maternal instinct and of her Eros. . . . As a sort of superwoman (admired involuntarily by the daughter), the mother lives out for her beforehand all that the girl might have lived for herself. . . . The daughter leads a shadow existence, often visibly sucked dry by her mother and she prolongs her mother's life by a sort of continuous blood transfusion." [12] (The only female with whom Hera seems ever to have joined forces is that other male-identified goddess, Athene: these two once joined Poseidon against Zeus; they were both strongly supportive of the Greeks during the Trojan War.) Hera's obsession with the other women in Zeus's life may reflect a subliminal recognition of how important they are to her, how in some way they represent otherwise unknown aspects of her own being.

Hera's gynephobia like her jealousy is part of what makes her unattractive to women and makes us reluctant to recognize her role in our lives. It may help to remember that Hera is pertinent to our lives not only if we see ourselves as identified with her, but also if we find ourselves in the world defined from her perspective. To recognize ourselves in her daughters, her sisters, or her rivals is to discover how inescapably her world is our world. I, for example, have much more often found myself to be the object of "the wife's" jealousy than the jealous wife; nevertheless, it is Hera's jealousy that has invaded my life. How reluctant I have been to acknowledge my participation in a too often repeated scenario, and to admit how my side (like Hera's) expresses a too little heeded misogyny. Because I have, for the most part, demanded that others live my jealousy for me, I have been nearly overwhelmed in those moments when my own jealousy flashes up and I receive intimation of the strength of my own possessiveness and fear of abandonment.

The divineness of Hera's jealousy is confirmed by Freud's conviction that we can understand jealousy best from its pathological manifestations because in all of us jealousy assumes some pathological characteristics. Perhaps there is no wholly "normal" jealousy, no jealousy that is "completely rational, that is, derived from the actual situation, proportionate to the real circumstances and under the complete control of the conscious ego." [13]

In its root sense, which Freud wants to return us to, pathology means woundedness. He hopes to bring us back in touch with that in each of us which has been wounded, hurt, and abandoned, that which still cries and rages. We have all been deprived of the mother's breast, we all have had to give up our claim for exclusive possession of her. Mostly, we have forgotten these childhood longings and losses, and especially how much feeling was attached to them. We have little sense of the strength of these jealousy impulses, of the tenacity with which they persist, and of the magnitude of their influence on later life.

Jealousy is "regressive," immature; but at some level every one of us is still a child, as well as the adult we pride ourselves on having become. The memories and the over-intense feelings persist. We continue to respond emotionally in ways that are exaggerated, are not appropriate to a rational response to situations, and are perhaps not even based on a realistic assessment of them. In us, too, there is something that wants to "kill" the one who has usurped our place (as in childhood we dream of murdering a father or younger brother) or the one who has proven "faithless" (as the mother was when we were infants). In all of us there still lives the child's unregarding possessiveness—the longing for an absolute, certain, and exclusive love. Each of us still experiences the child's greedy passivity, its conviction that love means receiving love. The child is "narcissistic," is unquestioningly its own preferred love-object, and so are all of us." [14]

We are more interested in what Hera's jealousy tells us about her (and about us) than in what it may reveal about Zeus. Much of its passion derives from the intensity with which she has repressed direct expression of her own sexuality: she projects onto Zeus the fulfillment of her own denied desires. Her jealousy may also include penis envy not just in the narrow sense of envy of Zeus's genital potency but its deeper meaning as resentment of his unrestrained freedom and aggressive power. In a sense her jealousy is an overt expression of her otherwise repudiated masculinity since in it she moves from feminine passivity to forceful activity. Her jealousy is a kind of fantasy activity that both expresses and disguises her deepest wishes and fears.

Freud refers often to the importance of the "third" in provoking psychic life. The dyad, whether it unites mother and infant or husband and wife, tends to be static. It is often characterized more by fusion than by genuine relating; the arrival of the third (father or mistress) forces differentiation, change, movement. Perhaps this is why the relationship between Hera and Zeus seems most alive when she is stirred to jealousy. It is her jealousy that provokes her to creative activity in the form of parthenogenetic procreation; it is also her jealousy that finally leads her to leave Zeus—not for another lover but for her own self-renewal, the re-creation of her virginity, her one-in-self-ness. In his essay "Marriage as a Psychological Relationship," Jung says: "Seldom or never does a marriage develop into an individual relationship smoothly or without crisis. There is no birth of consciousness without pain. . . . Disunity with oneself begets discontent, and since one is not conscious of the real state of things, one generally projects the reasons for it upon one's partner. A critical atmosphere thus develops, the necessary prelude to conscious realization." [15] From this perspective Hera's jealousy is a painful initiation into the realization that Zeus cannot bring her to fulfillment after all, that she has projected onto him her own unlived masculinity, her animus (and thence, Jung would say, stems the "animosity" between them).

Initially when Hera discovers that Zeus will not or cannot complete her, cannot be her animus, she looks to her male children to fulfill that role. Hera's and Zeus's relation to their children reflects the power struggle continually going on between them. From Hera's perspective, children express the bond between their parents, but when that bond is fragile there is a temptation to use them to strengthen the hold the parents have on each other; when the bond seems constraining, they are used in the parents' struggle to be independent of each other. Children born to such a marriage grow up resentful at not receiving the unstinted love from either parent for which they long; they are pulled into fighting on one side or another or into believing it is up to them to establish a reconciliation.

Though Hera's daughters are biologically Zeus's as well, they are clearly, as we have already indicated, psychologically completely identified with her—their bloodlessness suggesting what an exclusively feminine Hera, unshadowed by her masculine longings, might have been like. Concerning her sons' parentage there is, however, considerable ambiguity. According to Homer, Ares and Hephaistos are Zeus's children as well as hers, but in other accounts they (and also Typhaon) are hers alone. The twofold genealogies tell us that we stand here at the meeting of matriarchal and patriarchal culture. There is symbolic meaning in both accounts. Both Ares and Hephaistos represent the relationship between Zeus and Hera: Ares, its unmitigated tension; and Hephaistos, its creative possibilities. These sons image this relationship as experienced from *her* side. Even in those traditions which make Zeus their natural father, he rejects them as "really" Hera's—he flings Hephaistos out of heaven for siding with her and dismisses Ares for mirroring her mindless delight in battle for its own sake.

The stories that represent these gods as Hera's children alone view their creation as an expression of her rage at Zeus. They are both substitutes for her husband and part of her battle against him. No wonder that each of them suffers from some obvious deformity, that the parthenogenetic mother is the pathogenic mother as well.

This is most clear in the case of Typhaon, a horrible creature endowed with a hundred burning snake heads, who became Zeus's most dangerous adversary. That this monster is sometimes said to be Gaia's child rather than Hera's only underscores that here Hera is involved in trying to repeat her mother's and grandmother's attempts to use their sons to overthrow their husbands. In Hera's case the project failed (because of her bad luck or Zeus's good fortune—that is, because of luck-bringing Hermes' intervention). The fear of such a subjugation haunts Zeus—it lies behind his swallowing Metis and then giving birth himself to her first child, Athene, as though this were proof that

> *There can
> be a father without any mother. There she stands,
> the living witness, daughter of Olympian Zeus,
> she who was never fostered in the dark of the womb
> yet such a child as no goddess could bring to birth.*[16]

Hera's response to Athene's birth is to bear Hephaistos parthenogenetically. (The peculiarities of mythic chronology are evident in that Hephaistos is also represented as having split open Zeus's head with an ax to make Athene's emergence possible.) Much ambiguity is evoked by this god. In his artistry he makes manifest the sublimated creativity which in Hera herself remains frustrated. An Orphic hymn celebrates him as a gentle and gifted artist, creator of Achilles' intricately worked shield, the magnificent Olympian palaces, and of the first human female, Pandora. Steady and trustworthy, distressed by the strife between his parents, he longs to serve as a peacemaker between them. The *Iliad* shows him as acutely sympathetic to his mother's painful discontent, yet asking her not to allow it to possess her:

> All the Uranian gods in the house of Zeus were troubled. Hephaistos the renowned smith rose up to speak among them, to bring comfort to his beloved mother, Hera of the white arms: "This will be a disastrous matter and not endurable if you two are to quarrel thus for the sake of mortals and bring brawling among the gods. There will be no pleasure in the stately feast at all, since vile things will be uppermost. And I entreat my mother, though she herself understands it, to be ingratiating toward our father Zeus, that no longer our father may scold her and break up the quiet of our feasting. For if the Olympian who handles the lightning should be minded to hurl us out of our places, he is far too strong for any. Do you therefore approach him again with words made gentle, and at once the Olympian will be gracious again to us."
>
> He spoke, and springing to his feet put a two-handled goblet into his mother's hands and spoke again to her once more: "Have patience, my mother, and endure it, though you be saddened, for fear that, dear as you are, I see you before my own eyes struck down, and then sorry though I be I shall not be able to do anything. It is too hard to fight against the Olympian." [17]

This gentle introverted son who deliberately backs away from anything resembling strife echoes in exaggerated form Hera's own overt denial of the will to power. He represents all that is self-immobilizing in her, as demonstrated by the tale of his sending her a golden throne from which she cannot extricate herself. Animus-ridden women often seem drawn to such sensitive, creative men—but also drawn to destroy them. Hephaistos is her crippled animus, an expression of her own thwarted masculine energies. He was created in anger and born lame. One story has it that Hera found his disfigurement so disgusting that she threw him from heaven when he was born. She rejects this side of herself even in projected form. Whether thrown out by father or mother, he lands on Lemnos and grows up there. It cannot be accidental that the most noteworthy period in the history of this island was that during which it was ruled by bloodthirsty women who had slain their fathers and husbands—an anticonjugal (indeed, *post*conjugal) community, strikingly consonant with Hera's most vengeful fantasies. Hephaistos's marriage to Aphrodite who of course cuckolds him (most flagrantly by her affair with his brother, Ares) seems cruelly designed to make us discern in his crippledness some essential emasculation. Yet the tale, according to which he designed an invisible golden net which trapped the lovers in view of all the other gods, suggests a resourcefulness and a resilient sense of humor which allowed him to triumph over Ares after all. There is something about Hephaistos which inspires rejection, and yet his creativity remains unquenched. Aroused by his unsuccessful pursuit of Athene, he ejaculates against her leg; from the semen which falls to the ground grows Erichthonios, the progenitor of the Athenians.

Like his brother, Ares represents Hera's repressed masculinity but quite differently. As god of war, of delight in strife and destruction for its own sake, he is the embodiment of her instinctual rage allowed full sway.

> Lord, Ares, yours is the din of arms, and
> ever bespattered by blood
> you find joy in killing and in the
> fray of battle, O horrid one. [18]

The first being, mortal or divine, to be tried for murder, he is hated even by the gods, even by his own parents. Despite his lust for battle, he is represented as singularly unsuccessful, regularly defeated by the much more clearheaded Athene and also by less divine opponents such as Otus and Ephialtes, Herakles and Diomedes. Ares represents a self-defeating hypermasculinity. (Perhaps this underlies the man-hating Amazons' claims to be descended from him.) Although he has liaisons with many women and sires countless children, he never marries. The most important female in his life (as in his b other's) is Aphrodite—whose unfettered indulgence of her own sexuality makes her, in Jungian terms, Hera's shadow side. Though Aphrodite was married to Hephaistos, her union with Ares was more fruitful. Their children include Deimos (Panic) and Phobos (Fear) but also Eros and Harmonia—when united with love, Ares' instinctuality becomes creative.

Perhaps we should also at least refer to Hera's singularly complicated relation to one of her "stepsons," Herakles, whose whole life, as his name suggests, is defined by his relationship to her. It may well be that originally (before her cultic association with Zeus) Herakles was Hera's male counterpart, the son-lover-victim traditionally associated with the archaic mother-goddess. Despite her implacable enmity toward him, she was at one point tricked into suckling him at her breast. This episode may be a dim echo of an earlier tradition according to which she is his mother, a tradition also suggested by his marriage to Hebe, Hera's double-as-daughter, after the death by fire of all that is mortal in him. In any case, in the classical myths he is the paradigmatic hero, compulsively undertaking one trial after another in his hopeless attempt to fulfill the negative mother's expectations and demands. Like Ares and Hephaistos, he is both an extension of Hera and object of her persecution.

Hera's children, as we have already noted, cannot be understood as products of the Great Mother's boundless and essentially impersonal fertility. They are very clearly the children of this particular, highly differentiated Olympian goddess—the children of Hera-as-spouse, the children in that sense of Hera and Zeus. Hera is preeminently wife, her mothering is defined by that more fundamental (in her life) role. Zeus, from most perspectives, is more father than husband. He is the father of gods and men, the paradigmatic patriarchal ruler. Though essentially a political role, the fatherhood is also expressed in Zeus's having many biological children both divine and human. But, though his union with Hera is *the* marriage of Olympus, it is strikingly infertile. Hera *will* not see him as father, will not even allow him to be father to her children; she wants him simply as husband, as Zeus Heraios. When confronted by Hera, Zeus's dominance is never secure. They struggle continually. The classical accounts say plainly: if being wife means being dominated by a male, then being wife means being unhappy, jealous, and vindictive. Part of what emerges from reflection on those accounts is the conviction that if one stays in marriage as defined by patriarchy, one becomes *that* Hera.

Zabriskie speaks of Hera as a "restless matriarch in a patri-archal world." [19] To recover the full meaning of Hera for con-temporary women demands that we examine more carefully Hera's connection to the pre-Homeric matriarchal tradition.[20] What might have led an ancient mother-goddess to become Zeus's spouse? Sociologically, of course, we can explain this as the mythological correlate of the synthesis of two cults, but there is more to it than that: Hera is in some unique way the mother-goddess ready-to-become-spouse. This is one of those points where reflection on my own life experience opens me to an understanding of an aspect of the myth that had remained opaque apart from that correlation—in contrast to those many other times when it is recognition of the parallel to some mythic pattern that makes visible the significance of some fragment of personal history. I find I can understand Hera very well as an embodiment of that moment when a woman discovers intui-tively that she does not want only lover-victims. She does not want from a male only the phallus as the necessary instrument of her fertilization or for the experience of her own passion. She wants another who is "man" as fully as she is "woman"; in some sense she is only fully woman if thus met. We might speak of this as the move from the narcissistic world of dream to the world of actual others, the world of I and Thou. Murray Stein has this in mind when he speaks of Hera in terms of a "mating instinct" and asserts that "the *telos* of Hera is *gamos.*" [21] Though his language does not feel quite right to me, I agree with Stein that what pulls Hera to Zeus is not really sexual longing. The longing has a political element which represents Hera's hope for a matching of power. (We should remember that Hera's promise to Paris is sovereignty and wealth.) She wants to be fully met, matched, mated—sexually, yes, but more importantly, psychologically. (I am half-embarrassed to recall now how ripe I was for marriage when I was a bride, how though I had gone to college as Athene, I left, to my own surprise, as Hera.

Yet it seems important to remember and acknowledge that: to feel again what it was like to need to live being wife *now* as an imperative as impelling as is orgasm when one is at its brink, to recall the certainty of that conviction: "I am living exactly what I was created to live.")

To understand this longing is to understand Hera from within. We are introduced here to marriage not as something imposed by patriarchy but as something fulfilling a deep longing of women themselves. This understanding of marriage underlies the fact that in Greek cultic life the *gamos,* the wedding, was part of the Hera cult, not part of the Zeus religion. As Kerenyi observes: "The historical phenomenon is this. In Athens, a city that worshiped as its supreme goddess Pallas Athene—the virgin associated with the father and representing patriarchal ideas—the contracting of marriage . . . was a sacred act owed to Hera and performed in her honor. This was completely determined by a way of thinking dominant in matriarchal societies, a way of thinking that Hera embodied." [22]

Hera represents that moment of transition between matriarchy and patriarchy when both mother-right and father-right are honored. This is a moment the myths never catch; in a sense it is a moment that never happens except in Hera's fantasy. Because all that is ever visible is the move from one exclusive claim to the other, in the myths Hera is represented as the goddess who has capitulated. Somehow even in the myths both Heras are present: the one connected to patriarchy and the archaic one. Both are present in the myths—and in us: the one who chooses marriage and the one who works to undermine it. Inevitably this is confusing, to Hera *and* to Zeus, to husband and to wife. The fantasies of swallowing him and making his power her own or of losing herself in him are inevitably intermingled with the fantasy of being truly met. This does not mean that the first are somehow "realistic" fantasies and the latter pure illusion.

I see Hera as poised between the two worlds, as the goddess ready to move from the female-dominated world because it is a world which does not truly fulfill her as a female. She stands for the transition from in-one-self-ness to *hieros gamos,* in response to a vision of a *coniunctio* that is neither dissolution nor battle.

She is never just Hera Teleia but is also Hera Parthenos; the two belong together not as subsequent stages but as coexistent, mutually illuminating aspects of who Hera *is*. The narrative temporality of myth necessarily obscures this. Focusing on the married-to-Zeus aspect of Hera's life without recognizing how she is still also the virginal Hera misrepresents her. Cult with its recognition that the transition from one phase to the other happens repeatedly opens us to a deeper understanding. Ritually Hera renews her virginity annually when she immerses herself in the spring of Kanathos near Nauplion; ritually Hera is never only the Hera of Olympus but the pre-Olympian Hera as well. Kerenyi describes how at Paestum there were two sanctuaries belonging to the goddess used by the same cultic community; each was dedicated to one of the goddess's aspects, the rites involving a procession from one to the other.[23] (Hera's ability to rejuvenate herself, to recover her virginity is echoed in Hebe's restoration of the youth of Iolaus.)

Hera represents that in virginity which longs for conjunction as part of its own nature and that in *coniunctio* which looks back nostalgically toward in-one-self-ness as part of its own nature. Clearly, just as there are several different ways of being mother, there is more than one mode of virginity. Artemis's entire withdrawal from contact with the world of men is different indeed from Athene's sisterly ease in their company. That Hera's virginity is a virginity directed toward marriage is implicit in Kerenyi's reference to the union between Hera and Zeus as corresponding "to possibilities stored up in the original character of each of the two deities."[24] He also says that in the case of Hera: "Parthenos and Pais, 'virgin' and 'girl' . . . by no means had the simple meaning of being without a man, without the brother-husband! Rather these names meant secret lovemaking with him. . . . In Hera the *woman and wife* was always present from the beginning, in all the forms of a woman's loving fancy, without her thereby becoming polygamous."[25] Zeus thus is imaged precisely as the fulfiller of the virgin's "loving fancy," of her own fantasies—as the one who brings her to perfection as a consort unlike the passive males associated with the archaic mother-goddesses.

Hera's pathos is that after her marriage she finds that Zeus is not Zeus after all, is not the fully equal other, the perfectly matched other, she had imagined him to be. As Stein puts it: "Zeus thwarts Hera in a specific way, i.e., he will not allow her to find her 'perfection' and fulfillment in *gamos*. He will not be married to her in more than a token way, nor allow her to be deeply married to him." [26] The Hera-Zeus struggle appears inevitable, and yet one also feels that both really know better, both really mean something else, want something different. Reflection on their union brings us to an appreciation of the "dialectical content" of marriage, of its "progressive as well as regressive aspects, helps us see monogamy not simply as human oppression but as the attempt at a sustained relation between two people." [27]

It was only as I came to understand this that I began also to comprehend why there are not just two Heras but three. All coexist and mutually define one another. Hera is not only Parthenos and Teleia; there is also Hera Chera, Hera the solitary, unbound, widowed or divorced, no longer married. Hera represents not only the transition to marriage but the transition beyond. Here my reading of Hera (perhaps because I am a woman) is radically different from Stein's who sees Hera Chera as representing the ugly, unhappy phase of Hera's life. Though of course I agree with Kerenyi that this is its most dangerous phase— dangerous to men, that is, and to patriarchy. It is dangerous also to women as any phase that implies radical transformation must be, but many women would want to reinvoke "the increased religious valuation of this lowest phase" [28] which Kerenyi describes as occurring in the late classical period. Stein's interpretation seems to proceed from an entirely negative view of Hera's jealousy and possessiveness, which no longer seems adequate to me, and to issue in a therapy which would aim at making Hera content in her marriage. I have come to see journeys into dark places in a different way. Freud took the line which stands at the beginning of *The Interpretation of Dreams* from Virgil's Hera, Juno: "If I cannot bend the gods to my will, I shall move the underworld." This emphasis on the turn to the underworld thus marks the point of initiation into depth psychology.

The mythological version of Hera's separation from Zeus says that, when she could take his infidelities no longer, she left him and returned to her birthplace in Euboea. I understand her departure as providing the distance between them that might allow each to rediscover the fantasy, the hope that had brought them together in the first place. Perhaps Hera had only really discovered her essential aloneness *within* the relationship, and could only learn what genuine relationship might be in solitude. The separation can be understood as the necessary prelude to what Jung would call a genuinely psychological marriage. The divorce is thus an integral part of the shared history and, even more important, an essential aspect of Hera's being. According to the myth, Zeus and Hera come together again afterward. When he is unable to persuade her to return, he approaches Mount Cithaeron in the company of a veiled female statue and it is announced that he is about to marry a local princess. When Hera discovers the ruse, she is amused and reconciled to him. That smiling acceptance of him and of herself shows that something significant has changed between them.

Of course, such a return to marriage might not on the human level necessarily mean remarriage to the original spouse or remarriage at all. It may simply represent a recognition of how the pull to what Stein calls "deep marriage" continues to be important. On the other side of patriarchal marriage, the longing for a fully mutual and sustained primary relationship persists. It might lead toward a remarriage in which the partners can now truly accept and enjoy one another, or into a new marriage or deep love affair. It might lead into a genuinely fulfilling relationship with a woman rather than a man, or into an acceptance that something for which one deeply longs may not be granted. What Hera means is the strength not to pretend that some lesser gift is the fulfillment nor to deny the longing.

I suggested earlier how well Hera seems to fit Jung's picture of a woman with a negative mother complex. When writing of such women, Jung says:

> As a pathological phenomenon this type is an unpleasant, exacting and anything but satisfactory partner for her hus-

band, since she rebels in every fibre of her being against everything that springs from natural soil. However, there is no reason why increasing experience of life should not teach her a thing or two. . . . Her own masculine aspirations make it possible for her to have a human understanding of the individuality of her husband quite transcending the realm of the erotic. The woman with this type of mother complex probably has the best chance of all to make her marriage a success during the second half of life.[29]

Hera Chera is then still a Hera related to marriage, to deep relationship, *and* to in-one-self-ness, one who knows the costs of both. The in-one-self-ness on the far side of marriage is different from the maiden's innocent self absorption and immersion in her fantasies—it is an aloneness that includes within it being-with as both memory and hope. This is what I had in mind when I said at the beginning of this chapter that what began as a farewell to Hera became a greeting. Just when I had thought myself to be leaving her realm I found her waiting for me in a new phase of my life. Thereby I discovered not only a new understanding of Hera Parthenos and Hera Teleia as I viewed them from the perspective of Hera Chera but also learned something about myself for which I had not been prepared: how I am *now* and have always been related to Hera in all three of her aspects. I had not expected to experience at this point in my life an initiation into Hera's mysteries.

> *Here I sing of Hera*
> *She has a golden throne*
> *Rheia was her mother*
> *She is an immortal queen*
> *Hers is the most eminent of figures*
> *She is the sister*
> *she is even the wife*
> *of Zeus thunderer*
> *She is glorious*
> *All the gods on vast Olympos*
> *revere her,*

They honor her

even equal to Zeus
the lover of lightning [30]

NOTES

1. Edwin Muir, "I Have Been Taught," in *Collected Poems* (New York: Oxford University Press, 1965), p. 302.

2. Irene Claremont de Castillejo, *Knowing Woman* (New York: Harper & Row, 1974), p. 157.

3. Carl Kerenyi, *Zeus and Hera* (Princeton, N.J.: Princeton University Press, 1975), p. 114.

4. Jane Ellen Harrison, *Prolegomena to the Study of Greek Religion* (New York: Meridian Books, 1957), pp. 315ff.

5. Carl Kerenyi, *The Religion of the Greeks and Romans* (New York: E. P. Dutton, 1962), p. 231.

6. *The Orphic Hymns,* trans. Apostoios N. Athanassakis (Missoula, Montana: Scholars Press, 1977), p. 27.

7. M.I. Finley, *The World of Odysseus* (New York: Meridian Books, 1959), p. 140.

8. C. S. Lewis, *Till We Have Faces* (Grand Rapids, Michigan: Wm. B. Eerdmans Publishing, 1956), pp. 249, 253.

9. C. G. Jung, *Archetypes of the Collective Unconscious,* CW 9, pt. 1 (Princeton, N.J.: Princeton University Press, 1969), par. 172.

10. *The Homeric Hymns,* trans. Charles Boer (Chicago: University of Chicago Press, 1970), p. 154.

11. *The Iliad of Homer* 14. 346–51, trans. Richmond Lattimore (Chicago: University of Chicago Press, 1951), p. 303.

12. Jung, *Archetypes,* par. 169.

13. Sigmund Freud, "Certain Neurotic Mechanisms in Jealousy, Paranoia, and Homosexuality," in *Collected Papers,* vol. 2 (New York: Basic Books, 1959), p. 232.

14. Christine Downing, "Jealousy: A Depth Psychological Perspective," in *Jealousy,* ed. Gordon Clanton and Lynn G. Smith (Englewood Cliffs, N.J.: Prentice-Hall, 1977), p. 74.

15. C. G. Jung, *The Development of Personality,* CW 17 (Princeton, N.J.: Princeton University Press, 1954), pars. 331, 331b.

16. Aeschylus, *The Eumenides* 662–66, in *The Complete Greek Tragedies,* vol. 1, *Aeschylus,* ed. David Grene and Richmond Lattimore (Chicago: University of Chicago Press, 1959), p. 158.

17. *Iliad of Homer* 1. 570–600, trans. Richmond Lattimore, pp. 74f.

18. *Orphic Hymns,* p. 87.

19. Philip Zabriskie, "Goddesses in Our Midst," *Quadrant*, Fall 1974, p. 38.

20. I do not intend to imply that matriarchy in the strict sociological sense ever obtained in Greece; I am referring to a mythology dominated by female divinities.

21. Murray Stein, "Hera Bound and Unbound," *Spring*, 1977, p. 107.

22. Kerenyi, *Zeus*, p. 108.

23. Kerenyi, *Zeus*, p. 93. See also hexagram 54 of the *I Ching*, "The Marrying Maiden," which echoes this vision of transitional energy embodying itself in coexistent stages.

24. Kerenyi, *Zeus*, p. 93.

25. Kerenyi, *Zeus*, p. 129.

26. Stein, "Hera Bound and Unbound," p. 111.

27. Russell Jacoby, *Social Amnesia* (Boston: Beacon Press, 1975), p. 111.

28. Kerenyi, *Zeus*, p. 122.

29. Jung, *Archetypes*, par. 184.

30. *The Homeric Hymns*, p. 10.

·V·

DEAR GREY EYES
A Revaluation of Pallas Athene

They said:
she is high and far and blind
in her high pride
but now that my head is bowed
in sorrow, I find
she is most kind.

H.D.[1]

It seemed simple at first. I had been invited to write on "the
woman artist" and understood this to mean that it was
time to attend to Athene, the goddess of artist and artisan, the prototype of the artistically creative woman. It
quickly became less simple. James Hillman says that once we
know at whose altar a question belongs we will know better the
matter of proceeding.[2] Perhaps it is also true that we discover
what our question is by finding ourselves before a particular
altar, or discover that the real questions are the ones addressed
to us. I had not realized until I heard the owl hoot outside my
window, as it does every night, how unwittingly I (who live on
Serpentine Drive with an olive tree shadowing my patio) had
been prepared for this encounter with the goddess whose
emblems are snake and owl and olive. I had not known how
challenging her questions to me (as to all women who aspire to
creative accomplishments) would be. Kindly but unflinchingly
she demands that I review how in my life I have balanced my
loyalties to mother and father, women and men, to the so-called

99

feminine and the so-called masculine aspects of myself. She asks about the alternating pull of work and relationships, friendship and solitude, ego and soul, femininity and creativity. It is time to begin to answer, she indicates, this goddess whom I have known and avoided for so long.

Athene is a goddess I once loved—entirely and innocently as perhaps one can love only in adolescence. She was all I wanted to be and I gave my soul to her—self-confident and courageous, clear-eyed and strong, intelligent and accomplished, judicious and fair. I delighted in her ability to make full use of the given possibilities in any situation, in her gift for deep friendship unentangled with the confusions of passion, in her pleasure in struggle and challenge. Her dedication to the world of art and culture, of clear thought and realized accomplishment, were important testimony to me of how a woman might order her life. I coveted for myself the love and respect she was given by her father and her ease in the world of men, her erect carriage and her long proud stride. She was for me (as Walter Otto names her), "the ever-near." [3] Had I known it then, I might have chosen as my song the Homeric hymn dedicated to her, whose opening lines are: "I begin to sing of Pallas Athene, the glorious goddess, bright-eyed, inventive, unbending of heart, pure virgin, savior of cities, courageous Tritogeneia." [4]

She was singularly important to me in high school and in college—years when I felt close to my father and his vision of me and distant from a mother who did not share my intellectual interests and ambitions. Once I got married, I felt I had left Athene's realm: I came to look back somewhat disparagingly on that youthful period and the goddess who had dominated it. Athene now seemed too cool and distant, too suspicious of the emotional and sensual, too extroverted and ambitious—too "heady," in a word. I understood her birth from Zeus's head as the perfect mythological expression of what was wrong with her: her overidentification with men and seeming denial of her own femininity. I felt with Jane Harrison, "We cannot love a goddess who on principle forgets the Earth from which she sprang; always from the lips of the Lost Leader we hear the shameful denial:

Head of Athene (from Piraeus)

National Archaeological Museum, Athens, V. and N. Tombazi

There is no mother bore me for her child,
I praise the Man in all things
　　(save for marriage),
Whole-hearted am I, strongly for the Father." [5]

I could still accept the appropriateness of Athene's role in my life earlier on, but was sure I had now left her behind.

Goddesses are not so easily dismissed. I am only now beginning to see how Athene has been present all through my life. There were periods along the way when that presence was evident: not only the years of adolescence, but again when I entered graduate school seven years after my marriage. There I rediscovered the excitement of fully exercising my intellectual and creative capacities and the delight of having these recognized by the fatherly teachers I respected and by the brotherly colleagues who accepted me as one of themselves. Much later, after the traumatic ending of a love affair, I began to come back to life again in response to Athene's beckoning. She came (as she often did of old) in the guise of a man, recalling me to the deep excitement of shared intellectual concerns, the passion inherent in the kind of competitive rivalry where each partner urges the other to high achievement, to consummated accomplishment. In that meeting of spirit with spirit, I felt myself come to myself again. But again there came a time when I felt something in me was not being nourished by my attendance at this altar. I needed separation from Athene and from the relationship; I needed soul and not just spirit. And so (not suspecting that she may offer both), I left.

Or so I thought. Now I better understand the pertinence of Hillman's question, "Can one close the door on the person who brought one to the threshold in the first place?" and recognize the inevitability of the negative response. Athene is still there, has always been. The ambivalence she arouses in me is a clue to her own paradoxical nature. Such ambivalence, not the radical alternation between wholehearted celebration and passionate disparagement, is appropriate response to a complexity I had undervalued. I only now begin to understand that the ambiguity is hers, not just mine. In my transition from self-sufficient

maiden to mother, I had discovered darkness in what had earlier appeared as Athene's light side. Only more recently have I
discovered the light hidden in the aspect of her which is usually
obscured. There is an aspect of Athene which is minimized in
the classical accounts and which she herself is represented as
repressing. To recover this aspect is to see her, not as a goddess
who has renounced her femininity but as one who teaches us to
recognize courage and vulnerability, creativity and receptivity
as equally feminine qualities. Jung has taught us that we may
first encounter the gods and goddesses as our diseases, our
pathologies. I had wanted to be free of Athene because I did
not want to be the animus-ridden woman I took her to be. What
had once appeared as a splendid ego-ideal had come to look like
malignant shadow, because the heroic ego itself (of which
Athene seemed the exemplary female image) had come under
suspicion. But that, to borrow another phrase of Hillman's, was
"to confuse neurotic foreground with archetypal background"
and to forget that the goddess's power and the wounds she
inflicts and suffers are deeply intertwined. To see this is to
understand both her and myself very differently.

As I recognize not only that Athene has been present all
along but that her presence permeates every aspect of my life, I
recall Otto's words:

> Always divinity is a totality, a whole world in its perfection.
> This applies also to the supreme gods, Zeus, Athena, and
> Apollo, the bearers of the highest ideals. None of them
> represents a single virtue, none is to be encountered in
> only one direction of teeming life; each desires to fill,
> shape, and illumine the whole compass of human existence
> with his peculiar spirit.[6]

To open myself to Athene's illumination means, I see, re-
visioning my whole life through her: an overwhelming and awesome task. "The facts do not change, but their order is given
another dimension through another myth. They are experienced differently; they gain another tale." [7] The kaleidoscope is
given yet another shake. What belongs and what is extraneous,

what is important and what trivial, how the different parts relate—all this is to be understood anew. Not that Hera's illumination or Demeter's is to be discounted; there are seemingly endless ways the tale can be told, no one better or "more conscious" than the others.

That Athene is the goddess of weaving seems newly pertinent as I accept the necessity of unweaving the stories as previously told and weaving yet another. It is somewhat consoling to bring to mind Arachne whose beautifully woven account of the Olympians' more scandalous erotic involvements so enraged Athene that she tore it into shreds, beat Arachne with her shuttle, and so frightened the poor woman that she hanged herself. This serves as a reminder that it might be dangerous to aim for perfection in my telling. I think of Penelope (whose marvelous skill in weaving was a gift of Athene's) finding she had to unweave each night what she had so gracefully woven during the day. So, too, even this story may not be my final weaving: I see my present telling as the gift I bring to Athene's altar, as each year (on the occasion of the ritual observance of her birthday, the Panathenaea) she was brought a peplos, an elaborately worked shawl, which had been carefully woven and embroidered during the preceding nine months.

For the fourth time I return to Athene, for the first time, perhaps, ready to look her straight in the eyes and discover who she is and who I am in her light—hoping this time for recognition and not just repetition. To do this is more frightening than I would have imagined, for it means looking at the hitherto least explored aspects of my life: the negative side of my love for my father, my ever-repeated tendency to divert energy from my own creative work into relationships, the still present temptation to understand my assertiveness and intellectual acumen as masculine attributes. I understand now that Athene does indeed wear the Gorgon-head on her aegis. I remember that when Tiresias accidentally came upon her naked while bathing, he was struck blind. I remember, also, that in recompense Athene granted him second sight, soul sight.

To second sight Athene is to see her as one who gives soul. Cult and myth represent her as the one who gives soul to works of art. She is often associated with both Hephaistos and Prometheus as a cocreator, most notably perhaps in the accounts of the creation of the first human beings.

> In the strange myth of Pandora, one of the few in which Greek divinities are presented as creative powers, it is Athena and Hephaestus who fashion and embellish the form of the mysterious maiden; and Athena again who gives her the gifts of the arts wherewith better to beguile the souls of men.[8]

Man was born, so Hesiod and Ovid tell us, when Prometheus first mixed together earth and rainwater and fashioned it into the likeness of the gods, and then Athene breathed life into the soul. (How I would love to see the sarcophagus relief described by Farnell in which Athene is represented as inserting the soul in the form of a butterfly into the newly formed human body.[9])

Athene is thus soul-giver, soul-maker.[10] As an anima figure, she is appropriately present in the Homeric hymn to Demeter playing in the meadow and gathering flowers in the company of those other animas, Persephone and Artemis and the nymphs. Yet Athene is an anima figure who may help us get past seeing anima primarily in contrasexual terms. Athene is not just a goddess who takes on the role of being a man's anima—she serves also, I am coming to recognize, as an anima image for women, and thus as a goddess who provides us women with a singularly confirming understanding of our own creative powers as feminine powers.

At first, Athene seems to embody the presupposition that creativity, its cultivation and discipline, its coming into realized, visible form, is not really feminine. Yet these attributes are hers and she is a female god, a *goddess*. As we begin to explore Athene's relation to the masculine and feminine, we discover that even the image of the androgyne does not do full justice to her divine femininity. Such exploration calls for a close examination of her relationships to men and to women, to father and mother, to Ares and Hephaistos, to the polis and the underworld. There is a two-sidedness to Athene which is recalled when we remember to call her by her full name: Pallas Athene.

It is true that many of the stories told about her represent her as the friend and counselor of men. (In fact, as Athene Phatria she was seen as the goddess of the Athenian male brotherhoods.) Unlike Hera who challenges men to impossible heroic feats or Aphrodite who seeks to seduce them away from their worldly responsibilities to the pleasure of sexual passion or Artemis who entices simply by her unavailability, Athene helps the men whom she befriends with their own projects. (The temptation for such an anima, to which Athene herself does not fall prey, is, of course, that the satisfaction of being welcomed as sister and companion may lead to a subtle subordination of one's own creativity.)

Athene gives courage and confirmation, the sudden bright idea or the seasoned reflection. She does not actively take command over the men whom she supports but brings them into touch with their own highest potentiality. Thus, in the *Iliad,* when Achilles rashly moves forward to attack Agamemnon, Athene (visible only to him) holds him back and gives him that moment in which he can recall himself. As Walter Otto shows, in her affectionate care of Herakles, in her always appearing to him at the right moment as the true counselor and helper, she represents "the nearness of the divine at the moment of severest trial." [11] In a dream she offers Bellerophon the golden bridle which will enable him to capture Pegasus, the winged horse, for whom he had yearned since his youth. She advises Perseus how to go about fulfilling his rash boast of being able to overpower the Gorgon, Medusa.

Her closest involvement is with her protégé, Odysseus, whose integrity she helps to preserve as she gently encourages or restrains at every critical moment during the long years of combat at Troy. She is to him the one "who always stands beside me in all my tasks and always remembers me wherever I go." [12] She comes to him in many guises, as herself or as stranger or as friend. Not surprisingly, her favorite disguise is to come to him (as also to Telemachus) "likening herself in voice and appearance to Mentor," Odysseus's childhood friend. Indi-

rectly, she thus evokes the "brotherhood" they share and seems
to suggest a time "when we two were boys together." Her trust
sustains him during his many-yeared journey back to Ithaca,
even though she does not directly appear. She comes and
goes, ever near yet clearly distinct, with a life of her own apart
from him.

She wants Odysseus to remain true to himself, to maintain his
sense of balance, his reasonableness, his skepticism about
heroic glory, his optimism. Odysseus is a survivor. Adventures
have their appeal, but homecoming matters more. The concrete
pleasures of his everyday life in Ithaca have more power for him
than abstractions like glory and duty. He is prudent and daring,
resourceful and sometimes devious, skillful in practical arts, and
eloquent in debate. Though liable to outbursts of passion, he
has learned to temper feeling with reason.

In all this, he is much like the goddess who cares for him: her
masculine counterpart. Athene and Odysseus are, as she knows,
deeply bonded by a profound psychological similarity. "Of all
mankind thou art easily foremost both in counsel and speech,
and among all gods I win fame for my counsel and cleverness."
As she is at ease among men, so is he trusted by women and
comfortable with them. He is not identified with the masculine
world as this is represented by the heroic possibilities of the war
at Troy; he tries very hard to avoid going and is determined to
return home.

Because there is nothing possessive in Athene's love for
Odysseus, its naturally extends to include his son and his wife.
Thus her presence brings about Telemachus's transition from
youth to adult:

> For years he has been the young boy, observing in passive
> indignation the depredations of the suitors, childishly irri-
> tated with the ineffectual conduct of his mother but with
> no idea of ever asserting himself against her. Athene dis-
> guised as a visiting stranger, Mentes, awakens Telemachus
> to the thought that he is now a man by treating him as one.
> You ought to do something, she says. And Telemachus
> responds by following through with all her suggestions. He
> challenges the suitors, instructs his mother to return to her

own apartment while he takes care of what needs to be done, and sets out on a voyage to track down information about his father.[13]

She not only endows Penelope with her skill in weaving but with clear understanding and wit surpassing that of any other Greek woman. Athene appears to Nausicaa in a dream and thereby prepares this young maiden for the initiation into womanhood to be effected by her encounter with Odysseus.

Although Athene's intimate connections with women are often unnoticed, to disregard them is to identify her with an exclusive bonding with men that is (as the reference to Penelope and Nausicaa suggests) foreign to her. How easily we are pulled to overlook this, to pull her into our struggle about male identification, to project onto her our ambivalence about women bonding with women. We use her as our scapegoat, when she might instead offer us a more complex image of the creative woman than is otherwise available. That she spends her leisure hours, her own time, in the company of women is suggested by the account of her playing in the meadow with Persephone and the nymphs and by the tale that it was while she was bathing with her favorite nymph, Chariclo, that Tiresias accidentally came upon her naked. These accounts seem to imply that Athene's essential self is a with-women self—a vision of Athene that has only recently become apparent to me.

I therefore now attach much more importance than I had earlier to her close childhood friendship with Pallas, daughter of the sea god Triton by whom Athene was reared. One day as they were playing together, testing each other's skill at fencing, Athene inadvertently killed her foster sister. Grief stricken, she made a wooden image of Pallas which was at first set up on Olympus and later placed in the heart of the citadel of Troy. (Eventually the word "palladium" comes to refer to any statue of Athene in her aspect of protectress of the polis.) After the death of her friend, Athene becomes Pallas Athene. Pallas is more than an epithet or an attribute; as Guthrie says, "The one is her name as much as the other." [14] Though it may be that originally Pallas was a warrior goddess among the invading

Greeks who was then united with the Athene of Mycenean times, in classical Greece Athene *is* Pallas Athene. The double name suggests her two-sidedness: she is a goddess who has her own anima, who is spirit and soul.

"Pallas," so Kerenyi tells us, is a word for maiden but not just an equivalent of "Kore"; it suggests a robust, fierce maidenliness. "A distinct masculinity seems to adhere to this word even in its feminine form." [15] Kerenyi sees the term as referring to Athene's "androgyny," the androgyny celebrated in the Orphic hymn to Athene where she is described as "male and female, begetter of war, counselor, she-dragon of many shapes." [16] I, on the other hand, see androgyny as misrepresenting the inner meaning of Athene's being Pallas Athene. Perhaps the whole point of Pallas Athene is to help us transcend the facile equation of strength and courage and worldly wisdom with masculinity irrespective of the gender of the bearer of these attributes. I see Pallas's strength and independence as precisely womanly, related to her being a virgin in the sense made familiar by Esther Harding: in-one-selfness. (The emphasis on her virginity is confirmed by the festival of the Plynteria at Athens during which the palladium is annually taken to be bathed and thus to have its virginity renewed—as Hera's is renewed at Kanathos.) I am impressed that it is Zeus who is responsible for Athene's killing Pallas (and later for the palladium being thrown from Olympus). Zeus, watching the two maidens playing, becomes fearful that Pallas is about to strike his daughter, and so interposes his aegis. Pallas, startled, looks away, and is fatally wounded by her friend. It was thus his masculine misinterpretation of their assertiveness as aggression, their rivalry as destructive, that caused the death of the feminine Pallas.

The assumption which equates such courage and self-sufficiency as Pallas represents with the masculine is deeply embedded. It probably underlies the fact that the other Pallantes associated with Athene are all male. There is, for instance, a Pallas whom she kills in the Olympians' war against the giants, and out of whose skin she makes a shield; an Arcadian Pallas who is her teacher and the father of Nike, one of her own manifestations; and a Pallas who, in a variant account of her birth, is her father, a father who tries to rape her, whom she kills, and whose skin she again wraps around herself. In each case she takes their power and their name; in these versions it *is* an explicitly masculine side of herself that is represented by her Pallas aspect. She has become Pallas Athene through (in clinical terms) an "introjection of the father" (or of a father surrogate). This denies that both names, Athene and Pallas, refer to feminine ways of being in the world.

Those variants confirm that Athene's relationships to women and to her own femininity are mostly hidden and need to be uncovered by careful research and interpretation. Athene, in a sense, represents just this: the repression of the feminine and the undoing of the repression as a soul task. Really to understand Athene demands a courageous examination of our own participation in misogynous self-denial. To recover the Athene who is mothered by Metis and not only fathered by Zeus is to recover ourselves. We need to begin by recognizing that Athene's separation from her mother is not hers alone, and that we delude ourselves about ourselves if we self-righteously condemn her for it. To get to the Athene who can connect us to a fuller sense of what creative womanhood may encompass than our culture's pieties comprehend means beginning with the father and with the myth that Athene begins with the father. As usual we can only start with the most familiar features of a mythologem and, by reflecting on them, discover their unfamiliarity and strangeness, their prehistory. As L. R. Farnell noted almost a hundred years ago, Athene's character became "deeper and more manifold" the longer she was worshiped [17] —a truth whose pertinence I have only recently come to appreciate.

Because it is the dark side of the goddesses that is most intimately associated with transformation, fully to understand Athene is to enter deeply into the dark mystery of the father-daughter bond. Because for Athene Zeus is unquestionably the father, Zeus will appear very differently to her than he does to Hera who sees him preeminently as husband. Athene's ambivalence toward Zeus is not determined by the tension between his roles as brother, spouse, and patriarch, but by the ambiguities

inherent within fatherness itself. The power that fathers have
for their daughters lies at the very heart of patriarchal culture.
(Indeed, we might say that patriarchy appears when the daughter is felt to belong and feels herself to belong to the father, for
the son's identification with the father does not imply the same
radical devaluation of mother-right.) To understand ourselves
as women in a patriarchally ordered world like our own therefore necessarily means penetrating this mystery. It means trying
to comprehend as fully as we can how our creativity is released,
distorted, and inhibited by the power of the father—not primarily his outward power but his power in our own imagination.
The relationship between Athene and Zeus provides us with
the possibility of looking at the bond between daughters and
fathers in its purest essence, since (at least on first appearance) it
is uncontaminated by the daughter's involvement with mother
or siblings.

> *by the artifice of Hephaistos,*
> *at the stroke of the bronze-heeled axe Athene sprang*
> *from the height of her father's head with a strong cry.*
> *The sky shivered before her and earth our mother.*[18]

Thus is Pindar's account of Athene's miraculous birth. The
Apollo of *The Eumenides* concludes from this:

> *The mother is no parent of that which is called*
> *her child, but only nurse of the new-planted seed*
> *that grows. The parent is he who mounts. A stranger she*
> *preserves a stranger's seed, if no god interfere.*
> *I will show you proof of what I have explained. There can*
> *be a father without any mother. There she stands,*
> *the living witness, daughter of Olympian Zeus,*
> *she who was never fostered in the dark of the womb*
> *yet such a child as no goddess could bring to birth.*[19]

According to myth, Metis, who had helped Zeus in his battle
against his father by giving the emetic which forced Kronos to
vomit forth his swallowed children, becomes his first sexual
partner. Soon after Athene's conception, Zeus learns that Metis
is destined to bear a son who would eventually overthrow his

father. To prevent this Zeus swallows Metis and her unborn female child, as his father before him had out of a similar fear swallowed his newborn offspring. In due course, Athene is born, full-grown, out of Zeus's head. She had her beginning as all of us do within her mother, but then lived the time intervening before her emergence into womanhood within her father—as all of us live the equivalent years of our life within the patriarchally defined world (and often consciously bonded more with our fathers than our mothers).

Athene's identification with the father is most vividly expressed as she announces her judgment on behalf of Orestes in Aeschylus's play:

> *This is a ballot for Orestes I shall cast.*
> *There is no mother anywhere who gave me birth*
> *and, but for marriage, I am always for the male*
> *with all my heart, and strongly on my father's side.*
> *So, in a case where the wife has killed her husband, lord*
> *of the house, her death shall not mean most to me.* [20]

Athene defines herself as Zeus's inspired daughter. She takes on his attributes, is proud to be as dignified and as judicious as he, as brave and as commanding. He is her mentor, and she in turn delights in coming to Odysseus in the guise of Mentor. Her favorite among mortals is not a *puer,* like Bellerophon or Perseus, but the old Odysseus, further confirmation of the determining power in her life of that primary pull to the father.

As the mother-bound son of Rhea, Zeus is, of course, ready to foster his daughter's identification with him. Among the Olympians, Athene ranks second, immediately after Zeus. (Over and over again in the *Iliad* we hear the invocation, "O Father Zeus, and Athene and Apollo . . .") He is enormously proud of his gifted and courageous daughter and indulges her to a degree that utterly outrages Ares:

> *It is your fault we fight, since you brought forth*
> *this maniac daughter*
> *accursed, whose mind is forever on unjust action.*

For all the rest, as many as are gods on Olympos,
are obedient to you, and we have all rendered ourselves
submissive.
Yet you say nothing and you do nothing to check this
girl, letting
her go free, since yourself you begot this child of
perdition.[21]

Only once is their closeness disrupted. During the course of the
Trojan War, Zeus becomes furious at Athene's unyielding refusal to allow the war to end in any way short of the complete
destruction of Troy. Angrily he threatens utter wreckage of the
Greek forces, "so that the grey-eyed goddess may know when it
is her father she fights with." Yet even then Athene knows:

Yet now Zeus hates me, and is bent to the wishes
of Thetis
who kissed his knees and stroked his chin in her hand,
and entreated
that he give honor to Achilleus, the sacker of cities.
Yet time shall be when he calls me again his dear girl
of the grey eyes.[22]

(The latently incestuous element in their attachment is patent
here.)

Persephone comes to a creative relation to the dark, aggressive father when he approaches her in the guise of Hades
(chthonian Zeus) by marrying him. Athene's response is different; she defends against Zeus's potentially overwhelming masculine power by assimilating it in her own being, by being so
like him that in many ways she becomes a female Zeus. The
most exaggerated expression of that identification with the aggressor is the already twice-cited passage from the *Oresteia* in
which she denies any dependence on the maternal and fully
aligns herself with father-right, with the male order. (It seems
characteristic that even on the Acropolis, where she is the
dominating figure, she is surrounded by masculine divinities, by
Hephaistos, Hermes, Poseidon, Zeus.) This is the most trou-

blesome image of Athene; perhaps it echoes unwelcome and, therefore, denied misogynist stirrings. We either know we could not be Athene, could not be as confident and accomplished and creative as she—or are all too conscious of how easily we *could* be Athene, the Athene whose androgyny becomes a capitulation to her inner masculine aspect.

Hillman has written of the sense in which this inner Zeus is really Athene's own creation:

> We all know that fathers create daughters; but daughters create fathers too. The enactment of the maiden-daughter . . . draws down a fathering spirit. But its appearance and her victimization is her creation. Even the idea that she is all a result of the father (or the absent or bad father) is part of the father-fantasy of the anima archetype. And so, she must be "so attached" to father because anima is reflection of an attachment. She creates the figurative father and the belief in its responsibility which serves to confirm the archetypal metaphor of Daughter that owes its source, not to the father but to the anima inherent in a woman's psyche, too.[23]

In one sense, the power of the father over Athene is her fantasy—her attributing to him aspects of herself which are really her own and whose meaning in her life she distorts by this false understanding. Indeed, there is a positive way of understanding Athene's beginning life as a full-grown woman. It may be taken to signify her freedom from that crippling of full feminine capacity usually engendered by the process whereby (as Freud puts it) "a woman develops out of a child with a bisexual disposition." (Again I would want to dispute that the child's wholeness is best described in terms of bisexuality.) She has thereby escaped the agony of coming to believe that "creation and femininity are incompatible" that has so deeply afflicted many women. (Anaïs Nin, for example, refers to "the aggressive act of creation; the guilt of creating. I did not want to rival man; to steal man's creation, his thunder.") Tillie Olsen has written powerfully of the tragic acceptance

—against one's experienced reality—of the sexist notion that the act of creation is not as inherently natural to a woman as to a man, but rooted instead in unnatural aggression, rivalry, envy, or thwarted sexuality.[24]

Athene's emergence full-grown from Zeus's head may thus paradoxically represent her independence from him.

Historically, it is clear that Athene has her own existence apart from Zeus. Some forty years ago careful study of the archaeological and artistic evidence led A. B. Cook (in his monumental study of Zeus) to conclude that Hephaistos and Athene were the pre-Greek divinities of the Athenian Acropolis, and Zeus a later Hellenic arrival. The art-type of Athene's emergence from the head of Zeus represents her "conventional adoption," the subsumption of her cult under his, rather than "natural filiation." Cook sees Athene as antecedent to Zeus *and* his successor. Her birth out of his head represents the "departure of the indwelling divinity" from his moribund body. He "lives on in her younger, fresher life."[25] This may explain why it is Athene and not Zeus who in the classical period comes to be regarded as "the ideal incarnation of the many-sided Athenian life."[26] Even longer ago, in 1895, Farnell sought to show how the story of Athene's birth might have received its present shape.

The fact that in this earliest and half-savage form of the legend Athene is the daughter of Metis is a sign that for these primitive mythopoeic Greeks their goddess was no mere personification of a part of nature, but was already invested with a moral and mental character, and especially with the non-physical quality of wisdom; and of course her worship had long been in vogue, before it occurred to them to tell a myth about her origin. . . . Suppose that Athene was already, before this story grew, the chief goddess of wisdom, as in the most primitive legends she always appears to be: and was also the maiden-goddess of war, averse to love: also the goddess that protected the father-right rather than the mother-right: and that then like all the other Olympians, whatever autonomy each one of them may have once enjoyed, she had to be brought into some relation to Zeus. Then upon these pre-existing ideas the Greek imagination may have worked thus: she has abundant Metis (wisdom or counsel), and is the daughter of Metis; she has all the powers of Zeus, and is the very daughter of him; and she has no feminine weakness, and inclines rather to the father than the mother; therefore she was not born in the ordinary way; this might have been if Zeus swallowed her mother. Afterwards, as this swallowing-story gained ground, it received a new explanation, namely, that Zeus swallowed Metis to prevent her bearing any more children, as a son would else be born stronger than he.[27]

That Athene's existence comes to be seen as dependent on Zeus is one of those reversals in myth-work which interpretation-work must undo in order to rediscover the hidden truth. Such reversals, as Freud taught us, come up against powerful resistance. The truth that will give us back a lost part of ourselves is also one that takes away a self to which we have become deeply attached. Mary Daly names how the resistance to this recovery of Athene's true history is supported by Athene herself (and the Athenes among us):

> Since the twice-born Athena is now legion, having been reproduced over and over by xerox cloning (conditioning), she may not be able to feel her true condition as did Doctor Frankenstein's monster in Mary Shelley's tale. She may not be *able* to feel wretched, helpless, alone, and abhorred, "apparently united by no link to any other being in existence." Since she is a Self-suffocating shell, a figment of her bizarre father's imagination, she hides depth from the Self. But behind the foreground of false selves, of fathers' favorites, there is the deep Background where the Great Hags live and work, hacking off with our Dreadful double-axes the Athena-shells designed to stifle our Selves.

"Radical feminism," Daly affirms,

is not reconciliation with the father. Rather it is affirming our original birth, our original source, movement, surge of living. This finding of our original integrity is re-membering our Selves. Athena remembers her mother and consequently re-members her Self.[28]

The re-membering of Athene means the rediscovery of her relation to the feminine, to mother, to Metis. It leads into the discovery that her strength, her wisdom, her self-confidence are given her by her father, are expressions of her own masculine aspect, only because she sees them thus. For Metis is the original source of Zeus's wisdom, his *metis,* as well as her daughter's. An Oceanid, she is "the most knowing of the gods and men" and, like so many of the divinities connected to water in Greek mythology, a shape-shifter. To elude Zeus's grasp she takes many different forms—it is when she assumes that of a fly that he is able to swallow her. The swallowed Metis represents perfectly those silenced mothers and grandmothers of whom Tillie Olsen speaks, mothers who identify both proudly and resentfully with their more fortunate daughters. (In my own case, my mother could happily support my identification with Athene, including my adolescent bonding with my father, because she could remember being an Athene in her own youth.) Thus Metis's most important metamorphosis is her reemergence as Athene; here she comes forth full-bodied as a goddess. In this sense, Metis is the parthenogenetic mother of Athene as claimed by Robert Graves (and Daly): she creates Athene out of herself. But this insistence on parthenogenesis, this denial of the father, is the Furies' perspective. It forecloses the possibility that after one has rediscovered the mother one can acknowledge the father in a new way. Otherwise, we are back with Demeter and Persephone—a different story and a different pathology.

Metis represents, and bequeathes to her daughter, a "watery" wisdom—intuitive, attuned to subtleties and transformations, sensitive to nuances of personal feeling, poetic rather than abstract, receptive rather than commanding. The connection with water appears elsewhere in the traditions associated with Athene: for example, in the stories which tell of her competition with Poseidon for primacy in Athens, and in the epithet

"Tritogeneia" which recalls that Pallas (and perhaps Athene herself) is fathered by a god of the sea.

Metis is Athene's mother aspect. This means primarily that Athene *has* a mother, is connected to a maternal origin, not that she necessarily *is* one. Here my understanding clearly differs from Kerenyi's, as does therefore my interpretation of the birth of Erichthonios. The tradition is that when Athene defended herself against Hephaistos's attempt to rape her, he ejaculated against her thigh. She wiped off the semen with a handkerchief which she let drop on earth (Gaia). From this Erichthonios was born. Soon after his birth Gaia gave him into Athene's care. (Eventually Erichthonios grew up to become the Athenian king responsible for the establishment of the Athene cult.) Kerenyi understands this as an only slightly disguised statement that Athene is herself Erichthonios's mother.[29] I see the given, more complicated, account as yielding a deeper meaning. Athene may indeed once have been the local fertility goddess, one of the many embodiments of the Great Mother—this is her Gaia aspect and it is thus appropriate that the child be conceived in Gaia and issue from her. But by the time Athene is Athene she represents a different kind of creativity. (That we lose more than we gain by focusing on her as but another face of the Great Mother may be seen more readily by women than by men.) It is true also of Persephone that an important clue to her identity lies in the fact that she and Hades have no children: it is *souls* who are given life in the underworld, not children. Athene, similarly, is not a goddess of procreation, but of creation. She is Athene Ergane, the worker, the maker, and *as such* connected to soul, to soul-work. We have already seen how she puts soul into the work of art, into that which is made. Her relation to soul is a more extroverted one than is Persephone's. Athene is concerned to further the outwarding of soul, its expression and realization in what we do and make.

Athene is the goddess most identified with the work of civilization, the work that makes us human, the works that express our humanity. She is Athene Polias, the goddess of the polis, of the human community; "cities are the gifts of Athene."[30] She seems to have originated as the household goddess of the

Mycenean royal family, as the protectress of its citadel. Though she is to some degree associated with agriculture, she is not properly speaking a nature goddess but rather the goddess who taught humans the art of cultivation, particularly the cultivation of the olive. Though she is not associated with childbirth, with the biological creation of children, she is much involved in caring for young children and in their socialization.

Athene's virginity, her lack of susceptibility to Aphrodite's wiles, rightly understood, stems from her commitment to cultural activity, to what Freud meant by civilization (not from a regressive fixation on the father). Indeed, she initiates us into the difference between repression and sublimation. Her maidenhood seems to be a given so well established that it limits mythological development: though Hephaistos and Athene are closely associated in cult, their relationship cannot be imaged as a marriage. Athene's virginity carries an entirely different meaning from that of Artemis. It does not represent an untameable wildness, a withdrawal from the world of men, the choice of solitude. Athene is not a virgin in order to be alone but in order to be with others without entanglement. She represents a "being with" that fosters mutual creativity, that is based on soul and spirit rather than on instinct and passion. Athene's example raises serious questions about the connection between relationships and creativity, for from her perspective passionate relationships are diversion and self-betrayal. Yet Athene's in-one-selfness is not introverted: it encompasses deep friendship; it is dedicated to the outwarding of soul in creative activity.

The "monuments" of Athene worship, the sculptures, reliefs, vases, and coins depict her in two different ways: erect and threatening, brandishing her weapons; seated and tranquil, with shawl and spindle. One aspect represents her affinities with Ares, the other her closeness to Hephaistos. These two parthenogenetic sons of Hera are the masculine counterparts of Zeus's daughter; they are her brothers despite the myths' insistence that they and she have no common parent. When viewed in relation to Athene each could be regarded as her animus: as what her assertive or creative aspect might be like were it not integrated as part of her womanliness. There are many accounts of Athene and Hephaistos participating in joint projects and sharing delight in each other's creations, as there are tales of intense sibling rivalry between Athene and Ares. (The latter pair coexist more harmoniously in cult.) That Hephaistos and Ares are often associated with the same goddesses (Hera, Aphrodite, Athene) suggests that in a woman's consciousness they naturally appear as a complementary pair—the rejected creative animus and the overly aggressive, assertive one. The hope then would be that when creativity and assertion become consciously part of the feminine being, they will lose this negative dimension.

To understand why, among the iconic representations of Athene, the warrior-type predominates, we must recognize how her martial aspect relates to her civilizing function. It derives from her original commitment to the royal citadel and then to the polis and, consequently, to their defense. Athene Promachus is a protectress, the helper in battle, the instructor in the art of war, not a battle-lusty aggressor. A beautiful relief of her leaning on her spear, her head drooping, pervaded with sorrow, introduces us to a very different Athene: the warrior goddess herself touched by defeat and loss. Farnell believes she is mourning some terrible national disaster and the deaths of all those who were killed.[31]

When focusing on Athene's pathology we may see her as too much the defender, too well defended, but her transmutation of Ares' unrestrained aggressiveness into disciplined assertiveness is an important component of the process by which one brings creative insight to artistic expression. Virginia Woolf expresses her experience of the violence inherent in creation thus:

> Sometimes I am out of touch; but go on; then again I feel that I have at last, *by violent measures*—like breaking through gorse—set my hands on something central.[32]

Athene's patronage of the arts also derives from her original character as goddess of the household and thus of household crafts. Although the source of Athene's name remains a mystery, it may well derive from words connected to pottery; in any case, she is reputed to have made the first earthenware pot. She is also, in both senses, a "spinster" goddess, closely associated with the feminine arts of spinning and weaving. Homer refers to "the elaborate dress which she herself had wrought with her hands' patience." [33] She invented the trumpet and the flute (though, because blowing it made her ugly, she quickly tossed it aside in disgust). According to Graves, she also invented the plough, the rake, the ox-yoke, the horse bridle, the chariot, and the ship. [34]

Her role as goddess of art and artisan naturally brings her into association with the master artisan among the gods, Hephaistos. Her cult seems to have existed at Athens before his, yet Athens was his only major cult site; probably he was important there because, as Athene was more and more seen as the great city goddess, he seemed more directly available than she to the local craftsmen. The ritual connections between them are so extensive that Cook concludes that Athene and Hephaistos were originally the local Rhea and Kronos. [35] Athene's relation to Hephaistos antedates hers to Zeus. One myth has it that Hera conceived Hephaistos parthenogenetically in revenge against Zeus's parthenogenetic creation of Athene; another, that Hephaistos served as midwife at Athene's birth. It is he who releases Athene from the head of Zeus, from being contained by the masculine.

As Athene's relation to war differs from that of Ares, so her relation to artistic creativity differs from that of Hephaistos. That Athene and Hephaistos work together seems a more essential aspect of her creativity than of his. He generally does his work in private and then brings the finished marvels into the world of others. She is more extroverted, more able to combine creativity and human involvement. Athene's art is the art made within and for the human community; in her realm the distinction between the fine and practical arts fades away. It is art that issues from work, from discipline and training rather than from untutored, unfettered inspiration. She "finds place and gives image to the driving necessities"; she offers the Erinyes a cave where they may reside and be honored.[36] Hephaistos is only artist, whereas Athene is warrior as well. He is a crippled artist, and so represents the creativity that issues from woundedness. Proudly striding Athene is not crippled, unless *that* is her crippledness.

From the perspective of the underworld, the ever-conquering Athene may seem fatally flawed. But this image of Athene as invulnerable is radically inadequate. To know Athene deeply is to see beyond the Athene that Rose describes as "one about whom few if any unworthy tales are told." [37] Remembering her treatment of Arachne should liberate us from accepting the image of her as cold and passionless, always reasonable and fair. She strikes Tiresias blind. Cecrops's daughters go mad and kill themselves after they disobey her command not to peek into the infant Erichthonios's basket. She hounded the "lesser" Ajax to his death after he raped Cassandra at her shrine and gave Medusa her hideous petrifying face because she had yielded to Poseidon in a sanctuary dedicated to Athene. Athene is after all sister to Dionysos, Zeus's other parthenogenetic child, the god of madness and ecstasy, the male divinity most closely associated with the underworld. (One story has it that it was she who interrupted the Titans' banquet when they were feasting on Dionysos' dismembered body and rescued the heart and brought it back to Zeus.) Athene's bond to other divinities associated with the underworld is also closer than we usually recognize. The many ancient vases and coins representing a helmeted Athene holding a pomegranate suggest a connection to Persephone. A sculpture representing Demeter and Persephone greeted by Athene refers to that part of the Eleusinian ritual in which the priestess of Athene at the Acropolis is informed that the sacred objects have safely arrived at Eleusis.[38] Wheras Hera represents an antagonism to Demeter and her daughter, Athene represents an intimate complementarity. Persephone is involved with the soul's initiation into the underworld, Athene with its emergence into the human world.

There are other signs of Athene's connection to the realm of soul. As a Mycenean household goddess she seems to have been close cousin to the Minoan snake goddess. (This connection may explain why, to facilitate Athene's birth, Hephaistos is represented as cleaving Zeus's head with a double-edged axe, a tool peculiar to Minoan culture.) Even in the time of Herodotus, Athene was closely identified with the guardian snake believed to live in the Acropolis. Just before Salamis the snake deserted the sanctuary; the Athenians felt the goddess had abandoned it, too. A vase painting representing the judgment of Paris shows an indignant Athene accompanied by a snake equal to the goddess in height and majesty. "The artist seems dimly conscious that the snake is somehow the double of Athene." [39] The child Erichthonios is guarded by a pair of snakes in the closed basket in which he is kept during infancy. Even in Pheidias's superb statue sculpted in the age of Pericles she is represented with a snake at her side, a scaly aegis on her breast, and snakes around her waist. Cook connects these snakes to Athene's role as rock mother. Their salient characteristic in respect to this goddess is their emerging from the rocky surface of the Acropolis and then again disappearing. He speaks explicitly of these snakes as representing soul emerging from the underworld. [40]

Martin Heidegger helps us relate this theme of emergence from the rock to the particular understanding of the nature of the work of art represented by Athene. Heidegger speaks of the Greek temple rising from the rock (as the Parthenon rises from the Acropolis) as representing the "erection of a world" which occurs simultaneously with a "bringing forward of the earth" in which earth "becomes apparent as: undisclosable." [41] Heidegger's earth and world parallel what I have been calling soul and its outward expression in artistic realization. Under the aegis of Athene, art expresses its emergence from soul, from earth, *and* its dependence on its source.

The owl of Athene brings to mind similar associations. The owl was regarded as Athene herself in visible form, as her very soul, though Greek divinities are rarely represented theriomorphically. "With one exception Homer has no god in the form of animals: Athene, however, sometimes transforms herself into a bird and it is by this very transformation that the aged Nestor recognizes her." [42] She appears as pigeon, hawk, kite, vulture, swallow, gull, but (especially in Athens) she is

particularly identified with the owl.[43] She is also often represented as an anthropomorphic goddess with the wings of a bird;
later the owl becomes an adjunct, held in her hand or mounted
on her helmet (like the dove on the head of the Knossian snake
goddess). The conventional identification of the owl with wisdom is too simple. The owl is a bird of prey (and thus equivalent
to Zeus's eagle) and a night bird—associated with death and
darkness—but, like all birds, associated with winged flight and
also with spirit. The owl thus seems to suggest that bringing of
soul back into the upper air, which comes up again and again in
connection with Athene.

The ancient association of the owl and the serpent with
Athene suggests once again the ambivalence inherent in this
goddess, which we miss if we take her at face value and accept
her myth about herself. Yet the other truth, the other face, is in
plain view all the time. Athene wears on her breast the Gor-
goneion, Medusa's head. Although there is a well-detailed myth
rehearsing Perseus's decapitation of the Gorgon and another
version according to which Athene herself killed Medusa,
Medusa exists primarily (as Jane Harrison pointed out long ago)
as head, as face so terrifying that those who see it (or, Hazel
Barnes suggests, are seen by it [44]) are turned to stone. Harrison
represents it as the "Erinyes-side of the Great Mother";[45] Rose
explains it as a nightmare vision, "a face so horrible that the
dreamer is reduced to helpless, stony terror";[46] and Freud believes Medusa's head represents the terrifying genitals of the
Great Mother. Although Farnell rejects the notion "that the
Gorgon was originally merely the double of Athene herself,
personifying the darker side of her character,"[47] I am inclined
to accept it. The representation of Athene's shadow side by a
head is singularly appropriate to this daughter brought forth
from Zeus's head; the associations with the Erinyes and female
sexuality also fit. There is a powerful instinctual feminine side
of Athene which she does not really hide at all. When she wears
the Gorgon-head, it conveys the dark sources of her power but
it does not destroy or petrify. Once again we are in the realm of
reversal: the dark side is what redeems. The Furies through
Athene's intervention become the Eumenides. The blood

caught from the dripping head of Medusa is used by Athene and Asklepios to kill and to heal; Asklepios even uses it to raise the dead. The winged horse, Pegasus, often seen as a symbol of poetry, springs from the neck of Medusa when Perseus cuts off her head. The Gorgon which originally was conceived as an ugly demon becomes, in later sculptural representations, a beautiful angel; thus, there develops a new myth: it was because of Athene's envy of her beauty that Medusa was killed. Little wonder May Sarton can write a poem called, "The Muse as Medusa," which celebrates the Gorgon's capacity to inspire creativity:

> *I saw you once, Medusa; we were alone.*
> *I looked you straight in the cold eye, cold.*
> *I was not punished, was not turned to stone.*
> *How to believe the legends I am told? . . .*
>
> *I turned your face around! It is my face.*
> *That frozen rage is what I must explore—*
> *Oh secret, self-enclosed and ravaged place!*
> *That is the gift I thank Medusa for.* [48]

Athene as Pallas Athene, Athene as the two-faced goddess who wears Medusa's head on her aegis, embodies a much more profound mode of "realization" than the one implied by Murray Stein who says that she

> keeps us in the "real world"; she gives us the wherewithal
> to confront its problems, the joy of conquering ourselves,
> others, problems, and the sagacity and confidence to slay
> its dragons. She keeps us grounded in "real projects," out
> of vain and idle speculations. As a religious attitude,
> Athene is muscular and action-oriented; building, winning,
> marching. [49]

Otto, I believe, comes closer to seeing how profoundly Athene's "reality" is not that of the action-minded pragmatist but of the artist who has a clear sense of just which gesture, which word will most fully express an intended meaning. He speaks of "the spirit of brightest vigilance which grasps with lightning speed what the instant requires," of "the bright-eyed intelligence capable of discerning the decisive element at every juncture and of supplying the most effective instrumentality." He contrasts this to Apollo's indifference to the momentary, his investment in the abstract and the infinite, in pure cognition.[50] Hillman speaks of Athene as meaning psychological reflection, the energy directed to inner integration, as the goddess "who grants *topos,* judging where each event belongs in relation to all other events." [51]

Athene is related to Zeus and Metis, to Ares and Hephaistos, to the owl who is awake at night and to the serpent who creeps out of the rocks. More profound than the mother-maiden polarity Kerenyi focuses on, more comprehensive than the conflicting claims of patriarchy and mother-right, is the always tensive relation in Athene of soul and spirit. "Out of head comes body"; out of Zeus comes Athene. In the Athene we first know only as spirit is hidden a soul. For me this is most powerfully embodied in the image of Athene as Pallas Athene, and of Athene with the Gorgon-head. Both represent her as woman with woman, both soul and spirit are feminine. I am not sure we can even speak of either aspect as Athene's ego, for the very notion of ego seems relativized. Ego is perhaps the Athenian spirit when it is divorced from soul, when it is devoted to heroic success rather than artistic realization, when it forgets and thinks of itself as masculine. But as Pallas Athene, Athene is freed from that illusion, freed from having to understand her creativity as masculine, freed for psycho-poesis rather than psycho-logic. Athene herself has given soul to my image of Athene; I no longer look at her from the perspective of Apollo—or of the Erinyes. I see her as spirit emerging from the underworld, as soul made manifest in artistic realization.

Nevertheless, Athene is also still the one caught in the myth about being born of the father. I am strangely glad of that because it reminds me of my own continued entrapment. I had come to Athene this fourth time around wanting recognition, not repetition, and have found what I sought [52] but still found repetition. I had accepted that—in general. I believed I had learned long ago that the images of progress and growth do not apply to the course of my life, that I know from within what Jung means by the continued circumambulation of the same central themes. But somehow I had not seen what that meant concretely. Now I understand that balancing the claims of work and passionate involvements, keeping time-with and time-alone in creative proportion, finding ways of allowing the intellectual and the poetic to intermingle fruitfully—all of this is never going to be easy. I understand Athene's identification with her father as a reminder to me of how easily still I am pulled to disparage my mother, to forgive my father; how much harder still it is to do the reverse. I am forced to acknowledge how difficult it will always be not to fall back defensively at moments of stress on the masculine in myself—which *is* masculine when it loses its touch with its ground. I will always be susceptible to the danger of getting pulled into the underworld and lost there, or of getting cut off from the world of soul in the upper air. I see also how my very creativity as a female is stimulated and deepened by my continuing struggle with these issues. I think of Penelope, weaving and unweaving—and for today I bring this weaving to Athene's altar.

NOTES

1. H.D., "Pallas," in *Selected Poems* (New York: Grove Press, 1957), p. 23.

2. James Hillman, *Re-Visioning Psychology* (New York: Harper & Row, 1975), p. 139.

3. Walter F. Otto, *The Homeric Gods* (Boston: Beacon Press, 1964), p. 60.

4. Hesiod, "To Athena," trans. Hugh G. Evelyn-White, in *The Homeric Hymns and Homerica* (Cambridge, Mass.: Harvard University Press, 1914), pp. 453, 455.

5. Jane Ellen Harrison, *Prolegomena to the Study of Greek Religion* (New York: Meridian Books, 1957), p. 306.

6. Otto, *Homeric Gods,* p. 160.

7. James Hillman, "Senex and Puer," in *Puer Papers* (Irving, Tex.: Spring Publications, 1979), p. 7.

8. Lewis Richard Farnell, *The Cults of the Greek States,* vol. 1 (Chicago: Aegaean Press, 1971), p. 314.

9. Farnell, *Cults* 1:346. The relief is illustrated in Baumeister, *Denkm. des klass. Alterth.*, fig. 1568.

10. Cf. C. G. Jung, *Psychological Types,* CW 6 (Princeton, N.J.: Princeton University Press, 1971), p. 175, where Jung shows how, in Goethe's "Prometheus Fragment," Minerva (the Roman near equivalent to Athene) is soul to "the defiant, self-sufficient, godlike, god-disdaining creator and artist." Prometheus addresses her thus:

> *From the beginning thy words have been celestial*
> * light to me!*
> *Always as though my soul spoke to herself*
> *Did she reveal herself to me,*
> *And in her of their own accord*
> *Sister harmonies rang out.*
> *And when I deemed it was myself,*
> *A goddess spoke,*
> *And when I deemed a goddess was speaking,*
> *It was myself.*
> *So it was between thee and me,*
> *So fervently one.*
> *Eternal is my love for thee!*

11. Otto, *Homeric Gods,* p. 47.

12. Homer *Iliad* 10. 278–80, rendered by Otto, *Homeric Gods,* p. 46.

13. Hazel E. Barnes, *The Meddling Gods* (Lincoln: University of Nebraska Press, 1974), pp. 114ff.

14. W. K. C. Guthrie, *The Greeks and Their Gods* (Boston: Beacon Press, 1955), p. 108.

15. Carl Kerenyi, *Athene* (Zurich: Spring Publications, 1978), p. 26.

16. *The Orphic Hymns,* trans. Apostolos N. Athanassakis (Missoula, Montana: Scholars Press, 1977), p. 45.

17. Farnell, *Cults* 1:357.

18. *The Odes of Pindar,* trans. Richmond Lattimore (Chicago: University of Chicago Press, 1947), p. 20.

19. Aeschylus, *The Eumenides* 658–66, trans. Richmond Lattimore, in *The Complete Greek Tragedies,* vol. 1, *Aeschylus,* ed. David Grene and Richmond Lattimore (Chicago: University of Chicago Press, 1959), p. 158.

20. Aeschylus, *The Eumenides* 735–40, p. 161.

21. Homer *Iliad* 5. 875–80, p. 151.

22. Homer *Iliad* 8. 370–73, p. 192.

23. James Hillman, "Anima," *Spring,* 1973, p. 118.

24. Tillie Olsen, *Silences* (New York: Delta, 1979), p. 30.

25. Arthur Bernard Cook, *Zeus,* vol. 3, pt. 1 (Cambridge, England: University Press, 1940), pp. 732, 737.

26. Farnell, *Cults* 1:298.

27. Farnell, *Cults* 1:284ff.

28. Mary Daly, *Gyn/Ecology* (Boston: Beacon Press, 1978), pp. 72, 39.

29. Kerenyi, *Athene,* p. 53.

30. Farnell, *Cults* 1:301.

31. Farnell, *Cults* 1:350, pl. 20.

32. Virginia Woolf cited in Olsen, *Silences,* p. 160 (my emphasis).

33. Homer *Iliad* 8. 385–86, p. 192.

34. Robert Graves, *The Greek Myths,* vol. 1 (Baltimore: Penguin Books, 1955), p. 96.

35. Cook, *Zeus* 3: pt. 1, p. 201.

36. James Hillman, *Facing the Gods* (Irving, Tex.: Spring Publications, 1980), p. 28.

37. H. J. Rose, *A Handbook of Greek Mythology* (New York: E. P. Dutton, 1959), p. 103.

38. George E. Mylonas, *Eleusis* (Princeton, N.J.: Princeton University Press, 1969), pp. 193, 211.

39. Harrison, *Prolegomena,* p. 306.

40. Cook, *Zeus* 3: pt. 1, p. 764.

41. Martin Heidegger cited in Vincent Vycinas, *Earth and Gods* (The Hague: Nijhoff, 1961), p. 129.

42. Martin P. Nilsson, *A History of Greek Religion* (New York: W. W. Norton, 1964), p. 27.

43. Cook, *Zeus* 3: pt. 1, p. 781.

44. See "The Look of the Gorgon," in Barnes, *Meddling Gods.*

45. Harrison, *Prolegomena,* p. 194.

46. Rose, *Handbook,* p. 29.

47. Farnell, *Cults* 1:287.

48. May Sarton, *Collected Poems* (New York: W. W. Norton, 1974), p. 332.

49. Murray Stein, "Translator's Afterthoughts," in Kerenyi, *Athene,* pp. 74, 75.

50. Otto, *Homeric Gods,* pp. 55–59.

51. Hillman, *Facing Gods,* pp. 31, 29.

52. Among the recognitions has been a new understanding of why Lou Andreas Salome has for so long been an important self-image for me. She was an Athene in touch with both spirit and soul, in the prime of her life, as K. R. Eissler puts it (*Talent and Genius* [New York: Grove Press, 1971], pp. 24ff.), "probably the most distinguished

woman in Central Europe," a novelist, essayist, poet, and therapist. Her intellectual and emotional bond with Nietzsche (who called her "sagacious as an eagle and courageous as a lion") when she was in her early twenties might, had it continued, have enabled him to withstand the Gorgon's gaze. As Athene gave Bellerophon the golden bridle by which he might capture Pegasus, so Lou helped Rilke find his own personal poetic voice. Freud (probably the only man whose path she crossed who was never afraid of her and who did not fall in love with her) was Zeus ("the father face of my life") and Odysseus. Their friendship began when both were in their fifties and their mutual respect and deep affection ripened until she confounded and provoked not only wonder but envy; her synthesis of intellectual and artistic accomplishment with a life full of such deep and varied relationships looked like the assumption of a masculine prerogative.

·VI·

BEGINNING WITH GAIA

Earth isn't this what you want invisibly
to arise in us? Is it not your dream
to be some day invisible? Earth! Invisible!
What if not transformation is your
insistent commission?
Earth dear one, I will! Oh believe it needs
not one more of your springtimes to win me over.

Rainer Maria Rilke [1]

As we have seen, we first meet the goddesses of Greece as participants in a polytheistic pantheon, dominated by all-father Zeus, whose meeting place is high on Mount Olympus or in the sky. They are complex and vivid personalities, clearly defined, easily distinguished from one another, immediately familiar and very human creatures whose connection to aspects of the natural world is no longer directly apparent. Yet implicit in some of the myths in which they are involved and more visible in the cults devoted to them are evidences that each of these goddesses has some original connection to vegetation ritual, that they are highly developed and specialized forms of the primordial earth goddess, Gaia. To understand the role of the Great Mother in Greek mythology (in the Greek imagination and our own) means attending to her. As Jane Harrison proposes, we need:

> by an effort of the sympathetic imagination to think back of the many we have so sharply and strenuously divided into the haze of the primitive "one." Nor must we regard

Head of Gaia
Istanbul Archaeological Museum

this haze of the early morning as a deleterious mental fog, as a sign of disorder weakness or oscillation. It is not a confusion or even synthesis; rather it is . . . a protoplasmic fullness and forcefulness not yet articulate into the diverse forms of its ultimate birth.[2]

The most familiar goddesses are, as we are so often reminded, the mothers of patriarchy. They are the equivalent of the mothers of what Freud has taught us to call latency, the period that begins when the presence and primacy of paternal power has been acknowledged. Perhaps a reason these goddesses seem so familiar is that we can so easily recognize our own mothers (and ourselves) in them. Yet we half-know they are not adequate representations of the original mother; something has been lost. As we heed that presentiment, we discover that what has been lost is precisely: the mother. These ancient goddesses have all been cut off from their own mother—as our mothers, too, were cut off from this source. Demeter, Hera, and Hestia were swallowed by their father immediately after birth; Aphrodite was born (at least according to Hesiod's account) out of the semen that surrounded her father's severed genitals after Kronos had thrown them into the surging sea; Athene (according to the same source) emerged full-grown from father Zeus's head.

Of the major Olympian goddesses only Artemis—whom we shall consider more fully in the next chapter—had a mother: a mother whom Artemis seems to have mothered from almost the moment of her own birth. The newborn daughter immediately set about assisting with the delivery of her twin brother Apollo. On many other occasions she rescues Leto from insult or danger. There is much that is instinctively motherly in Artemis, especially her tender solicitude for all that is young and vulnerable, animal or human. Indeed, at Ephesus, she was worshiped as the many-breasted Great Mother. Yet the classical Artemis is a virgin who never literally mothers a child of her own; she shuns the world of men, lives in the forest on the fringes of the inhabited world. She represents the persistence of the natural, the untamed, even within the Olympian hegemony—but a naturalness that has become infertile.

Nor are any of her sister goddesses more whole in their mothering. Like Artemis, Athene and Hestia are childless. Though Hestia can love generously and impartially, and in Rome as Vesta she is a prototype of the good mother, she seems (perhaps in consequence of the early loss of her own mother) to be deeply suspicious of close personal attachments. Athene is a devoted and dependable friend, protectress of the generation of young children on whom the future of the polis depends, but she carefully protects herself from sexual passion. Remember how in Aeschylus's *Oresteia* she explicitly avows her allegiance to father-right and implicitly accepts Apollo's declaration "that the mother is no parent of that which is called her child." Aphrodite's marriage to Hephaistos is sterile; her children are the incidental consequences of the self-indulgence of her passionate attraction to an Ares or an Anchises. She loves Aeneas, the issue of the latter liaison, and tries to protect him as best she can during the Trojan War and his subsequent journey to Italy, but she takes no part in rearing him. In her mothering, she seems to display the same kind of adventitious dispensation of favors which characterizes her sexual involvements. Hera is preeminently wife, not mother. As we have seen, her daughters, Hebe and Eileithyia, are but pale shadows of herself; her sons, Ares and Hephaistos (who, at least according to some accounts are parthenogenetic offspring), serve her primarily as pawns in her incessant battles with her husband. Her stepson and namesake, Herakles, is the prototype of the hero who must take on one impossible task after another in the never-quenched hope of receiving her blessing. Demeter's boundless love for her daughter, Persephone, seems at first glance to represent an idealized version of maternal devotion—yet a closer reading suggests it may be her very overinvestment in her child that makes Persephone's abduction by Hades a necessary denouement.

Thus these goddesses seem to represent precisely the mothers with whom we are all too familiar—the mothers whom we see as having failed us in the variety of ways articulated by Adrienne Rich in *Of Women Born* (and less subtly in Nancy

Friday's *My Mother, Myself*)—the mothers who leave us feeling "wildly unmothered." In these goddesses we see in divine proportions the mother who abandons her children or holds them too tight, the mother who uses her children as agents in her marital struggles or as fulfillment of her own frustrated ambitions.

But there is in Greek mythology a "great" mother in the background—Gaia, grandmother to Demeter, Hera, and Hestia, great-grandmother to Athene and Artemis, and ancestress also of Aphrodite who is born of the severed genitals of Gaia's son-lover, Ouranos. Gaia is the mother of the beginning, the mother of infancy. She is the mother who is there before time—a recognition given mythological expression in Hesiod's *Theogony* where she is represented as coming into being at the very beginning, long before Kronos.[3] In Freud's terms Gaia is the mother of primal fantasy, the mother who is the correlate of what he called primary narcissism. She is a mother whom we come to know only as we begin to long for a mother from whom we are not separated, as in time, in consciousness, we find ourselves to be separated from the mother of the present. She is a fantasy creature behind the personal mother, construed of memory and longing, who exists only in the imagination, in myth, archetypally—who is never identical with the personal mother. Although she is there from the beginning, our discovery of her is always a return, a re-cognition.

But to effect that return is to see the later goddesses (whom we inevitably know first) and our own mothers differently. For to recognize Gaia's presence in the background is to return them to their source, to their mothers, and thus to their own primordial stature and power. To see them matrilineally is to discover aspects hidden in the patriarchally shaped classic presentation. We have already seen how more richly pertinent to the self-understanding of contemporary women Athene becomes when we appreciate what it means that she is Metis's daughter and not only Zeus's—and when, as we seek to interpret the complex story of Erichthonios's birth, we discover that Athene herself has a Gaia aspect. Hera, too, becomes fully herself when, seeking to free herself from being possessed by the anger and jealousy that Zeus's infidelities inspire in her, she returns to her birthplace. There, in the land of her mother, she immerses herself in the spring of Kanathos and recovers her virginity, her in-one-self-ness. Probably each of the Olympian goddesses was originally a pre-Hellenic local earth goddess— Hera in Argos, Athene in Attica, Artemis and Aphrodite somewhere in the Near East. In this sense, each *is* Gaia. Nevertheless, I see Hesiod's attempt to distinguish the Olympians from the original mother as deriving from a genuinely mythopoetic sensitivity. It is of the essence of the first mother (of these first undifferentiated "protoplasmically full" mothers) to give birth to a rich variety of daughters. So remembering Gaia's relation to these later goddesses does not mean saying they are really nothing but Gaia herself under other names, but rather that she is the ground out of which their figures emerge.

Discovering the archetypal character of the Great Mother who lives in the imagination of each of us also makes possible a different relation to our personal mother. We can forgive her for not being what she could not have been—the transhuman all-giving source—and can understand how she, too, began as an unmothered daughter. As we are able to return our mother to her source, to see her in relation to but distinct from the archetype, as its necessarily frail and fallible carrier, we may at last be able both to bless what is communicated through her and to forgive her for what she could not give. For we now see her as standing in exactly the same relation to Gaia as do we.

It is perhaps inevitable that we notice the figures in the foreground first. I know it has taken me a long while to get to Gaia. I am only now beginning to see why. The history of my search among the goddesses has proceeded along the course of an inexorable psycho-logic—though I understand that only in retrospect.

My search began several years ago following my dream of the *She,* so palpably but invisibly present in the cave. I had thought of that vision as peculiarly my own until I found this passage in which Susan Griffin describes the experience in eerily exact detail—except that where I said "I," Griffin more beautifully and truly says "we":

The way we came here was dark. Space seemed to close in on us. We thought we could not move forward. We had to shed our clothes. We had to leave all we brought with us. And when finally we moved through the narrow opening, our feet reached for ledges, under was an abyss, a cavern stretching farther than we could see. Our voices echoed off the walls. We were afraid to speak. This darkness led to more darkness, until darkness leading to darkness was all we knew.

The shape of this cave, our bodies, this darkness. This darkness which sits so close to us we cannot see, so close that we move away in fear. We turn into ourselves. But here we find the same darkness, we find we are shaped around emptiness, that we are a void we do not know.

The shape of a cave, this emptiness we seek out like water. The void that we are. That we wash into as sleep washes over us, and we are blanketed in darkness. We see nothing. We are in the center of our ignorance. Nothingness spreads around us. But in this nothing we find what we did not know existed. With our hands, we begin to trace faint images etched into the walls. And now, beneath these images we can see the gleam of older images. And these peel back to reveal the older still. The past, the dead, once breathing, the forgotten, the secret, the buried, the once blood and bone, the vanished, shimmering now like an answer from these walls, bright and red. Drawn by the one who came before. And before her. And before. Back to the beginning. To the one who first swam from the mouth of this cave. And now we know all she knew, see the newness of her vision. What we did not know existed but saw as children, our whole lives drawn here, image over image, past time, beyond space.

The shape of a cave, the bud, the chrysalis, the shell, what new form we seek in this darkness, our hands feeling these walls, here wet, here damp, here crumbling away; our hands searching for signs in this rock, certain now in this darkness, what we seek is here, warm and covered with water, we sweat in this effort, piercing the darkness, laying our skin on the cool stone, tracing the new image over the old, etching these lines which become clear to us now, as what we have drawn here gleams back at us from the walls of the cave, telling us what is, now, and who we have become. . . .

This cave, the shape to which each returns, where image after image will be revealed, and painted over, painted over and revealed, until we are bone. Where we touch the ones who came before and see their visions, where we leave our mark, where, terrified, we give up ourselves and weep, and taken over by this darkness, are overwhelmed by what we feel; where we are pushed to the edge of existence, to the source which sounds like a wave inside us, to the path of the water which feeds us all.[4]

Although I at first thought of my search as a more solitary one than it has since proven itself to be, I did know, as I woke from my own dream, that I must begin tracing the faint images etched on the walls, for I sensed that beneath those were older images, images that would take me back to the beginning, to Her.

The image closest to the surface was Persephone and so I began with her, as I have begun this book with her. As the Greek divinity whose cult persisted far into our own era, long after the service of Zeus Olympios had fallen silent, she is connected to a more recent past than the other goddesses. I did not know that then nor did I consciously know that—since to attend to Persephone is evitably to attend also to Demeter—I had begun not only at the end of the story of the Greek goddesses but close to its beginnings as well. For of all the pre-Homeric offshoots of Gaia, Demeter resembles the primordial mother most closely.

I began with Persephone and then, as I have already described, found there were other goddesses demanding my attention: first, Ariadne; soon thereafter, Hera and Athene. I had always thought of Athene as Zeus's daughter but when she reappeared she showed herself also as daughter to Metis, the ancient Titaness whom Zeus had swallowed to make her wisdom his own. Behind the father, I discovered, was the original, the primal mother. The morning after I had finished writing about my reengagement with Athene, I had a dream just before waking:

A telephone call had come for me from my parents' home three thousands miles away. I picked up the receiver in a room filled with a small holiday gathering of my children and their lovers and my own: "Chris, your father has just died." I went to take the call in another room. The message was still the same: "Chris, your father has just died." I knew somehow it had been a sudden and easy death; it felt timely. I had no sense of regret, no feeling that though perhaps timely for him it was premature for me. I lay face down on the bed and wept, simply, naturally, with full release (as I would long to be able to do when this "really" happened).

It was time—is time—to turn to Gaia, the mother before the father (and before the literal mother). One cannot after all begin with Gaia—though when we come to her we recognize "we have arrived where we started and know it for the first time." Farnell suggested that "of all the religious conceptions of primitive man," Gaia might be most available to contemporary consciousness. The irreducible anthropomorphism of the Olympian deities makes them seem alien, whereas "the latent secretion of this most ancient belief is in our veins . . . source and measure of the warm affection with which we attach ourselves to external nature." [5]

So it is time now for Gaia, for Ge-ology in the truest sense: the word she will draw forth from me. The Homeric hymn "To Earth," which begins:

> *The mother of us all,*
> *the oldest of all,*
> *hard,*
> *   splendid as rock*
> *whatever there is that is of the land*
> *   it is she*
> *   who nourishes it*
> *   it is the Earth*
> *   that I sing.* [6]

is such a Ge-ology.

For Gaia is *not* simply mother, she is *earth* mother. Indeed, she differs from the later goddesses in that she *is*—and remains earth, earth recognized as animate and divine. Gaia is never wholly personal, never entirely humanized—not even in Homer, not even in Hesiod. This is not deficit, does not mean she is thereby somehow less than the so completely anthropomorphic Olympians (who may wield the thunderbolt or drive the chariot of the sun but are not themselves the lightning flash or the solar disc; who may take on the shape of a bull in sexual pursuit or of a swan in flight but without forfeit of their humanlike personalities).

Gaia reminds us that the divine is transhuman and prehuman—there from the beginning—not simply human projection. Because of this she is source as no humanlike mother can be. She is the answer to that deep longing for homecoming which no mother (and no lover as mother surrogate) can assuage.

Yet she is not earth as an abstraction, not *the* earth but earth, especially that particular expanse of earth which for us *is* earth, from which we know the earthiness of earth—though that we *have* such a piece of earth is perhaps no matter-of-fact reality. It has certainly not been for me. Uprooted from my motherland, when I was very young, I can go back to Germany now and find it beautiful, feel that my feet are somehow treading on familiar soil, and yet know that, nevertheless, this is not quite home. Yet neither is America, though I think and dream (mostly) in English and even in my dreams move (mostly) through American landscapes and dwellings.

Not until I went to Greece for the first time, twice seven years ago, did I know what it is to be at home on earth. There, to me earth showed herself. I experienced a truth I later found articulated in Henry Miller's *The Colossus of Maroussi:*

> Greece is what everybody knows, even *in absentia,* even as a child or an idiot or as a not-yet-born. It is what you expect the earth to look like given a fair chance. It is the subliminal threshold of innocence. It stands as it stood from birth, naked and fully revealed.[7]

It was not only that I found myself in places I had heard spoken of with reverence from the time I was a child, not only that this was the land that had inspired so much of the poetry by which I have been most touched (from Homer to Hölderlin and on to H.D.), but because there I directly felt how a particular image of the divine emerges from sensitivity to the sacredness of a particular place. Once there it seems self-evident that there would be a temple to Poseidon on the ocean-washed cliffs at Sounion, and one to Athene atop the rocky Acropolis. To know Persephone one must only be in Greece in April when the peach blossoms cover the meadows and hills with a soft pink cloud and the brilliant red poppies are everywhere underfoot.

Here, earth happens—and especially so at Delphi. I knew I was at the center of the earth the first time I was there. Recently, I found again the account I wrote then, not having remembered how similar that experience had been to my cave vision (and only now understanding why):

> In the midst of the temple's ancient upward-thrusting pillars, surrounded by the sternly unapproachable mountains, and under a sky alternately bluely brilliant and dark with thunderous clouds, one could not help but recognize the god's presence. It was overpowering. Yet it was a presence that never condensed into a shape, a speaking that never focused into word, not even into the ambiguous words of the most famous of the oracle's pronouncements.[8]

Delphi affected me on that visit much as it did May Sarton:

> *The site echoes*
> *Its own huge silences*
>
> *Wherever one stands,*
> *Whatever one sees—*
>
> *Narrow terror of the pass*
> *Or its amazing throat,*

Pouring an avalanche of olives
Into the blue bay.

Crags so fierce
They nearly swallow
A city of broken pillars.
Or Athene's temple,
Exquisite circle,
Gentled on all sides
By silvery leaves.

Eagles floating
On high streamers of wind.
Or that raw cleft,
Deep in the rock,
Matrix
Where the oracle
Uttered her two-edged words.

Wherever one stands,
Every path leads to Fate itself:
"Speak! Speak!"

But there is no answer

Choose the river of olives.
Chose the eagles.
Or choose to balance
All these forces,
The violent, the gentle
Summon them like winds
Against a lifted finger.
Choose to be human.
Everyone stands here
And listens. Listens.
Everyone stands here alone.

I tell you the gods are still alive
And they are not consoling.

I have not spoken of this
For three years,
But my ears still boom.[9]

Yet Sarton at least knew enough to speak of "the gods,"
whereas I, after that first visit, spoke only of "the god." When I
returned to Delphi seven years later it was with a deeply loved
woman friend. I had hoped so much that this place would be as
self-evidently sacred for her as it had been for me, but it was
summer and the path to the shrine was filled with noisy, hurry-
ing tourists. "They go up and they come down and they are not
changed," she observed. Wordlessly, we turned off from the
sacred way and, a few hundred yards into a pine grove, sat
down. I have no idea how long we sat there, several feet apart,
still silent. In some ways it seemed forever. I had never had
such a sense of a deep communion with another human being.
It seemed to me as though my soul had entered her body as hers
had entered mine. Much later, we both arose, knowing it was
time to go. We embraced and I began to speak. "There's no
need to ask," she gently said. "It really happened." But that
evening I spoke. "I don't understand," I said, "why this should
have happened here at Apollo's shrine and not rather at Eleusis
which is dedicated to the deepest bonds that unite woman with
woman."

I *thought* of it still as Apollo's place though we had *experienced*
another presence. I know now that it was Gaia's and know who
Gaia is, in part, by virtue of that appearance of the goddess. For
Delphi, I have since learned, was first Gaia's; as navel of the
earth it is preeminently the place where humans and earth come
together. The omphalos may originally have been a grave
mound, clear evidence of a connection to some chthonic cult.
When the oracle was Gaia's it probably took the form of dream
inculcation in which initiates sought for the kind of knowledge
that emerges from hidden depths. Aeschylus suggests that the
transition from Gaia to Apollo was a peaceful evolution (via
Themis and Phoebe). Hesiod and the Homeric Hymn to
Pythian Apollo present a more violent struggle. Python, a
female dragon created by Gaia as guardian of the shrine, was

slain by Apollo to make possible his usurpation of the oracle. Gaia responded by sending dreams to all those who might otherwise have come to consult Apollo's wisdom, until Zeus was persuaded by Apollo to order her to desist. So goes the story. I am not sure she ever really did what Zeus commanded.

I first encountered Gaia, the divine presence of earth, there at Delphi, and only afterwards discovered that one does not have to go to Greece. Some friends had wanted to share with me a place sacred to them in the desert at the far eastern edge of the southern California county in which I now live.

They left me to explore it in my own way, alone. It had not occurred to me I would know so immediately, I am *here,* that I would so surely know this place had a power I had felt in only one other place: Delphi. I knew I was here and I knew, my body knew, just where to go. I climbed up some cliffs remarkably like those in the goddess dream vision of two years earlier, though I did not consciously recognize the similarity then. Some fifty feet perhaps from the summit was a small grassy plateau, just large enough for me to lie down in, completely ringed with low, fairly flat boulders. Ritually, carefully, I took off my clothes and neatly folded them and lay down in the prepared space, aware of that wonderful sun in the sky above me, of the earth beneath my body, the encircling stones, the mountain behind me, the other mountains to my left and before me. At some point I began caressing my body in that loving, knowing, unhurried way in which women make love to women. And at some point my fingers in their wanderings came across the moist spot and followed the channel whose opening it marked, deep, deep down into the center within—her sacred place. And *then* the vision flashed back and I knew I was there. I found it strange that as often as I had thought of that vision, and even told it, I had never really thought of the cave within the cave as my womb—not until then when I simultaneously entered and was entered.

Recognizing that I had now *lived* what I had earlier imagined, I knew that this was in some very deep way a moment of completion, of finding Her. Some while later I sat up to look around me and discovered that behind the spot where my head had been laid was the opening of a cave. I moved toward it unbelievingly, and of course utterly believingly, for it was the cave of my vision. Except that in the middle of it lay the stone Mother, Ungit,[10] lying on her side, knees somewhat drawn up, with ripe, ripe breasts. Waiting. There was room, barely, for me to lie down beside her, my stomach to her back, my hands caressing her warm round belly—and room, barely, for me to tuck myself in the half circle made by her breasts and belly and thighs and to feel myself in the Mother. And room, barely, for me to turn around and make love to her and she to me. Laughing and smiling all the time. Knowing exactly what we were up to. The sweetness of woman with woman and the dark, dark mystery. Then when it was over, I knew I needed to leave a sign, and knew what it had to be, and knew it was impossible for I had stopped flowing the day before. But on the hand which had been within Her/me at the beginning of the afternoon I saw a faint marking of dried blood (which I didn't wash off until I got home). I returned to the sweet source and found there the rich ripe drops of blood with which I marked the cave. And then I left, and climbed down the mountain, and walked for hours in the desert until I felt ready to be with others again.

I learned that day what Heidegger means when, in response to Hölderlin's "Homecoming," he speaks of "learning at home to become at home."[11] Gaia had home-d me as no literal mother could. Gaia is the recumbent rock I had embraced and the boulders within whose clutches I had sat, the landscape at which I had gazed, and the earth itself. She is the earth, recognized as animate and divine—a goddess and yet never wholly personal, never entirely humanized. (Hestia, too, is a goddess who makes us feel at home, centered; she, too, is associated with the omphalos and like Gaia is less fully personified than the other Olympian goddesses. But her space is domestic—the family hearth, not the volcano; the house, not the landscape. I associate Hestia with the secret chamber of my earliest dreams which has always been "home," whereas Gaia had made me feel at home in the universe.)

Gaia is the living presence of earth; she reminds us of the time "when matter was still rebellious,"[12] long before one could imagine it as *terra firma*. She reminds us that matter is *still* rebellious, alive and eruptive. Gaia is earthquake and volcano, molten lava and shifting rock. She is earth as it is in itself, not earth as subdued by humankind. She may be goddess of all that grows but she is never the goddess of agriculture. (Indeed, in Greece the agriculture rites are so entirely civic, political affairs that a goddess as far removed from being a fertility goddess as Olympian Athene can be their patron.) Gaia is earth, not polis; the potential tension between mother earth and father land is powerfully displayed in Aeschylus's *Seven Against Thebes*.

To know Gaia is to be deeply attuned to the irony implicit in this passage from Griffin's *Woman and Nature:*

> The land is brought under his control; he has turned waste into a garden. Into her soil he places his plow. He labors. He plants. He sows. By the sweat of his brow, he makes her yield. She opens her broad lap to him. She smiles on him. She prepares a feast. She gives up her treasures to him. She makes him grow rich. She yields. She conceives. Her lap is fertile. Out of her dark interior, life arises. What she does to his seed is a mystery to him. He counts her yielding as a miracle. He sees her workings as effortless. Whatever she brings forth he calls his own. He has made her conceive. His land is a mother. She smiles on the joys of her children. She feeds him generously. Again and again, in his hunger, he returns to her. Again and again she gives to him. She is his mother. Her powers are a mystery to him. Silently she works miracles for him. Yet, just as silently, she withholds from him. Without reason, she refuses to yield. She is fickle. She dries up. She is bitter. She scorns him. He is determined he will master her. He will make her produce at will. He will devise ways to plant what he wants in her, to make her yield more to him.[13]

Gaia reminds us of all that cannot be brought under control. She is divine; she transcends the human. She is that very transcendence, but as an earthly, shaped, present, appearing reality.

Yet to understand Gaia as *only* earth, to reduce her to a personification of an aspect of the natural world (à la Max Müller's reductionist interpretation of mythology) is to miss the point. Gaia is earth made invisible, earth become metaphor, earth as the realm of soul. She is more then vegetal fertility, more than earthquake and volcano. There is a with-in-ness to Gaia; souls live in her body. The Greeks understood that soul-making happens in earth, not in sky. Soul (unlike spirit) relates to the concrete imagination.

One cannot understand Gaia entirely in human or psychological terms. The very name, earth, serves to remind us of that and yet she is nature moving toward emergence in personal form. The most usual artistic representation of Gaia expresses this beautifully—she is shown as a human woman emerging breast-high from the earth itself. Gaia arises from the earth but does not leave it. It is only a later conception that imagines Dionysos *rescuing* Semele (a Gaia figure) and taking her to heaven, or that is disappointed by Orpheus's failure to bring Eurydice up from the underworld.[14]

A week after the West Coast volcano erupted at Mount Saint Helens, I had a devastating vision from which I could not free myself.

> I felt myself to be the mountain, felt energies long, long repressed or ignored, entirely unfamiliar, to be gushing forth, with tremendous force and heat. There was no stopping them. I knew myself also to be the slopes steaming with lava, the trees topped by the fierce wind, the bare trunks consumed by the fire, the fields covered with ash.

Freud called the force I had experienced *das Es* (usually and misleadingly translated as the id)—some primal "that" in us, sheer raw instinctual energy, nature alive within, nature just on the way toward being given human form. These psychic forces within that so clearly transcend the individual, that are an aspect of the unconscious that is inexhaustible and unassimilable but without which we could not live—these forces are Gaia. Strabo may have known how the volcanic deposits left by eruptions of

Vesuvius and Etna enriched their slopes and the nearby plain, and Jung can speak of the collective unconscious mostly in terms of its creative potentiality—but neither would minimize the destructive potentiality of the erupting energies. Jung had personal experience of moments when he felt himself about to be shattered and smothered by an avalanche of rock; he knew the Gaia that shows herself in the Mount Saint Helens eruptions.

For the Greeks, Gaia is always first the earth; all that she means as goddess follows from that. This is clear in Homer where, though Gaia has a definite shape and is more than a vague, inchoate conception of the whole earth as animate and conscious, she is not as concrete and personal as her Olympian offspring and not personally active. She is the presupposition. Because earth is always near at hand and cannot be escaped, she is the guarantor of the most serious oaths. Even the gods swear by her. When Erichthonios establishes the Athenian cult, he declares that every other sacrifice must be preceded by a preliminary offering to Gaia in gratitude for her nurturing. Likewise, in Aeschylus's *The Eumenides* Apollo's priestess dedicates her first prayer to earth.

Though in Hesiod, too, Gaia is still clearly *earth,* she is represented anthropomorphically. According to his *Theogony,* in the beginning there was chaos, by which he means simply emptiness, pure potentiality, a yawning abyss. Then, by a process of spontaneous emergence, appear Gaia and Tartaros (along with Eros, Erebos, or Darkness, and Light). This doubling in the Greek conception of earth reappears at later stages of the divine genealogy. Tartaros represents the within-ness of earth, its dark unknowable interior; Gaia its giving forth; Tartaros its chthonic aspect, earth's relation to death and soul; Gaia its relationship to vegetation, physical life, fertility. (Persephone's relation to Hades is a later representation of the chthonic dimension; her relation to Demeter represents the fertility aspect.) But the two cannot really be separated. Tartaros is Gaia's within-ness, Gaia is Tartaros's self-externalization. (The genealogy suggests an understanding of darkness within darkness. Tartaros is the darkness within Gaia, Erebos the gloom of Tartaros, and then there is Night itself. There is also an understanding of light and life as necessarily born of darkness. Thus, the mating of Erebos and Night produces Light and Day.) To be generative is Gaia's very essence. To be Gaia is to give birth to something other than herself, to heterogeneity. To honor Gaia is to celebrate otherness and polymorphousness. Her first creations are her parthenogenetic offspring, sea, and mountain, and sky. Though she then mates with her own dark double, Tartaros, and with sea and sky, she is still their origin. All things begin with the mother, even fathers. Of these primal divine beings only Gaia has a cult. The others belong to mythology, to cosmogonic reflection, but are not experienced as living still active principles as is she. The others are supplanted, Ouranos by Zeus, Pontus by Poseidon. She is not; indeed, she participates in the supplantation.

Ouranos and she coparented not only the twelve Titans but also a race of one-eyed Cyclopes and of hundred-handed monsters. Because Ouranos found these latter creations ugly and terrible, he hid them in Gaia's depths and did not allow them to emerge. But it is Gaia's very nature to give forth. Thus, she is in great distress at having to contain these creatures within her. She solicits the aid of the youngest of the Titans, Kronos, to accomplish their release. When next Ouranos comes to make love to her, Kronos springs forth from his hiding place and, using the sickle his mother had fashioned precisely for this task, cuts off his father's genitals. The falling drops of blood are received by Gaia who conceives and later gives birth to the Erinyes, the giants, and the tree nymphs. From the foam surrounding the sea-tossed member, Aphrodite emerges. Castrated Ouranos has lost his physical potency but not his life—Hesiod is well aware that the primal powers can never really be eliminated. Ouranos is henceforth relegated to the sky, and serves there as the very figure of distance, uninvolvement, abstraction. Kronos (with his sister Titan, Rhea, as consort) takes his father's place and gives birth to six children. But Gaia and Ouranos warn that he is fated in his turn to be overcome by one of his children. So, one by one as they are born, he swallows them. Once again it is Gaia who intervenes on behalf of the emergence of life. She deceives Kronos into swallowing a stone instead of his last-born child, Zeus, and herself secretly brings up her grandson.

When Zeus grows up, he tricks Kronos into disgorging the swallowed stone and children and then fights against his father with his siblings, the Cyclopes, the Hundred-handed, and one of the Titans, Themis, as allies. The battles are of truly cosmic proportions—sea and earth and even the wide heavens are shaken by them. Hesiod's descriptions of the clamor, the heat, the confusion are magnificent. But, though Gaia had sided with Zeus against the Titans, when he next begins to battle the Giants, she sides with them. The Titans are Ouranian; they seek to contest the Olympians for heavenly supremacy. The Giants win her support because they are truly earth-born (not at all the huge ogres of fairy-tales). It seems to her that Zeus intends to deny his common origin with all her other creations and off-spring. This so enrages her that she proceeds to engage in the creation of new monstrous forces to pit against him, most nota-bly the fearsome dragon, Typhoeus, from whose shoulders grow a hundred snake heads.

Gaia shows herself here as always for life and against any stifling order. Gaia cannot be subdued nor can her responses be predicted. She deceives and betrays. She is ever fertile: a drop of Ouranos's blood or of Hephaistos's semen impregnates her; but she is as likely to give birth to the monstrous as to the beautiful.

The Olympians represent immutability and deathlessness. They would not have understood Rilke's song:

> *Because to be here is much, and the transient Here seems*
> *to need and concern us strangely. Us, the most transient.*
> *Everyone once, once only. Just once and no more. And we*
> *also once. Never again. But this having been once, although*
> *only once, to have been of the earth, seems irrevocable.*[15]

Gaia is for life but for ever-renewing life and so for life that encompasses death. Gaia rituals included animal sacrifice as well as offerings of cereal and fruit; in archaic Greece as in many vegetation cults, worship of her may have included human sacrifice. The Orphic hymn addresses this goddess thus:

> *Divine Earth, mother of men and of the blessed gods,*
> *You nourish all, you give all, you bring all to*
> *fruition, and you destroy all.*[16]

Guthrie distinguishes between *ge* and *chthon* as between "furrows" and "graves" and associates Gaia only with the fruitful earth and speaks of *chthon* as its cold dead depths.[17] But this is to force a distinction that is foreign to the Greek conception; the depths are not dead in that sense: the depths are where the dead live, the realm of soul. There are many evidences that Gaia is a chthonic as well as a fertility deity, goddess of grave and furrow. On the Areopagus her statue stands with those of Hermes and Hades. At Athens, Mykonos, and probably Delphi she was worshiped in association with the dead. The Attic Genesia (also called a Nekyia—a descent into the underworld) was an All Souls' festival when offerings were brought to kinsmen's graves. The Anthesteria which, in classical times, was celebrated in honor of Dionysos was probably originally a mournful festival consecrated to Gaia and the dead; even in the classic period Gaia was still involved.[18]

Gaia is the giver of dreams and of mantic oracles, of soul knowledge and soul food. The elusive, fragmentary, often unfamiliar and sometimes bewildering or terrifying character of dream consciousness seems appropriate expression of Gaia. Dream consciousness is primary consciousness: earthy, concrete, self-sufficient. Dreams ground us, give depth to our experience. Hermes may be the divinity most closely associated with the interpretation of dreams; Gaia returns us to their source. Her prophecies come not from being able to read the stars or the entrails of bird or beast, but from her deep knowledge of what is really and inevitably going on. Her warnings to Kronos and to Zeus stem from such insight. (When Zeus is seen as having oracular power, as at Dodona and Olympia, it is only by virtue of his association with her.) Though Zeus intervenes on behalf of Apollo's usurpation of the Delphic oracle, the style of prophecy remains hers. Apollo's victory seems a surface truth. Near the Castalian spring her temple still stands. She remains.

Gaia remains also in her emanations. Farnell says Gaia "must disguise herself under other names that do not so immediately betray the material fact (as *Ge* does)—in order to develop into active personality."[19] Gaia is indeed the source of polytheism. She is the incarnation of the polytheistic imagination which tends inevitably toward a multiplication of forms. In contrast to Kronos who swallows his progeny in order to feel safer, it is in her very nature to generate, to bring forth variety, heterogeneity. Gaia groans and protests, feels essentially thwarted when Ouranos forces her to contain her own children in her body. Gaia's emanations are projections of her own being, each catching one aspect of her own protoplasmic fullness. To know her fully is to see her in that which emerges from her.

Among the pre-Homeric offshoots of Gaia the most important are Themis, the Erinyes, Demeter, and Persephone. What a different aspect of earth each reflects—and yet there is no conflict between them (as there is among the Olympian goddesses). Themis, daughter of Gaia and Ouranos, shares many of her mother's functions and attributes, including her foreknowledge of the future. (It is she, for instance, who warns Zeus against the threat posed by any son born to Metis.) Delphi was hers after it was Gaia's and before it became Apollo's. As bride of Zeus she is mother of, among others, Dike (Justice) and the Fates. She comes to be associated particularly with righteousness and communal order. For an earth goddess to represent righteousness suggests that right order in the human realm means harmony with the natural order.

The Erinyes also represent the forces which insist on such right ordering and emerge to reestablish it when it is disregarded. They come into appearance especially to extract retribution for the most heinous crimes—matricide and oath breaking. But Aeschylus has it all backward in having them become the Eumenides only within the patriarchal order as given shape by Athene. The aboriginal conception associated them not just with retribution but also with marriage and childbirth (though these, too, are bloody events). It saw them as bringers of a gentle death (as to Oedipus), not only as avengers.

Demeter and Persephone in their essential bond with each other represent the two aspects of Gaia, the vegetative and the chthonic. Demeter is more associated with cultivation than is Gaia; she is the corn mother, not really the earth mother. She is more human, too, especially in her bereavement and grief, than Gaia ever is. Persephone is the goddess of the underworld but never just a goddess of the world of soul; she is always also the beautiful young goddess of spring as it manifests itself in tender leaf and half-opened bud, in the rushing streams and the freshness of bird song. To hold soul and earth together, the hidden and the appearing—that is Gaia's gift (which may explain why she does not intervene to protect Persephone from Hades' abduction).

Gaia's rituals, like other chthonic rituals and the rituals of the mystery cults, suggest the possibility of a different kind of identification between the worshiper and the goddess than we find in the worship of her Olympian offspring. Ecstatic, perhaps orgiastic, possession (as in the cult of Gaia's byforms, Rhea and Cybele) has no place in the worship of Athene or Hera. The Olympians may be seen as humans writ large, in whom we can recognize ourselves; whereas to be taken over by Gaia is to be overwhelmed by a clearly extrahuman force, to be taken out of ourselves.

Gaia is the all-mother, the mother not only of the gods but of human beings as well. There are many different tales of how the primordial human sprang directly from earth: one speaks of Erichthonios whom Gaia conceived when Hephaistos's semen fell to earth, another of Cecrops who was born from the earth with a snake's body. There is a story to the effect that once in anger Zeus determined to destroy the whole human race with a flood. Only Deukalion and Pyrrha were saved; as they longed for other human companionship they were told to throw over their shoulders the bones of their mother. They picked up stones and tossed them behind them: Deukalion's stones became men, Pyrrha's women.

All humans have their source in Gaia but Pandora, the first

woman, is Gaia in human form. Her very name, "rich in gifts,"
"all-giving," a name also of earth itself, suggests this. In
Hesiod's account she is fashioned by Hephaistos of earth and
water. In vase paintings, where she is often represented as a
creation of Prometheus, her art-type is indistinguishable from
Gaia's—she is Gaia emerging in human form from the earth, an
earth worked up by Prometheus's (or Epimetheus's) hammer.
In Hesiod she is associated with the letting loose of many evils
into the human world, including sickness and death. It is easy
(and proper) to attribute this to Hesiod's misogyny, but it is
important to see the truth as well. Pandora is indeed Gaia's
manifestation: the giver of all gifts, those we welcome and those
we would rather decline.

For Gaia represents a protection against those feminist rein-
terpretations of goddess religion that seek to deny or explain as
patriarchal overlay the dark side of the goddesses. I would repeat (and somewhat change) Sarton's verse:

> *I tell you the goddesses are still alive*
> *And they are not consoling.*

Gaia is not benign: she is generative—that is her only principle.
The Python and Typhaon, the Furies, the Giants, the Titans, the
Cyclopes, the Hundred-handed are terrifying—and there are
ever new forms of terror. No kiss transfigures them into fairy
princes. There is, irreconcilably, that which does not conform
to human scale, that which is not moral or purposive. Gaia is
never present as a model for human being—but she is a reality
never to be ignored.

The humanization of the Olympian goddesses is both gain
and loss. They represent much more clearly differentiated versions of female possibilities; they are closer to our own lives and
experiences, more reflective of our own pathologies. But just
because of this it becomes vitally important to remember their
connection to Gaia. For she reminds us that they are indeed
goddesses, more than oversized human beings acting out very
human scenarios. To remember her is to be protected against
inflated identifications. We need an earth goddess to bring them

down from Olympus and to bring us down. As we return each goddess to the mother we rediscover her fullness. They do not thereby lose their particularity but they do lose their pathology. Their very dark aspects come to be visible as transformative. Thus Hera becomes not simply the jealous wife but the threefold goddess who pertains to all aspects of a woman's life. Athene becomes not just a female who has identified with patriarchal power but representative of a fully feminine strength and creativity.

To see the Olympian goddesses in relation to Gaia is also to be reminded that we do not get to choose among them—we are, like it or not, involved with every one. One or another may initially seem closer to our experience or temperament than the rest, but the others, too, must be met. As Persephone, Hera, and Athene led me to Gaia, she in turn leads me to the others. To return to the beginning, to Gaia, is not to finish but precisely to begin. It is to be back in the cave where Artemis and Aphrodite are still shapeless presences and where one senses still unfamiliar aspects of those goddesses one thought one already knew. The relation between Gaia and the later goddesses is twofold. In relation to her, they are seen as who they truly are. But she is also seen as who she truly is in relation to them. Ge-ology can never be a monotheism. Gaia really is mother; she mothers children; more importantly she mothers mothers. We are not called to be children in relation to her, but to be birth-givers—who make of every drop of semen or blood that falls on us something vital, though not necessarily something easily valued.

As I begin again after coming at last to Gaia, I hope to remember her as I turn to the others—to Artemis, to Aphrodite, to the child. And like the poet of Homeric hymn, I invoke her:

> *Now,*
> > *mother of the gods*
> > > *bride of the sky*
> > > > *in stars*
> > > *farewell*
> > *but if you liked what I sang here*

give me this life too

then

in my other poems
I will remember you.[20]

NOTES

1. Rainer Maria Rilke, *Duino Elegies,* trans. C. F. MacIntyre (Berkeley: University of California Press, 1961), pp. 71f.

2. Jane Ellen Harrison, *Prolegomena to the Study of Greek Religion* (New York: Meridian, 1957), p. 164.

3. Kronos is, of course, not really identical with Chronos, but it is an ancient conceit to speak as though he were.

4. Susan Griffin, *Woman and Nature* (New York: Harper & Row, 1978), p. 159ff.

5. Lewis Richard Farnell, *The Cults of the Greek States,* vol. 3 (Chicago: Aegean Press, 1971), p. 2.

6. *The Homeric Hymns,* trans. Charles Boer (Chicago: Swallow Press, 1970), pp. 5f.

7. Henry Miller, *The Colossus of Maroussi* (New York: New Directions, 1941), p. 153.

8. Christine Downing, "A Thank Offering," *Inward Light* 30, no. 72 (Fall 1967): 22.

9. May Sarton, *Collected Poems* (New York: W. W. Norton, 1974), pp. 258ff.

10. The name "Ungit" was explicitly included in my associations then; it comes from C. S. Lewis's novel, *Till We Have Faces* (Grand Rapids, Mich.: Wm. B. Eerdmans Publishing, 1956).

11. Martin Heidegger, *Existence and Being* (Chicago: Henry Regnery, 1949), p. 245.

12. Robert Graves et al., *The New Larousse Encyclopedia of Mythology* (London: Hamlyn, 1968), p. 93.

13. Griffin, *Woman and Nature,* p. 53.

14. Jane Ellen Harrison, *Epilegomena to the Study of Greek Religion* (New Hyde Park, N.Y.: University Books, 1962), p. 420.

15. Rilke, *Elegies,* p. 67.

16. *The Orphic Hymns,* trans. Apostolos N. Athanassakis (Missoula, Mont.: Scholars Press, 1977), p. 37.

17. W. K. C. Guthrie, *The Greeks and Their Gods* (Boston: Beacon Press, 1955), p. 218. (Cf. discussion in James Hillman, *The Dream and the Underworld* [New York: Harper & Row, 1979], pp. 35ff.)

18. Farnell, *Cults* 3:23.

19. Farnell, *Cults* 3:28.

20. *Homeric Hymns,* p. 6.

·VII·

ARTEMIS
The Goddess Who Comes from Afar

None of us ever sees Her in the dark
or understands Her cruel mysteries.
Euripides [1]

So speaks Iphigenia after years of devotion to Artemis. Even Hippolytus, who prides himself as alone among mortals having the privilege of conversing with her, confesses, "True I may only hear. I may not see God face to face." [2] For one like myself who has fought to evade such devotion, it cannot help but be even more true. Artemis claims me now, calls me to her cruel mysteries with a power I can no longer withstand. The other goddesses who have presented themselves to me seemed to come forward out of the past, out of my childhood and youth and the early years of my marriage, or like Gaia as a reminder of some even more remote, prepersonal, transhuman past. They helped me to re-member who I have been and am; whereas Artemis seems to beckon from the future, to call me toward who I am now to become.

Until now Artemis has always been "the other." I have honored her as manifest in the life of the woman who has been my dearest friend, ever since we each gave birth to our first child. I have shared with this friend as intimately as with anyone I know, yet I sense in her a self-enclosedness, a pure inviolability, which I have never broached. There is a space around her which compels respect. Though we are dear friends, it would seem profanatory to say we are close. This woman stands tall and essentially alone as does Leto's daughter:

Artemis (from a fifth-century vase painting)
The Louvre, Paris, Photographie Giraudon, Paris

The heart of Leto is gladdened
for the head and the brows of Artemis are above all others
and she is easily marked among them, though all are lovely.[3]

My friend embodies Artemis's fearless self-sufficiency; she is beautifully serious, committed, utterly uncompromising. Her passion is neither repressed nor sublimated, nor does it leak away. Neither protective nor seductive in her care for me, she expresses one woman's deep trust in another. She inspires, she does not enchant. She has never said, "Choose me" but always, "Choose yourself." From the beginning of our friendship I have recognized her difference from myself, her at-home-ness with a goddess of whom I am more than a little afraid.

When Artemis beckons now, she appears as a stranger, as one hitherto unknown. Yet, of course, that is a lie. She has always been there—as the strange one, as remote, mysterious, unapproachable, and nevertheless there: *unheimlich*, uncanny, and *therefore*, as Freud taught us to recognize, *heimlich*, very well known, deeply familiar.[4] It is tempting to lie about that familiarity, to deny it or to transpose it into a more comfortable key. Artemis, "the Wolf-One,"[5] like other wolf goddesses seems to prompt lies such as those Diane di Prima lists in her "Some Lies About the Loba":

> *that she is the goal*
> *that she knows her name . . .*
> *that she is black, that she is white*
> *that you always know who she is*
> *when she appears . . .*
> *that you can hear her approach . . .*
> *that you can remember the first time you met*
> *that she is always with you*
> *that she can be seen without grace*
>
> *that there is anything to say of her*
> *which is not truth*[6]

The lies, however, never entirely persuade.

When I read in Nilsson, "Artemis was the most popular goddess in Greece," [7] I disbelieve. Those worshipers must have
been lying, or engaged in some apotropaic ritual. Perhaps they
were responding to a much diminished version of this awe-
inspiring figure—or else they must have overcome fears which
still assail me. Di Prima represents the transition in another
poem, "DREAM: The Loba Reveals Herself":

> *she came*
> *to hunt me down . . .*
> > *she came to hunt, but I did not*
> *stay to be hunted. . . .*
> *she came, she followed, she did not*
> *pursue.*
> > *But walked, patient behind me. . . .*
> > *only a step or two*
> > > *behind me.*
> *I turned to confront*
> > *to face*
> > > *Her:*
> > > > *ring of fur, setting off*
> *the purity of her head.*
> *she-who-was-to-have-devoured me*
> *stood, strong patient*
> > > > *recognizably*
> *goddess.*
> > > *Protectress*
> *great mystic beast of European forest.*
> *green warrior woman, towering.*
> > > > > *kind watchdog I could*
> *leave the children with.*
> > *Mother of sister.*
> > *Myself.* [8]

Now I, too, must turn to face the one in whose name (so Otto
tells us) "the Greeks undoubtedly detected the meaning, 'She
Who Slays.'" [9] Turning to Artemis is, I know, a turning to face
myself—not, as with the other goddesses, turning to face the

soul meaning of mother or children, father or husband, lover or work—not as in my earlier evasions of this goddess a turning away from one who has power in my friend's life but none in my own. The present task is simpler and more difficult; it involves only the goddess and myself. I feel before Artemis what Rilke felt before her brother, Apollo:

> For there is no place
> that does not see you. You must change your life.[10]

I understand the turning toward Artemis as another ritual observance, this time of my forty-ninth birthday. Endings and beginnings have always been important to me, perhaps naturally so for someone born at just that moment in the astrological calendar (on the cusp between Pisces and Aries) when one year ends that another may begin. Every birthday invites celebration, but this one has for several years loomed as singularly significant. Seven times seven suggests a completion and a turning around, a birth into the rest of my life. I had looked to this birth as an easy one, like the ("only symbolic") rebirth of a snake shedding its skin or the emergence of a butterfly from its chrysalis. I had imagined it as a sloughing off of what was worn out and used up, so that what was viable and vital might emerge less fettered. Perhaps I had forgotten it would have to be a human birth, a birth into the human. Or perhaps I had expected the birth to be assisted by gentle Eileithyia rather than by Artemis. Though Artemis is a skillful and compassionate midwife, in her realm childbirth is painful and difficult and always accompanied by the threat of death. (The priestess of Artemis inherited the clothes of those who died in childbirth.) The first labor she attended (her mother's delivery of Artemis's own twin brother, Apollo) took nine desperately agonizing days (though her own birth had been without travail). I (whose literal birth-ings were all so easy) am now discovering what it is to be engaged in a giving birth that one resists, twists away from in pain, despairs of being done with. (Another image that describes this in-between place perfectly comes from May Sarton: "I feel like a river when the tide changes and for a while the waters flow in crosscurrent, with no direction, only a pulling from all sides."[11])

I had thought at first I could easily name what was being born. A few months before my birthday an annual checkup suggested I might have cancer of the uterus. "So, it is my death I am to give birth to," I thought. "Perhaps the reason I have for so long looked forward to this birthday is that somewhere deep inside me something knew it was to be the last." That very literal threat was proven illusory before it led me to call on Artemis whose arrows bring a swift and gentle death to women. Then a love affair which I had felt from its beginning was in some way a last time around seemed to be coming to an end. "So that's what it is," I mused; "I am going to be abandoned into an evaded solitude for which I have always known myself to be destined." I recalled a poem by Sarton evoked by a similar threat of abandonment which begins:

> If I can let you go as trees let go
> Their leaves, so casually, one by one

and goes on:

> Twice I have set my heart upon a sharing,
> Twice have imagined a real human home,
> Having forgotten how some fiercer caring
> Demands this naked solitude for loam.[12]

Again I did not consciously think of Artemis, "the mercurial queen of solitude," during the interval before I realized that in my love affair it was a time for changes, not for endings. Again, I felt both relieved and cheated. What *was* going to happen? For a time it seemed that a job I knew I would not stay with much longer might come to an end earlier than I would have chosen; for a time my former husband and I considered remarriage. Both possibilities would have represented genuinely significant transitions, but I knew even before they dissolved that neither was what this birthday was really "about." It was not so much that these changes would have been too partial or too concrete as that they were too passive. Di Prima has it right. The transition I anticipated would not happen until I turned around to confront "Her." This huntress insists on being hunted; she will never overtake. It is just that which makes it so difficult. *I* have to give birth—or struggle to be born; neither giving birth nor coming to birth are things that happen *to* one.

I understood that when I discovered that the most adequate name for this particular liminal space is simply: Artemis. The name does not eliminate the mystery; it honors it with an appellation that suggests its complexity and depth.

I must admit some puzzlement and even resentment at the youth of this goddess who stands so powerfully before me now. "What does *she* know?" I want to ask. Though I could have accepted the appearance of some divine child (for after all the child is symbol of all new beginnings), the archetypal image I really expected at this point in my life was that of the wise old woman. Finding myself under Artemis's tutelage at first made me feel somewhat embarrassed to be learning at fifty what others learn young. Like Slater and Pomeroy I saw the youth and virginity of the classic version of some of the goddesses only in negative terms; I believe it expressed male fear of mature femininity.[13] I now see that because Artemis has been the youthful virgin forever, she is, in her own paradoxical way, herself a wise old woman. I realize how truly timely it is to be pulled to doing therapy now (in the full ancient sense of *therapeia*) with this ancient huntress who surely and fearlessly follows any scent and who trusts us to learn to do the same. My familiar evasive games lose their efficacy in her wilderness; she will not be seduced into a relationship nor diverted by my storytelling skill. This ever-evanescent goddess appears only to say: "Here you are alone, as you have said you were ready to be."

As Walter Otto saw, manifold as Artemis's manifestations may be, we discover their unity and thus apprehend her essence, when we know her as the goddess who comes from afar, whose realm is the ever-distant wilderness. To this primary remoteness he appropriately connects her virginity, her solitariness, and her strangely cruel solicitude.[14]

Though others have found Artemis more accessible, I have learned by now that I need to start with what is darkest, with what I like least but which cannot be eluded: Hera's jealousy, Athene's misogyny, Artemis's otherness. I agree with James Hillman:

> . . . that each archetype has its pathological themes and that each pathologized theme has an archetypal perspective. Archetypal psychopathology finds the pathological inherently necessary to the myth: Christ must have his crucifixion; Dionysus must be childish and attract titanic enemies; Persephone must be raped; Artemis must kill him who comes too close.[15]

I have come to trust that the meaning of her remoteness will be transformed as I am willing to acknowledge it. So long as I deny that she is, indeed, "She Who Slays," I am still evading Artemis.

Artemis is the Lady of the Wild Things, a title that encompasses much more than is acknowledged in the post-Homeric image of her as the shaft-showering huntress.[16] As Aeschylus reminds us, she is not only the hunter but protector of all that is wild and vulnerable:

> *Artemis the undefiled*
> *is angered with pity*
> *at the flying hounds of her father*
> *eating the unborn young in the hare and the*
> *shivering mother.*
> *She is sick at the eagles' feasting.*
> *Sing sorrow, sorrow: but good win out in the end.*
> *Lovely you are and kind*
> *to the tender young of ravening lions.*
> *For sucklings of all the savage*
> *beasts that lurk in the lonely places you*
> *have sympathy.*[17]

Artemis represents the mystic, primitive identity of hunter and hunted.[18] There are indications that the worship of Artemis in Arcadia and Attica included an initiation cereomoy for prepubescent girls in which the goddess, her worshipers, and the bear whose skin the maidens wore were "considered to be as of one nature and called by the same name." [19] Artemis is intimately associated with the wild beasts of the field, the animals of the chase: the hare, the lion, the wolf, the wild boar, the bear, the deer. The earliest artistic representations show her holding one or another of these animals in her hands, often wearing the fruit of some wild tree on her head or with the branches of a wild fig tree above her. Artemis is herself the wilderness, the wild and untamed, and not simply its mistress.

She is uncivilized nature in quite a different sense from Gaia. Gaia is *there* before gods or mortals; she represents the ceaseless, irrepressible fecundity of nature. As Auden puts it, "Earth, till the end, will be Herself":

> *why we should feel neglected on mountain drives*
> *unpopular in woods, is quite clear. . . .*
> > *what*
> *to Her, the real one, can our good landscapes*
> > *be but lies?*[20]

Artemis by contrast is wilderness within the Olympian and human world. In this world, as Nilsson puts it, what "interests man is not Nature in herself, but the Life of Nature in the measure in which it intervenes in human life and forms a necessary and obvious basis for it." [21] Although Artemis may originally have been an oriental goddess, may have come from the fringes of the Greek world, in the classical period she is particularly identified with Arcadia, the wild, mountainous, forested center of the Peloponnesus. This reinforces my discovery that though we may first know her as the other without, she is more truly the other within. She herself insists on that inclusion; witness her anger at Oeneus and Agamemnon for ignoring her when sacrifices to the Olympians are due. Yet she is not at home on Olympus; she has no friends there except Herakles who waits patiently at the gate to welcome her return from the chase. Clearly out of her element on the battlefields of Troy, her skill with the bow in the wilderness avails her little in that scene of interhuman strife. Hera scolds her contemptuously:

"How have you had the daring, you shameless hussy, to stand up and face me? It will be hard for you to match your strength with mine even if you wear a bow, since Zeus has made you a lion among women, and given you leave to kill any at your pleasure. Better for you to hunt down the ravening beasts in the mountains and deer of the wolds, than try to fight in strength with your betters. But if you would learn what fighting is, come on. You will find out how much stronger I am when you try to match strength against me.". . .

She caught both of her arms at the wrists in the left hand and with her right hand stripped away the bow from her shoulders, then with her own bow, smiling, boxed her ears as Artemis tried to twist away, and the flying arrows were scattered. She got under and free and fled in tears, as a pigeon in flight from a hawk wings her way into some rock-hollow and a cave, since it was not destiny for the hawk to catch her.

In that realm Artemis is a clumsy child who runs whimperingly to her father:

The maiden took her place kneeling at the knees of her father and the ambrosial veil trembled about her. Her father Kronides caught her against him, and laughed softly, and questioned her:

"Who now of the Uranian gods, dear child, has done such things to you, rashly, as if you were caught doing something wicked?" Artemis sweet-garlanded lady of clamours answered him:

"It was your wife, Hera of the white arms, who hit me, father, since hatred and fighting have fastened upon the immortals." [22]

Born on unpeopled Delos, Artemis is really only at home in the wilderness, far from the haunts of men. A different logic, a different strength and wisdom, rules there. The romantic view of Arcadia as an idyllic pastoral realm inhabited by nymphs and shepherds does not do full justice to the Arcadia of ancient mythology: a wild and dangerous, rude and barbarous land.

Arcadia is an imaginal realm, set apart from the everyday world, where things are as they are in themselves, not as shaped and manipulated by humankind. Artemis represents the form of imagination most foreign to me: the one connected to the psychological realm Jungians call sensation (as opposed to thinking, feeling, or intuition). There is nothing spiritual or sentimental or even sensual in Artemis's response to the wild things in whose company she lives. She does not respond to them as vehicles of symbolic meaning nor on the basis of their capacity to bring pleasure or displeasure. She knows each tree by its bark or leaf or fruit, each beast by its footprint or spoor, each bird by its plumage or call or nest. Only such carefully attendant seeing allows one to know why the black poplar that bears no fruit should be emblem of the underworld goddesses, the rose Aphrodite's flower, or the wild fig the fruit of Artemis; why the migratory quail should be Artemis's bird while the night-preying owl is Athene's. The woods and fields belong to Artemis and her nymphs: each tree, laurel or myrrh, oak or ash, is truly recognized only when we know with which nymph(s) to associate it; each wild flower, each brook and stream, also evoke a particular sacred presence. Artemis's imagination is concrete and specific, bespeaks a loving respect for the unique essence of everything as it lives in its natural state. It would be a wrong to mis-take her mode of perception for literalism: her response is animistic, anima-istic. Each creature—each plant, each wood, each river—is to her a Thou, not an it. Unlike Aphrodite she never confuses this I-Thou relation with merging. To know Artemis is to understand what Buber means by "*distance* and relation."

Artemis is what Jungians call an anima figure—one who helps us recognize that anima is not to be equated with contrasexuality or a gift for relationship or with the functions of feeling or intuition. Rather, anima is, as Hillman puts it, what gives events (or persons or "things") the dimension of soul.[23] Soul making is not confined to the making of our own soul but to the re-creation (or rediscovery) of the world within which we live as a realm of souls, of living, meaning-full-in-themselves, beings.

Artemis also reminds us of the necessary and profound connection between soul and solitude. In the interhuman world of the polis we necessarily respond mostly on the basis of ego and persona; in the wilderness those are as dysfunctional as is Artemis's wilderness on the Trojan battlefield. In her *Journal of a Solitude* Sarton celebrates the reality and depth made possible by the stripping down that is correlate of true aloneness:

> I am here alone for the first time in weeks, to take up my "real" life again at last. That is what is strange—that friends, even passionate love, are not my real life unless there is time alone in which to explore and to discover what is happening or has happened. Without the interruptions, nourishing and maddening, this life would become arid. Yet I taste it fully only when I am alone here.[24]

Solitude attracts Sarton as a needed and healing complement to her life within the human world. From the perspective of the Olympian pantheon Artemis represents such complementation. From her own perspective she represents a much more radical and wholehearted choice of the lonely wilderness—and a more terrifying one. There is risk in Artemis's world of losing one's capacity for human communication, danger of being caught helplessly within one's anima-lity. Ovid describes Actaeon's horror at discovering the horned stag's head which the pool reflects back to him:

> (he) tried to say "Alas"—but no words would come. He sobbed; that at least was a sound he uttered, and tears flowed down his new-changed face. Only his mind remained unchanged.[25]

and Callisto's pain at her transformation into an ugly, lumbering, grinning bear:

> Her power of speech was lost, with no prayers or entreaties could she win pity, and a hoarse and frightening growl was her only utterance. Yet her human mind remained even when she had become a bear; with never-ceasing moans she made known her suffering.[26]

I know that my own fear of Artemis is connected to a fear of such radical solitude and of unprotected confrontation with self. For as long as I have attended to my dreams they have suggested that my true destiny is associated with a primary aloneness that I not only accept but in some measure choose. This is the theme of the very earliest dream I remember, one that recurred repeatedly while I was a child:

> The dream begins with my leaving my bed after everyone else in the household is asleep and making my way to a small and secret door at the back of my closet. It opens onto a steep, narrow, dark and uneven flight of stone stairs which lead down to a landing far, far below the cellar of our house. There is another door, massive and beautifully paneled, with heavy iron hinges and a lock to which only I have the key. Within is a spaciously elegant chamber, plush velvet carpet and drapes, sparkling chandeliers and sconces, a room empty but for (and this varied) either a gilded, cushioned throne or an ornately worked bejeweled treasure chest.

I knew as a child, even in my waking hours, that this room was always there, that no one else had access to it, and that it was my real home.

Years later as a young married woman I had a dream in which the world I really belong to, though again a place apart, was more clearly "outlandish" than the safe enclosure of that early vision of the interior:

> In this dream I enter an elegant room whose mirrors and appointments suggest the ballroom at Versailles and am led to a table evidently reserved for me. There opposite me sits a young man, the one for whom I am destined. He is not the prince of my fantasies, yet I know I have only to stretch my hand across the table toward his, and he will immediately be transformed into my ideal. I know it will take only this gesture and then I will forever after look upon him as a true fulfillment. But I cannot settle for that. I get up from the table and walk to one of the French doors and step out—out into boundless space—floating

alone and yet somehow feeling supported and in my own element.

A decade or more later still I had another dream in which I chose solitude despite the beauty and joy of creative relationships with others:

In the center was a pond, in its center a spring which lifted itself only a few inches above the level of the water, not a spectacular fountaining of water, only a continually renewing source. We were all around this pond. I had always been there. They had just come. They were all not yet known to me and for the most part it seemed they did not see each other either. We went around the circle, and one after another sang that song which expressed himself, his gift and the pattern that enclosed him and his longing. Then as in a progressive circle dance, each of the men came before a woman and sang to her what could only come from him to her and she responded, and this we all heard for it belonged to what was happening in our midst. Then each couple made love in that couple's way and that was a private happening which concerned only those two. And then the men moved on around the circle to the next girl. I was included in this singing, this lovemaking, this dancing, and wanted and responded to and cared about each of the men who came to me in the way created by his particular being-there. And all of us came to know each other, to know what we might be hoping to hear in *This* one's song the next time he sang, to know how we hoped we might be able to love *That* one when he came to us and how we hoped he might turn to us and what he might bring to song in us which was waiting but which only he could draw forth.

Then we had come around full circle and one by one they came to me, the men and the women, and kissed me on the face and left. I didn't know until all were gone and I sat there before the spring how important and wonderful it was that all had gone—had been strong enough to go and willing to go, though it had been difficult to hold some of them back—but all had gone, and as I sat there before the spring I knew that if when the time was over they had not gone, the spring would no longer spring and I would have been left there before a dead and dried-out pool.[27]

Some receptivity to Artemis's call has been alive in me all along. And yet, and yet . . . I fear the loneliness and isolation of truly responding. I also know how some of the attraction is itself pathological, inspired by a fear of intimacy and commitment, of losing myself in *that* way. How instinctively I call on Aphrodite to help me against Artemis; how spontaneously Aphrodite seems to appear to lure me away. A more recent dream put this clearly:

At the beginning (and even within the dream there was the sense of being at a mythological beginning point) I was with my lover, together with him in a wondrously sensuous, profoundly beautiful, though not explicitly sexual way. There was a connection between us at the level of soul like an orgasm which leaves one feeling utter fulfillment. We knew that for the moment there was nothing more we could give each other, though (at least on my side) there was also a kind of smiling blissful welcoming of later moments when we would turn to each other again to give and to receive.

But then somehow (though not in words) my lover communicated to me that it was time for me to go off and take care of myself, to do what I needed and wanted to do for myself. Only if I really did that, did it just for me and not for the sake of some later reconnection between us, might we be together again in this so important to both of us way at the end of the evening/at the end of our lives. (That ambiguity, too, was present within the dream: this was the task of the evening, the task of my life.)

Though my lover sent me off it nevertheless felt that the going was right *for me,* not imposed by him nor undertaken simply for the sake of our relationship. And so I went; I did many things, some by myself, some with others, and each thing I did was symbolized by some beautiful concrete artifact (a small very old and worn prayer rug, some jewelry, a stone from a beach); these I collected in a small suitcase that I took with me everywhere. From time to time I would think, "And some time I will see my lover again," but that was for its time; it did not seem to inform how I was in this time.

Then the evening/my life/our lives came to their foreordained end. Without having looked for him, without going to him, my lover was there. I was filled with joyous anticipation of sharing with him all the beautiful things in my suitcase and the story that went with each. But he said, or somehow communicated, "No, I don't want to see. You did it for you, didn't you, not for me, not for the sake of being together again or in order to have something wonderful to share with me?"

I was devastated—and not sure of my answer. I knew that, yes, I had done it all for myself. There was nothing I had done that wasn't just for me, that I had done to win his praise or gratitude, nothing I would have done differently had I known we would never be together again. I also knew there had never been an assurance that we would reconnect; no promises had been made; there had been no betrayal, yet at some level I had always taken it for granted that we *would* reconnect and that he would love what I had brought to share with him.

The dream suggests how deeply intertwined appear the call to solitude and the recall to relationship. I seem able to bear being with Artemis only on condition of an eventual return to Aphrodite's realm.

Contemplation of Artemis's solitude provokes not only fear of loneliness but of savagery, wildness, of a passion entirely different from Aphrodite's sensual indulgence of feeling. In Artemis's realm, feelings do not issue in creative expression or in sexual involvement. One does not do anything with them; one simply comes to know them, discriminatingly, unflinchingly. "So this is me." The very taming of feeling is beside the point. The feelings evoked in her realm are of many hues— vulnerability, solicitude, rage, instability. They include the painful sense of implacable otherness, and even the ache of not having access to one's deepest feelings. Each is pure, entire, for the time all-encompassing.

In Artemis, passion and virginity are strangely intertwined, as
are the wildness and remoteness of her woodland habitat. Artemis and her wildness both invite and resist violation. We long,
like Callisto, to enter "a woods that no one throughout the
years has touched"; yet, once we have entered it, it is no longer
a virgin forest. The wilderness becomes an ever-receding and
even more fantasmal reality. Artemis becomes the hunted. The
sad quixotic character of this search for the other is powerfully
communicated in Lévi-Strauss's *Tristes Tropiques.* He describes
there the experience of being "the first white man to visit a
particular native community":

> They were as close to me as reflections in a mirror. I could
> touch them, but I could not understand them. I had been
> given at one and the same time, my reward and my
> punishment. Was it not my mistake and the mistake of my
> profession to believe that men are not always men? That
> some are more deserving of interest and attention because
> they astonish us by the color of their skin and their cus-
> toms? I had only to succeed in guessing what they were
> like for them to be deprived of their strangeness: in which
> case I might just as well have stayed in my village. Or if, as
> was the case here, they retained their strangeness, I could
> make no use of it, since I was incapable of even grasping
> what it consisted of.[28]

Lévi-Strauss believes that otherness is either illusion or impossible barrier; so long as we see the other as other we will seek to
destroy it—or her. Compare Susan Griffin's "The Hunt":

> She has captured his heart. She has overcome him. He
> cannot tear his eyes away. He is burning with passion. He
> cannot live without her. He pursues her. She makes him
> pursue her. The faster she runs, the stronger his desire. He
> will overtake her. He will make her his own. He will have
> her. (The boy chases the doe and her yearling for nearly
> two hours. She keeps running despite her wounds. He
> pursues her through pastures, over fences, groves of trees,
> crossing the road, up hills, volleys of rifle shots sounding,

until perhaps twenty bullets are embedded in her body.) She has no mercy. She has dressed to excite his desire. She has no scruples. She has painted herself for him. She makes supple movements to entice him. She is without a soul. Beneath her painted face is flesh, are bones. She reveals only part of herself to him. She is wild. She flees whenever he approaches. She is teasing him. (Finally, she is defeated and falls and he sees that half of her head has been blown off, that one leg is gone, her abdomen split from her tail to her head, and her organs hang outside her body.) [29]

Artemis demands that we allow her to be other, to remain the goddess who comes from afar, as she allows each creature in her world its own otherness. Artemis's virginity means this insistence on inviolability, on separateness, on in-her-self-ness.

How often I welcome rather than resist what Artemis would experience as violation, how little protective I often am of my own soul space. Nevertheless, at some of the most important moments in my life, I have fought as fiercely as Artemis herself for such privacy. At those times the pull to be alone has been felt as an instinctual, animal necessity. To live these moments—when I was brought in touch with the deepest rhythms of feminine biological being fully, imaginally— demanded being allowed to live them alone. The instances that come most immediately to mind are three: keeping my first pregnancy an unshared secret (even from my husband) for the first three months—this was *my* child; arranging to deliver my last child when my husband was far away—this was to be *my* bringing forth; at the time of deepest turmoil in my life saying with all my strength to the husband who wanted so much to help, "Get out of my way—I have to do this myself." Though I did not recognize her, Artemis, in whose realms birth and death are feminine mysteries, was clearly present in each of these moments. Otto, as often, says it superbly: "The bitterness and danger of woman's most difficult hours come from Artemis, who . . . works her mysterious effects upon womankind from the wilderness." [30]

Artemis is, indeed, closely associated with feminine being, especially with those aspects of feminine experience connected to biological femaleness: menstruation, conception, parturition, nursing, menopause, death. (The last may not seem to us a peculiarly female mystery, yet to the Greeks it was self-evident that, though Apollo's arrows bring death to males, it is Artemis who brings about the death of women.) A goddess of all women, she is related to all the phases of female existence, yet very differently than Hera. Hera is a threefold goddess, simultaneously maiden, wife, and postconjugal solitary one. She represents female being oriented toward (and away from) fulfilling relationship with male being. Artemis represents female being in its own essence, without respect for male being in fact or fantasy, longing or refusal. Thus she is and remains virgin. Her chastity, her physical virginity (though probably not part of the most archaic conception of Artemis), is a central element in the Greek vision of Artemis long before Homer or Hesiod. Originally, Artemis was probably a mother-goddess—as the many-breasted Artemis of Ephesus still is even in classical times—whose virginity simply meant that she belonged to no one, that she had never been confined in a monogamous marriage. We should not move too quickly to understand the virginity of the later Artemis as only symbolic, but rather try to understand the meaning of this virginity as an essential aspect. It seems appropriate that a goddess as involved as is Artemis with the biological dimensions of feminine experience should express her own essential femininity by stressing that her feminine being has never been violated.

In his somewhat sentimental "Hymn to Artemis," Callimachus suggests that as a mere three-year-old Artemis already had a precocious sense of her own essence. In response to her father's asking her what gifts would most delight her, she immediately pleaded: "Pray give me eternal virginity." Athene's virginity allows her to move comfortably and unthreatened in the world of men, her girdle securely knotted like a warrior's. As understood by Homer and the tragedians, it represents a transcendence of gender, a way of preventing sexual attraction from disrupting heterosexual companionship. Artemis, on the other hand, wears the untied girdle of the maiden. She is unwilling to disown her femininity, but also unwilling to succumb to masculine approaches. Her power lies in this enticement—and in her inviolability, which often makes her seem cold and cruel, disdainful of those who are more susceptible.

Artemis embodies a profound denial of the world of patriarchy, the world where some persons have power over others, the world of dominance and submission, where one can be hunter *or* hunted. Although in Homer and Callimachus she is represented as Zeus's childishly winsome daughter, usually Artemis is presented as intensely identified with her mother. Zeus is relegated to the role of the anonymous procreator like the father in the original matriarchal family. Leto, Apollo, and Artemis appear, says Kerenyi, as the characteristic matriarchal triangle.[31] Leto's children protect her from rape by Tityus and Python and from Niobe's insulting boasts. (Artemis's own near-compulsive virginity can, at one level, be understood as response to her mother's so often threatened sexual vulnerability.)

In Artemis's realm, as in the matriarchal world generally, the connection with the brother is more important than that with father or husband. Her twinship with Apollo is not aboriginal; Apollo plays no part in the primitive Arcadian cults devoted to Artemis, and Artemis has no early relation to Apollo's oracle at Delphi. Cook suggests Artemis might once have been worshiped as Apollo's mother [32] (and Farnell that, as Cyrene, she may have been his lover [33]). By the time of Homer, however, their twinship is well established. Mythological twinship may be derivative of the notion of two-faced divinity and, like it, represent the essential complementarity of lightness and darkness, divinity and mortality, masculinity and femininity. How difficult it is to know which of the points of affinity or contrast between the two divinities led to their association and which resulted from it. It may well be, for instance, that Artemis's association with the moon (which despite popular assumptions almost all scholars agree to be post-Homeric) derives from Apollo's with the sun. Otto sees the relation between the two becoming more important as we recognize how essential to each is purity, sublimity, remoteness. Other scholars lay less stress on Apollo's significance for a full appreciation of Artemis.

My own sense is we must take Artemis's sisterliness seriously and understand how it differs from that of Athene or Hera. Hera's sibling relationship to Zeus is clearly subordinated to the spousal; their marriage (at least ideally) represents an incestuous *hieros gamos* in which male and female are brought together in perfect fulfillment of each. Athene's brothers, Ares and Hephaistos, are crippled, fractional incarnations of masculine potentialities she herself realizes more fully and wholly. Athene's virginity is determined by the sublimation of father-daughter incest, whereas that of Artemis receives its definition from the matriarchal taboo on brother-sister incest.[34] The twin-ship with Apollo establishes Artemis's virginity even more clearly as a confirmation of her femininity rather than as a rejection of it.

As indicated earlier, Artemis's virginity (like Hera's marital fidelity) seems to invite violation (as Athene's rarely does). With some assistance from Apollo, she easily repulses Orion's and Otus's sexual advances. (Orion may have been a valued hunting companion until he misunderstood the terms of their friendship; if so, he is an anomaly in Artemis's life, otherwise so singularly devoid of supportive relations with men.) Artemis's reaction to Actaeon represents more vividly that she is, indeed, She Who Slays. (After a day's hunting, Actaeon left his fellow huntsmen to find a quiet place to rest. Accidentally, he comes upon Artemis bathing with her nymphs. Outraged at being seen naked, she flings water at his face and thus transforms him into a stag. Catching the animal's scent, his own hounds relentlessly pursue their erstwhile master and tear his body to shreds.) To hide from this story is to hide from Artemis herself. Artemis is all decisiveness; she is hard and cruel, ruthlessly singleminded. Athene, as we have noted, responded as automatically by striking Tiresias blind when he saw her bathing with Chrysippe but, repenting the extravagance of that gesture, later granted him prophetic foresight, long life, and the preservation of his intelligence in Hades. Artemis exhibits no such second thoughts. When Actaeon's glance turns her the huntress into the hunted, she naturally makes him experience the same transformation from hunter into victim. In her world, as in Sartre's, the voyeur is a thinly disguised rapist. She is the other who comes from afar as Thou; she is not willing to submit to being made into the other who is the transfixed object of my gaze.

I had at one time understood Artemis's dramatic rejection of any male other than her brother (and perhaps a few brotherly companions like Herakles and Orion) as simply the obverse of her devotion to women. I had imagined that the most promising access to this most woman-identified of the Greek goddesses would be by way of an exploration of her relation to the nymphs in whose company we so consistently find her. Indeed, Nilsson suggests she is essentially nymph epitomized, *the* nymph who rises to prominence from amidst the company of nymphs.[35]

Here was Artemis prodding me to look honestly at the role in my life of deep and passionate friendships with women. Even this Artemis threatened me, portended a judgment from which I flinched. I saw her as having wholeheartedly chosen the love that women share with women, and as disdaining someone like myself who cannot say that friendships with women are the only ones really needed, the only ones that truly nurture. Even the patriarchally determined classical versions of the myths reveal Artemis as a woman who loves women. (Perhaps the most compelling evidence is to be found in the story of Zeus's rape of Callisto, the most beautiful of Artemis's nymphs, the one most dear to her. To win the nymph's love Zeus disguises himself as Artemis; in that guise Callisto welcomes his embrace.) But to see the relationship between Artemis and her nymphs primarily in sexual terms is simplification and distortion. It transposes their relationship into an Aphroditic key and thus ignores the testimony of the Homeric hymn to Aphrodite that alone among gods and mortals, Hestia, Athene, and Artemis are immune to Aphrodite's power. Artemis does not say, "Choose women," but "Choose yourself." The meaning of her primary association with women is that in loving women we are loving our womanly self. (Thus, though the Amazons are worshipers of Artemis, they may—at least in the well-known accounts of them—represent a somewhat different attitude. They are both antimale and as ruthless and bellicose as any man; Artemis represents a more profound femininity, one that is not essentially defined by a relation, positive or negative, to the masculine.)

Fully to understand Artemis's connection to women demands relating it to that virginity so essential to her nature. Even in her association with women Artemis points to a communion not identical with sexual union and possibly subverted by it. The deep bonding of woman to woman which Artemis encourages may, indeed, encompass passionate attraction, sensual delight, and sexual consummation. Yet she reminds us that the sexual may be surrogate for a more profound affirmation of one another and of our shared womanliness than we quite know how to express, an evasion of spiritual connection more fearful than the physical one. We mis-take Artemis's chastity if we interpret it only as patriarchal culture's attempt to suppress her lesbianism, her refusal of men and her love of women. Her chastity represents something more essential to her nature. It surely does not mean that she is not stirred by feminine beauty; it does not necessarily mean that she refuses sexual intimacy with women; it does mean that she never wholly gives herself to another, female or male. Artemis's axial self-enclosedness is captured in Farnell's description of a Praxitelean sculpture:

> The face is high, the features maidenly and noble. The hair is carefully drawn away from the forehead and temples, the eyes are long and rather narrow, the line of the eyebrows is straight and pure; the wall of the nose near the eyes is very large, as it is in the Hermes' head; the upper lip is slightly curved and the lower lip is very full; the chin is large and the cheeks are broad. The eyes are full of thought, with a distant inscrutable look in them, and the proud reserved expression accords with the self-centred life of the goddess.[36]

When Otto speaks of Artemis as one who "compels delight but cannot love," he captures her remoteness but not, I believe, the beautifully dispassionate caring it expresses. Artemis's refusal to give herself bespeaks her respect, not her rejection, of the other; it is an expression not of frigidity but of passion. She gives herself to her own passion, her own wildness. Though invoked as the "frenzy-loving" goddess, Artemis is not driven mad by her passion as are the maenads when they leave their husbands' beds for their mountaintop orgies. Neither does she feel the need to find some appropriate sublimated expression for it, as might bright-eyed Athene, nor to transpose it immediately into the interpersonal erotic realm as would Aphrodite. Because Artemis is at home in the wilderness, she is comfortable with her own wildness. As René Malamud so sensitively perceives, the spear of the goddess is a spear of passion, "for all passion means fundamentally a search for self." [37]

Artemis is who she is with an ease and simplicity that indeed seems divine. She does not suffer self-doubt or inner division and has little patience with those of us who do. Thus she often appears as a harsh judge of women. She attacks not only the Chiones or Niobes who boast that they are more beautiful than she or richer in progeny than her mother, but also women who betray their lovers. She does not punish the breaking of marital bonds per se; after all, she supports Aegisthus and Clytemnestra against Agamemnon. When she kills Koronis and Ariadne it is because they have betrayed an immortal lover (Apollo or Dionysos) with a mortal one (Isychys, Theseus) and thereby in some profound sense betrayed themselves.

She Who Slays confronts even the nymphs she loves most dearly, for her care for women never issues in uncritical affirmation. She expects them to be as true to their self-sufficient virginal womanliness as she is to hers; when they fail there is no forgiveness. Most of the myths about her nymphs recount such failure; many suggest that the nymph in question is simply a byform of Artemis herself, as though such inviolability could not really be maintained eternally. The nymphs resist, but to no avail. Thus, as Ovid describes it, Callisto (whose name, "most beautiful," is often an attribute of Artemis herself)

> fought against (Jupiter) with all a woman's strength—
> Juno's anger would have been lessened could she have
> seen her—but what god is weaker than a girl, and what god
> can overcome Jupiter? He won, and to the heavens he flies
> and she hates the wood that knows her shame.[38]

Artemis never gives Callisto a chance to explain how passionately she tried to fight off Zeus's advances; when Callisto's pregnancy is discovered, banishment is immediate and irrevocable. (Though it is Hera, not Artemis, who turns her into a bear whom years later her son nearly kills.)

Myths about such resistant but ravished nymphs abound. Britomartis (a Cretan Artemis whose name means "sweet nymph") flees from King Minos's advances for nine months until, caught on a steep mountain crag, she leaps in desperation into the sea below—some suggest in shame because she had been despoiled despite all her resistance. Arethusa, spied upon by Alpheius as Artemis was by Actaeon, turns into a spring in Ortygia (an island close to Delos often designated as Artemis's birthplace) to avoid his advances; he becomes a river whose waters flow under the sea and then rise to the surface on the island to mingle with those of the stream. Artemis turns Taygete into a doe to help her escape Zeus's embraces, but he ravishes her nonetheless. Even Persephone's abduction by Hades can be seen as another variant of this same scenario.

Atalanta is a human version of the young female deeply but unavailingly committed to remaining a virgin. Exposed as an infant because her father had wanted only boys, she is raised by a she-bear. She grows up to love hunting above all else and to be fleeter afoot than any other mortal. Yet even her speed cannot protect her from being caught by Aphrodite's protégé, apple-dropping Melanion. Another human Artemis, pictured only as a young, self-enclosed girl on the edge of womanhood, is Nausicaa:

it was Nausikaa of the white arms who led in the dancing;
and as Artemis, who showers arrows, moves on the mountains
either along Taygetos or on high-towering
Erymanthos, delighting in boars and deer in their running
and along with her the nymphs, daughters of Zeus of the aegis,
range in the wilds and play. . . .

so this one shone among her handmaidens, a virgin unwedded.[39]

Because Artemis is the goddess of unspoiled virginity, she is especially associated with nine- to twelve-year-old prepubescent girls, with maidens in "the years of fugitive bloom." The transition from childhood to womanhood is her particular province; she is the maiden; she is the transition. Artemis is a tender nurse of all that is young and vulnerable, be it human or animal; but she has no patience with those who remain childish, who stay dependent and needy, as adult women. Because Artemis represents a transition into womanhood that is not defined by an entrance into monogamic marriage, a sacrifice to her is part of the young girl's prenuptial ritual. Before her marriage the girl takes her dolls and the clothes she has worn as a child and in propitiation dedicates them to Artemis. The ritual reminds the girl of all that she is giving up by marrying. She may also be imploring Artemis to be present, nevertheless, in the peculiarly feminine pains and dangers that still await the bride, particularly those associated with childbirth. (The premarital ritual was once more bloody, as is implicit in Clytemnestra's first painfully innocent question to Agamemnon. When she still believes that she has come to Aulis to see Iphigenia wed to Achilles, she asks:

> Now I ask this, have you slain the victims
> to Artemis the goddess for our child? [40]

Little does she know that the victim will be Iphigenia herself or that much later, as Artemis's priestess in the bloody rites of the Taurians, Iphigenia, the slain one, will become the slayer.)

As I look at each aspect of Artemis in turn, again and again I discover She Who Slays, she who comes from afar, she who is other. Paradoxically, the reaffirmation of Artemis's otherness has made me more aware than ever of the power of Aphrodite in my life. How spontaneously, when confronting Artemis's claims on me, I respond by pleading, "Let's play Aphrodite instead." I have never been so aware of my tendency to devote my energies to love affairs rather than to soul, to discriminate on the basis of what I find pleasing or displeasing; how naturally I seek to transform all feelings into sexual passion, all potentially transformative experience into well-shaped story, and to make all my therapists, including Artemis herself, fall in love with me. That attending to Artemis should bring Aphrodite so prominently into view seems surprising, until I remember the story of Hippolytus and how it is his monolatrous devotion to Artemis that provokes Aphrodite's disastrous intervention. It is as though exclusive attention to Artemis—which she plainly demands—inevitably stirs Aphrodite. I understand better now how it can be that so many of the oriental and Cretan goddesses—Cybele, Bendis, Astarte, Ariadne, to name but a few—are associated with both Artemis and Aphrodite, as though they are so essentially complementary as to be one.

I have seemingly always known I am no monotheist. Yet it is too simple to leave Artemis with that affirmation—and denial. I know that she is still *the* goddess to whom I now must attend. Her wilderness may indeed be a liminal space, but it is precisely the character of such "betweens" that while one is in them *that* is where one is, that is all there is. This is a time for me to turn away from that reliance on Aphrodite's ways which have for so long sustained me. I must begin to learn what is meant by the phrase "monogamy of soul." The cruel mystery inherent in that phrase led me to this attempt to expose myself to Artemis's mysteries. The birth into the rest of my life which she midwifes still feels incredibly painful. I still find it unspeakably difficult to join my voice with Iphigenia's as she, from her funeral pyre, cries:

> Dance!
> *Let us dance in honor of Artemis . . .*
> *O lift your voices*
> *Lift them to Artemis*
> *In honor of my fate*
> *And of my dying.*[41]

NOTES

1. Euripides, *Iphigenia in Tauris* 476–77, trans. Witter Bynner, in *The Complete Greek Tragedies,* vol. 3, *Euripides,* ed. David Grene and

Richmond Lattimore (Chicago: University of Chicago Press, 1959), p. 361.

2. Euripides, *Hippolytus* 86–87, trans. David Grene, p. 166.

3. *The Odyssey of Homer* 6. 100–108, trans. Richmond Lattimore (New York: Harper & Row, 1977), p. 105.

4. Sigmund Freud, "The Uncanny," in *Collected Papers,* vol. 4, trans. Joan Riviere (New York: Basic Books, 1959), pp. 368–407.

5. In the months before Artemis's birth her mother, seeking to hide from Hera, moves through the world as a wolf; Artemis herself, we are told, was born in that hour before dawn when only the wolves can see.

6. Diane di Prima, *Loba* (Berkeley, Calif.: Wingbow Press, 1978), p. 76.

7. Martin P. Nilsson, *A History of Greek Religion* (New York: W. W. Norton, 1964), p. 28.

8. Di Prima, *Loba,* pp. 81ff.

9. Walter F. Otto, *The Homeric Gods* (Boston: Beacon Press, 1954), p. 86.

10. R. M. Rilke, "Archaic Torso of Apollo," in *Translations from the Poetry of Rainer Maria Rilke,* trans. M. D. Herter Norton (New York: W. W. Norton, 1938), p. 181.

11. May Sarton, *Journal of a Solitude* (New York: W. W. Norton, 1973), p. 129.

12. May Sarton, "The Autumn Sonnets," in *Collected Poems 1930– 1973* (New York: W. W. Norton, 1974), pp. 385ff.

13. See Philip E. Slater, *The Glory of Hera* (Boston: Beacon Press, 1968), p. 12; Sarah B. Pomeroy, *Goddesses, Whores, Wives, and Slaves* (New York: Schocken Books, 1975), p. 10.

14. Otto, *Homeric Gods,* p. 82.

15. James Hillman, *Re-Visioning Psychology* (New York: Harper & Row, 1975), p. 108.

16. Martin P. Nilsson, *Greek Folk Religion* (New York: Harper Torchbook, 1961), p. 16.

17. Aeschylus, *Agamemnon* 132–43, trans. Richmond Lattimore, in *The Complete Greek Tragedies,* vol. 1, *Aeschylus* (Chicago: University of Chicago Press, 1959), p. 39.

18. W. K. C. Guthrie, *The Greeks and Their Gods* (Boston: Beacon Press, 1955), p. 100.

19. Lewis Richard Farnell, *The Cults of the Greek States,* vol. 2 (Chicago: Aegaean Press, 1971), pp. 435f.

20. W. H. Auden, "Ode to Gaea," in *Collected Poems* (New York: Random House, 1976), pp. 423f.

21. Nilsson, *History of Greek Religion,* p. 49.

22. *The Iliad of Homer* 21. 479–95, 506–13, trans. Richmond Lattimore (Chicago: University of Chicago Press, 1951), pp. 431ff.

23. James Hillman, "Anima," *Spring,* 1973, pp. 97–132.

24. Sarton, *Journal,* p. 11.

25. Ovid, *The Metamorphoses,* trans. Mary M. Innes (London: Penguin Books, 1955), p. 79.

26. *Metamorphoses,* p. 63.

27. Christine Downing, "A Thank Offering," *Inward Light,* Fall 1967, pp. 24f.

28. Claude Lévi-Strauss, *Tristes Tropiques* (New York: Atheneum, 1974), p. 333.

29. Susan Griffin, *Woman and Nature* (New York: Harper & Row, 1978), p. 103.

30. Otto, *Homeric Gods,* p. 87.

31. Carl Kerenyi, *Zeus and Hera* (Princeton, N.J.: Princeton University Press, 1975), p. 51.

32. Arthur Bernard Cook, *Zeus,* vol. 2, pt. 1 (Cambridge, England: University Press, 1925), p. 457.

33. Farnell, *Cults* 2:447.

34. Kerenyi, *Zeus,* p. 53.

35. Nilsson, *History of Greek Religion,* p. 112.

36. Farnell, *Cults* 2:543.

37. René Malamud, "The Amazon Problem," in *Facing the Gods,* ed. James Hillman (Irving, Tex.: Spring Publications, 1980), pp. 56ff.

38. *Metamorphoses,* p. 61.

39. *Odyssey* 6. 101–6, 109, p. 105.

40. Euripides, *Iphigenia in Aulis* 719, trans. Charles R. Walker, in *The Complete Greek Tragedies,* vol. 4, *Euripides,* ed. David Grene and Richmond Lattimore (Chicago: University of Chicago Press, 1958), p. 332.

41. Euripides, *Iphigenia in Aulis* 1479–80, 1466, p. 377.

·VIII·

AND NOW YOU, APHRODITE ...

Last night

I dreamed that
you and I had
words: Cyprian.
          Sappho [1]

I t has been possible to speak in the third person of each of the goddesses who has come before me since I first found myself in Her presence in the dark underground cave. Even as I have named their powerful presence in my life and invoked their varied blessings, I could address them as *She.* But you, smile-loving, wile-weaving Aphrodite evoke from me (as you did from Sappho) a more direct address.

You are to me not only a you but that in me which is you-directed, which comes into being as it is shared with another, a you apart from whom I cannot imagine myself. Saying that, I understand better than I had before the appeal to me of lines from W. S. Merwin which I have had tacked up next to my desk for the last year or so:

> *The long way to you is still tied to me—but it*
> *brought me to you*
> *I keep wanting to give you what is already yours* [2]

lines which I have transposed to read:

Crouching Aphrodite (from Rhodes)
Hirmer Verlag, Munich

The long way to me is still tied to you—but it
brought me to me
I keep finding you give me what is already mine

You are so close to me, Aphrodite, that I have often not been aware of your presence as that of another. Now that it is time to begin to discover who I am apart from you, I realize I must confront you directly. To speak of you in the third person would be to evade. I also know how easily, in the seductive realm of the personal, you and I can avoid the disentanglement for which I think I am ready and yet resist, a disengagement I sometimes despair of accomplishing. As I discover how you are interwoven into the very fabric of my life, I begin to understand why the Athenians identified you with Clotho, the Spinner, oldest of the Moirae. Your relation to me is not simply a matter of particular situations, of particular behaviors or particular roles, as I used to believe when I thought I could define and delimit your place in my life.

Perhaps just because you are so close, it has often been easier for me to see you in others than in myself, positively in those whose beauty I find compelling, negatively in those whom I see as too ready to play the enchantress. (This tendency to see you more clearly in projected form has been at work especially in my relation to my own younger sister. How right was C. S. Lewis's decision to retell the tale of Psyche from the perspective of the ugly, jealous, self-righteous older sister who only at the end of her life discovers, "You, too, are Psyche." [3]) When others have seen my Aphroditic aspects, I have tended to deny them or to admit only to the negative elements implicit in the identification or to say, "That was once true, but. . . ."

Though I have come to recognize you as the goddess with whom I am most intimately entangled, I was certainly not raised to know that. You were hardly spoken of; yet somehow I learned that you were to be viewed with supsicion because you had the power to lure one from one's chosen path. My parents communicated their certainty (or hope?) that Aphrodite was not my goddess. Yet I also sensed that they accepted you as the goddess most perinent to the life of my young sister. Through all my growing up, and to some extent always, I have both envied and disparaged her Aphroditic bond—and for a long while relegated you, Aphrodite, to the shadows of my life. It was easier for me to do that, of course, so long as I saw you only in reference to physical beauty and unfettered sexuality—a reductive vision of your powers I have now relinquished.

When you first appeared so powerfully that I could no longer deny you, in the sexual urges and pull to passionate intimacy of late adolescence, I confused your workings with those of Hera. When I married I did not see that the life-infusing warmth in any marriage is your work, not hers. Hera herself knows that her beauty and her longing for mutual commitment and trust are both insufficient without your magic, without the "grace and desirability" only you can bestow. Thus (as the *Iliad* recounts), when Hera wanted to reawaken Zeus's passion for her, she came to borrow your magic girdle on which are figured all beguilements and loveliness, the passion of sex, "and the whispered endearment that steals the heart away even from the thoughtful." When Zeus saw her thus adorned,

desire was a mist about his close heart
as much as on that first time they went to bed together
and lay in love, and their dear parents knew nothing of it.

He says to her:

Now let us go to bed and turn to lovemaking.
For never before has love for any goddess or woman
so melted about the heart inside me. . . .

So speaking, the son of Kronos caught his wife in his arms,
There
underneath them the divine earth roke into young, fresh
grass, and into dewy clover, crocus and hyacinth
so thick and soft it held the hard ground deep away from them.
There they lay down together and drew about them a golden
wonderful cloud, and from it the glimmering dew descended.[4]

As Kerenyi sees, Zeus is enchanted with love, not the love that binds, "but rather the sort that is Aphrodite's gold." [5] Recognizing the absolute appropriateness of your coming to Hera's aid has put in perspective an almost forgotten memory from the early years of my own marriage: at moments when unconsciously I must have known I needed you because, too full of Hera's seriousness, I took on the role of an alter ego whose presence delighted both my husband and myself. She even had a name: Gay Abandon.

I became more conscious of you a few years later when, as a lover's Ariadne, I was initiated into the rewards and cost of being an anima woman. I began then to attend to you more deliberately, for I hoped to learn from you how to love in ways that would be genuinely creative and responsible. I came to bless your presence in my life; I believed I was most fully realizing my own gifts and potentialities as I turned to others in ways that stirred to life in them potentialities hitherto hidden and dormant.

The aspect of you I so joyously discovered then is one more visible in the cults devoted to you than in the myths about you. I knew you as creatrix, a life force, the source of all reproductive energy in the universe; I understood why Empedocles called you "the giver of life," Sophocles, "the goddess of abundant fruits." [6] It is as creatrix that you are associated with flowers (the generative organs of vegetal life) and with fruits (the progeny) and that the Horae, the seasonal processes of birth and growth, are your attendants. I could imagine your first stepping-forth from the cockleshell that bore you to Cyprus with grass growing up beneath your shapely feet. I loved the Homeric hymn's description of your arrival at Mount Ida, filled with yearning for Anchises and stirring yearning in all you met:

> *She went right up the mountain*
> *to the sheepfolds. Behind her moved grey*
> *wolves, fawning on her, and bright-eyed*
> *lions, bears, and quick, insatiable panthers.*
> *When she saw them she felt joy in her*
> *heart, and she put longing in their breasts,*

and immediately they all went into the
shade of the valley in twos to sleep
with each other.[7]

I remembered the tale of Pygmalion's falling in love with the beautiful ivory statue he had carved. Though all his passionate devotion and unrivaled skill could not bring the sculpted Galatea to life, your blessing could. I felt myself in touch with that same life-infusing warmth.

But then I discovered in what I had regarded as a creative relationship an unacknowledged destructive aspect; upon discovering our relationship, the wife of my lover felt her whole world destroyed. The Furies descended on her and she sent them on to me. They tore from me all that I had loved and trusted in myself; there was nothing beautiful, nothing living, left. I did not expect ever to trust you again. It took a long while for me to rediscover you as a creative power. To allow myself to love again, and to be loved, seemed too dangerous. Yet until it happened, I did not really live again.

Only on the far side of the apparent loss of our connection, only when I became aware that you were again present, did I begin to realize how much more extensive your role in my life has been all along than just as the nurturer of erotic relationship. My conviction that it is time, Cyprian, that you and I have words comes from my feeling that I need to understand more consciously than ever before all the manifold ways in which you participate in my life. Only thus can I know who I might be apart from you.

I see now how you enter into and shape the most spontaneous, most taken for granted, most me-feeling ways in which I respond to events and persons. To see you only in terms of beauty and sexual enchantment is to ignore that your presence in my life is more significantly evident in my almost instinctual reliance on what Jung calls the feeling function. How naturally I orient myself in the world on the basis of what I value and like rather than on the basis of what can be logically established or empirically verified. How dependent I am on being liked and admired. To begin to admit that is to begin to sense how little I have controlled my life, how goddess-ruled I truly am. This frightens and dismays. Oh, Aphrodite, just because you are so intimately connected with what I value and trust most, it is difficult really to look at you. Nor does it help that some of those who love and know me best cherish and bless precisely the you in me and so encourage this present sorting through but little. And the you in me depends so on their support or understanding or, at least, acceptance. . . .

Perhaps their hesitations bespeak an appropriate suspicion of my own initial tendency to understand this transition as a rejection, a leaving behind, rather than a transformation of the relationship between us. It may not have been apparent enough that I do not at heart aim to deny you. I trust the many myths pointing to the dangers inherent in such a foolish project. That you are here in each of us, irrespective of our more conscious allegiances and despite our overt denials, is the presupposition of H.D.'s "Hippolytus Temporizes." Though Euripides presents Hippolytus as one attacked by you only from without, H.D. discerns (as hidden counterpoint to the youth's praise of Artemis) an encomium to you:

> I worship the greatest first—
> (it were sweet, the couch,
> the brighter ripple of cloth
> over the dipped fleece;
> the thought: her bones
> under the flesh are white
> as sand which along a beach
> covers but keeps the print
> of the crescent shapes beneath
> I thought:
> between cloth and fleece,
> so her body lies.). . . .
>
> I worship the feet, flawless,
> that haunt the hills—
> (ah, sweet, dare I think,
> beneath fetter of golden clasp,

of the rhythm, the fall and rise
of yours, carven, slight
beneath straps of gold that keep
their slender beauty caught,
like wings and bodies
of trapped birds.). [8]

The Homeric hymn dedicated to you makes plain that, except for Athene, Artemis, and Hera, "nobody else, none of the blessed gods, no mortal man, no one else can ever escape Aphrodite." [9] So I do not seek to escape you nor would I wish for a life no longer touched by your blessings. But with you as with each of the other goddeses, I must confront more directly what I call the dark side. With you, Aphrodite, this means acknowledging your implication in the difficulty I have in separating myself from you. Perhaps my inability to discern you as a distinct presence derives in part from your very nature as the available goddess. You are *Aphrodite Automata,* spontaneously giving—and yet unpossessable. To recognize you as other—but as another who refuses to be kept at a safe distance: that is the task.

My sense of you is itself still confused. I know the myths in which you play a part, the cult titles most frequently associated with you, the locus of the dramatic sites on which your temples are built—but the various aspects of you thus brought into view still blend and fuse. I know that I need to understand more clearly what it means to speak of you as the goddess of beauty and how your beauty differs from that of the other goddesses. I need also to learn what distinguishes love in your realm from love as those others represent it. It is time to apprehend more precisely the mode of consciousness associated with you and, of course, time to look at the dark Aphrodite, at your integral connection with death and loss.

The temptation to reduce your scope, to minimize your potency, is not mine alone. It is already evident in Homer's attempt to present you as only an effeminate goddess of love (though he clearly knows your powers are more manifold). He would have us see you, not as born from Ouranos's sea-tossed genitals, but as daughter of Ouranos's grandson, Zeus, and of Dione (an otherwise mostly ignored wife of Zeus). He pictures you running to Dione for comfort, after you have been wounded by Diomedes, trying to rescue your son, Aeneas, from his attack. Dione gathers you into her arms, while Zeus chides you:

> No, my child, not for you are the works of warfare. Rather concern yourself only with the lovely secrets of marriage, while all thus shall be left to Athene and sudden Ares.[10]

How unconvincing is this diminution of you. Nevertheless, it is true that in the Hellenistic period you became little more than the divinity of love and desire, a personification of human beauty, a goddess of the courtesan world. Thus reduced in scope, you cannot be brought fully into consciousness until all the repressed aspects are acknowledged.

What shines through even Homer's vision of you is that beauty itself is somehow divine. "What is beautiful appears blissful in itself." [11] The divinity of your beauty is expressed in your unself-conscious acceptance of it. Only a goddess could so naturally and entirely delight in her own loveliness. "The austere and elemental quality of your awe-inspiring loveliness" is communicated in Pheidias's sculptural representations. Farnell describes a fragment now in the Louvre:

> It has, in fact, all the prominent forms of the Pheidian type of head: the great breadth of cheek and depth of skull, the full chin, the simple grandeur of the line of eyebrows, and the large circles of the eye-sockets, the striking breadth of the forehead and the space between the eyes, the simplicity in the rendering of the hair. The lips are full, the upper high-arched. The eyes are gazing upward, and the whole countenance is full of thought and power without severity. For warmth of spiritual expression, perhaps, no head of ancient sculpture surpasses this. It is the head of a goddess, and the bright look on the face and the faint smile speak of Aphrodite.[12]

All Greek goddesses are beautiful; the mysteriousness of what distinguishes your beauty from that of the others is conveyed in H.D's description of how Achilles responds to Helen (one of your human byforms) as she appears on the ramparts of Troy:

> *it was not that she was beautiful,*
> *true, she stood on the walls,*
>
> *taut and indifferent*
> *as the arrows fell;*
> *it was not that she was beautiful,*
>
> *There were others,*
> *in spite of the legend,*
> *as gracious, as tall;*
>
> *it was not that she was beautiful,*
> *but he stared and stared.*[13]

Your beauty is connected to a particular kind of energy, to your goldenness, your warmth, your availability. That energy is *charis,* grace, "a loveliness which is at the same time receptivity and echo," harmony and consummation, unpossessable yet self-giving: "The bewitching one is eager to surrender, the image of loneliness voluntarily bends toward the love-stricken with an undisguised yearning which is itself irresistible."[14] That energy is charisma, personal magic.

Your magic is intrinsic to your being, "an immediate divine power, not something artificial, not a sorcery":

> Even if deceiving in its transient splendor—deceiving like
> happiness which for us mortals contains eternity only in its
> depths and not in its duration—that magic is nevertheless
> warm and genuine, like the rays of the sun. It is the warmth
> and truth of passion that shine through Aphrodite's nature,
> as sunlit gold shines through her whole appearance.[15]

Warmth and truth conjoined; that is your magic, a magic which enhances natural beauty, which makes a hidden truth more evident through exaggeration. You are the only goddess who is willing to be seen unclothed and the one most skilled in the cultivation of beauty, the use of cosmetics and perfume, of ornament and gorgeous dress. Perhaps an intuition of this complementation of natural and artistic beauty underlies the tradition which marries you, the epitome of inherent loveliness, to Hephaistos, the ugly but skillful artisan who fashions your golden ornaments, including the coveted ornately worked girdle which makes any wearer irresistible. The poets delight in describing your golden jewels and lovely gowns. They picture your arrival on Cyprus:

> On her immortal head
>   (the Hours) placed a crown
>   that was carefully made,
>   beautiful and in gold,
> and in the pierced lobes of her ears
>   they placed
>   flowers of copper
>   and precious gold.
> On her delicate neck
>   and her silver-white breasts
>   they arranged
>   necklaces of gold,
>   which they have themselves made. . . .
>
> And then,
>   when they had placed
>   all this decoration
>   on her body,
>   they led her
> to the immortals.[16]

I have only reluctantly recognized that my own mode of enhancing natural beauty is one of the primary ways in which you work through me. The magic of the imagination is also *your* magic. You are at work in me, not only in the still present temptation to play anima or the still powerful reliance on the feeling function but also in what had felt even more *me:* my particular way of making conscious, of "giving events the dimension of soul": the transposition of experience into story. The gift of storytelling, which has given me the deepest happiness I have known, has also often been the way through which I have most creatively touched the lives of others. I sense, however, that it is important for me to put storytelling aside for a while. I have been enchanted by my own enchantments; I am not sure I any longer know how *not* to tell stories.

A similar need to let go of being the enchantress is expressed by Helen of Troy as she momentarily glimpses that her magic is your work. She protests against your attempt to persuade her to come to Paris's bed after his near defeat by Menelaus:

> *"Strange divinity! Why are you still so stubborn to beguile me?*
> *Will you carry me further yet somewhere among cities*
> *fairly settled: In Phrygia or in lovely Maionia?*
> *Is there some mortal man there also who is dear to you?*
> *Is it because Menelaos has beaten great Alexandros*
> *and wishes, hateful even as I am, to carry me homeward,*
> *is it for this that you stand in your treachery now beside me?*
> *Go yourself and sit beside him....*
>
> *Not I. I am not going to him."* [17]

Though, of course, you easily persuade her to go. Getting out of your clutches is no easy matter.

As goddess of beauty you have been more subtly and significantly pertinent to my life than I have always understood. So, too, as goddess of love you are present in many facets beyond those immediately connected with sexual infatuation, though being the beloved has certainly also been (and still is) important in my life. I remember all too well, and with some embarrassment, how I delighted in my power to stir love in others, how difficult it was for me to acknowledge my responsibility for what I evoked and not only for how I responded. As I learned to be more conscious in my loving, I felt I had freed myself from you. Though no longer enchanted by you (or so I thought), I knew you were still present. I knew there to be a sensual dimension underlying all my important relationships, homosexual or heterosexual. The possibility of a sexual consummation was never *essentially* excluded (as it would be in Athene's realm or that of Artemis or Hera), even though there would often be a mutual agreement not to literalize that possibility.

I also know full well that the erotic dimension is present in those encounters between me and my students or patients that are genuinely effective. Having learned from Socrates and Freud how important to learning and healing is love, if we can allow it to do its work without self-indulgence, I have come to welcome and almost trust your presence in those relationships. Or perhaps it was directly from you that I learned that such love has an aim different from literal gratification—and that it is to be blessed, not denigrated. I can honor the dreams others have of me, dreams which seem to invest me with some magical life-giving or truth-telling power, when I understand that the power such dreams project on me is really yours.

How much until now, soul making, as I have been engaged in it, has occurred under your tutelage. Others keep journals intended only for their own perusal, in which they wrestle with their most intimate demons and record their most private joys; my most honest, most risk taking, most genuinely exploratory attempts at naming have always taken the form of letters, addressed to a particular other who seems in some way to make possible and confirm that self-unfolding.[18] I know I in part invent those others, have always known how, in large measure, I am writing to myself. Nevertheless, it does not work to write directly to myself. I need the sense of the other. Such letters seem to function as an exercise in what Buber called "imagining the real"; the half-imagined others seem often to feel confirmed in their own deepest sense of who they potentially but essentially are; they are able to respond from that evoked-into-being self.

There was a period in my life when I felt all my real living put into the letters I wrote. A lover and I, separated for two years, wrote weekly. I felt my life became real as I shared it with him—as I looked at it carefully enough to describe it, as I savored it, touched it, made a whole of its fragments. I felt I was attending to my life more lovingly, in more detail, so that I might show it to him. I came to believe that an initially dreaded separation had actually led to a deepening and strengthening of our relationship, and that through these letters I had discovered and created myself as an adult. Eventually it became possible for us to live in the same part of the country again. When we met to celebrate our reunion, he told me how he had ritualized the ending of our separation. On a secluded riverbank sacred to him, to which he had often retreated during the years apart, he had carefully burnt all my letters and then thrown the ashes into the river. I understood even then how important and appropriate the ceremony had been to him—but I was devastated, as though, like an Indian widow, I myself had been burnt and my ashes dedicated to the river. I burst into racking sobs in the middle of the exquisite restaurant in which we sat while he told me his tale, mourning what felt like my own death.

You are not the only Greek divinity associated with love; what distinguishes love in your realm is its celebration as a self-validating cosmic power. Yours is the love that begets life, a creative energy that far transcends human sexuality. You are a reality prior to Zeus, unparented, self-sufficient. Hesiod describes you as born from the foam surrounding your father's severed genitals. Beginning life already full-grown, you are attended from your first appearance on earth by Eros, love, and Hemeros, desire. Because you are feminine being in its fullness, there are no tales of your infancy or childhood. Because you are the ripe self-sufficiency of feminine sexuality, there are no accounts of the loss of your virginity. You need no man to initiate you into your own sexuality; you are from birth, so Hesiod tells us, member-loving, *philommedes,* because you sprang from your father's members. Even Anchises is not really duped when you come to him pretending to be not only a mortal but a virgin with modestly lowered eyes:

> *I beg you . . . take me,*
> *virgin that I am, ignorant of lovemaking,*

as I am, and present me to your father
and your good mother and to your brothers,
born from the same stock as you. I won't be
a daughter-in-law unfitting for them, but very fitting.
Send a messenger immediately to the Phrygians
with their fast horses to tell my father
and my worried mother. And they'll send back
gold and plenty of woven garments, and you,
you receive these splendid things as a dowry.[19]

You are not only the beloved but also the loving one. You are object and subject, the enchantress who is herself enchanted. Like all Greek divinities, you yourself suffer what you impose. You represent the free giving and receiving and returning of love. There are no accounts of your being raped or seduced, taken against your will, nor of your teasing someone by enticing his love but then withholding your favors. When Ares comes to sweet-garlanded Aphrodite in the house of Hephaistos, you are well pleased to sleep with him. Because passion is your essence, it does not overwhelm you. The Homeric hymn to Aphrodite says that when you first see Anchises "a terrifying desire" seizes your heart, but all that follows suggests it is really simply the "pleasant longing" Zeus had intended you to feel for a mortal, since you had so often led him into similar entanglements. You unhesitatingly take the initiative. You hurry to Cyprus where you bedeck and perfume yourself. You present yourself so beguilingly to Anchises that, despite his initial awed reluctance, he quickly yields:

No one, no god,
no mortal man will stop me right here and now
from making love to you immediately. . . .
Why I would even
consent to disappear into the house of Hades
after mounting your bed, lady.[20]

You are the goddess of all physically passionate love, marital and adulterous, heterosexual or homosexual. Thus, at Delphi and elsewhere, you were recognized as the goddess who joins together in matrimony:

> The honor and charm, and mutual love and trust, that grow up daily (in a happy marriage) prove the wisdom of the Delpheans in calling Aphrodite the goddess who joins together.[21]

It is the quality and intensity of the relationship that marks it as Aphroditic—its existence for its own sake, for the pleasure and fulfillment of both partners, rather than for power or offspring. In your sphere, reaching toward the other is an essential activity of the self. Unlike Hera, you do not need a sustained relation to a particular other for your own fulfillment; rather, you need to be turning toward others to be yourself. What means completion for Hera, genuine marriage, represents an impossible constraint for you. (No classical texts, except Demodokos's lay in the *Odyssey,* represent you as married; even that account which describes your cuckolding of your ugly lame husband Hephaistos only serves to underscore the ridiculousness of imagining you confined to any marriage.) Turning toward the other constitutes your essence. To understand you thus is to apprehend why I feel you so closely intertwined with my own being. Such turning has been so natural an ingredient in my own way of being in the world that I have little sense of who I am except as I share myself with others.

Love in your realm most intrinsically generates love, not progeny. Thus, you are recognized as patronness not only of heterosexual desire but also of lesbian and male homosexual love. Because homosexuality is explicitly not reproductive, it was sometimes viewed as the more genuinely Aphroditic sexuality. Plato's *Symposium,* for example, speaks of an Ouranian Aphrodite who is innocent of any lewdness, and sponsors that desire of the soul rather than the body which he believes characterizes legitimate homosexual love.

You, most feminine of goddesses, were worshiped as the bearded Aphrodite on Cyprus; you are also the mother of Hermaphroditos. Aside from Ares, the men you are attracted to are often in conventional terms effeminate: beautiful lyre-playing Anchises, gentle Adonis, sly-spoken Hermes. Farnell found this aspect of you ("the strange confusion of the sexes, the blending of the male and female natures in one person") mysterious and distasteful.[22] Kerenyi appreciates it as another sign of your self-sufficient wholeness:

> Shining in golden purity, Aphrodite, the male-female wholeness, makes pale every sort of partialness. She is present when wholeness emerges from the halves and when the resolved opposites become the indissolvable goldenness of life.[23]

Really to understand you and our relation to you seems to imply appreciation of that indissoluble golden wholeness. Walter Otto speaks of your world as one where "all that is separated desires blissful fusion into oneness." [24] Nevertheless, to associate you with nondifferentiation and dissolution is a misunderstanding provoked by our inability to appreciate the particular mode of consciousness you embody: consciousness with respect to feelings and to relationship. We may learn from you a way of knowing ourselves and the world that comes only through turning in love toward another. Through feeling, as you teach it, we may win redemption from what T. S. Eliot called "the general mess of imprecision of feeling." You represent a trust of feeling, an intelligence about feeling, an ability to discriminate within the realm of feeling. Your true work is education in feeling. You inspire feeling, and curse those who seek to evade it. Because your world is the world of feeling, even those moments when we feel cut off from feeling, feel frigid, callous, frozen, dead, happen within your sphere. (Both Plutarch and Ovid refer to *Aphrodite Parakuptousa,* the figure of a hardhearted female turned to stone because she had looked unfeelingly at the corpse of a lover.) We can learn from you only by trusting ourselves to you. That is why I need to address you as *you,* why I need to allow this invocation of you to be shaped by feeling.

I see your connection to the dangers of dissolution expressed in your intimate connection with the sea. The attempt to derive your name from *aphros,* foam, may be but a pretty etymological conceit; nevertheless, it conveys how genuinely sea-born a goddess you are. Herodotus reports that you came to Greece from across the water by way of a series of islands: Cythera, Cyprus, Crete. Many of the birds sacred to you are water birds; the tortoise on which you are pictured riding is an amphibian creature. You represent not so much the dangers of destructive immersion but their transcendence. You are the divinity of the calm summer sea, the goddess of prosperous voyaging, the savior from shipwreck. In your waters we do not drown, but discover reflections which add depth to our experience.

I have come to see the tendency to understand you in terms of the pull to an undifferentiated consciousness as representing an inability to differentiate you from the Great Mother. How essential it is to remember that in truth you are not she; you are one among the many highly differentiated Olympian goddesses whose distinction from the all-absorbing Great Mother is forcefully indicated in your being yourself motherless. Nevertheless, it is important to come to terms with the fact that you are sometimes spoken of as She Who Lulls to Sleep, sometimes represented as yourself an immobilized sleeping beauty. One of the plants most often associated with you is the sleep-inducing poppy. Among your byforms are Circe who transforms men and women into beasts or stone, and Calypso whose love is potent enough to keep Odysseus with her for seven years, though not forever.

My sense is that you are often seen as representing the pull toward dissolution because you imply a reconciliation of what are usually seen as contradictions or mutually exclusive choices. What you make possible is not logical resolution or synthesizing compromise but mediation at the level of feeling. Your bringing together what is ordinarily kept apart is not fusion; it represents an intense valuing of both poles. Yours is a loving consciousness, a connecting, not a dissolving, consciousness. It is a transformative consciousness, responsible for all the metamorphoses Ovid relates to us; a metaphorical consciousness which brings two entities together, not to proclaim their identity nor to establish some abstract *tertium quid,* but for the sake of the tensive bond itself.

I understand you, Aphrodite, to be the divinity who, by causing us to experience the seductive or overpowering lure of
unconsciousness, leads us toward a new appreciation of consciousness and to a new mode of consciousness—a consciousness peculiar to you. You bring us to reject the Apollonian
claim that there is only one mode of consciousness, that of
Logos, of the thinking function.

My sense that we need to recognize you as representing a
form of consciousness is confirmed by your affinity with the
sun, with daylight, rather than with the moon and night. You
are, after all, the golden Aphrodite, a sunlit goddess who un-
ashamedly makes love to Anchises in midday, a goddess not
embarrassed at being caught in view of all the gods passionately
embraced by Ares. (It is only recently that I have learned that
the Greeks perceived in you a "joy-creating *sun-like* magic" and
in the sun "a mysterious femininity, that sisterly helpfulness and
goldenness of young women." [25] Yet to someone like myself
whose native language is German and who therefore grew up
knowing the sun as feminine, *die Sonne,* the association of the
sun with you seems entirely natural, more so actually than its
association with Apollo.) Kerenyi describes your sunlit-ness
thus:

> under the sign of Aprodite we are not dealing with some-
> thing heavy and darkly earthy, with an unconscious disso-
> lution into a state of fusion, but rather with something
> bright and lucid. The images of Anadyomene rising up out
> of the depths of the sea, is the transparent purity of com-
> plete union become visible. Through Aphrodite the whole
> world becomes pellucid and thus so brilliant and smiling. [26]

Your willingness to be seen unclothed also suggests that seeing and being seen are essential aspects of your divinity. Athene
and Artemis severely punish anyone who spies them naked,
whereas you tease Anchises for fearing impotence because of
having had intercourse with you. For you to be the only Greek
goddess who can be represented nude in sculptures or vase
paintings suggests it is an essential quality of your divinity to be
seen thus. [27]

Aphroditic consciousness is consciousness in your realm, the realm of relationship and feeling. Despite the title, the focus in Apuleius's "Amor and Psyche" is really on the relationship between you and Psyche. Erich Neumann and other commentators have seen you, Aphrodite, as representing a pull to unconsciousness against which Psyche must struggle in order to achieve individuation. I, however, agree with Bachofen in seeing Psyche as an aspect of you (as those who worshiped her—initially, simply because of her physical loveliness—recognized). It is you, after all, who impose the tasks by which she comes to that psychic realization which makes possible a renewed and newly conscious relationship with Eros. In Psyche, as Bachofen recognizes, you yourself achieve the highest stage of consciousness "that women's materiality can attain." Though the chauvinism implicit in this description annoys, Bachofen is surely correct in discerning that consciousness in your realm is not spiritual but earthly consciousness "exalted to the highest purity." [28]

It is your genius to move into the heavens without losing your connection to earth and sea. Jane Ellen Harrison sees this to be the very essence of your power and vitality:

> Aphrodite the earth-born Kore is also sea-born, as becomes an island Queen, but more than any other goddess she becomes Ourania, the Heavenly One, and the vase-painter sets her sailing through heaven on her great swan. She is the only goddess who in passing to the upper air yet kept life and reality. Artemis becomes unreal from sheer inhumanity; Athene, as we have seen, becomes a cold abstraction; Demeter, in Olympus, is but a lovely metaphor. As man advanced in knowledge and in control over nature, the mystery and the godhead of things natural faded into science. Only the mystery of life, and love that begets life, remained, intimately realized and utterly unexplained; hence Aphrodite keeps her godhead to the end. [29]

In your realm sensuousness and consciousness cannot be severed from each other. As Farnell persuasively demonstrates, one of your most prevalent titles, Ourania, points to you as a heavenly goddess and recalls your closeness to eastern Queens of Heaven like Ishtar and Astarte, Cybele and Tanit. In the *Symposium* Plato contrasts Aphrodite Ourania, a heavenly Aphrodite who blesses the intellectual communion of one soul with another, with Aphrodite Pandemos, an earthly Aphrodite concerned only with the sensual love of the body. But from the cultic perspective the title Ourania always included a recognition of your most sensuous aspects; for instance, the Corinthian Aphrodite bore this title, and Corinth was the only place in Greece proper where you were served by what Pindar calls "daughters of Persuasion" (that is, by prostitutes). In cult, Pandemos had a serious religious meaning; it pointed to you as a goddess worshiped by the whole community. This revelation of the subtle intertwining of the physical and spiritual is among your most important gifts. Kenneth Clark in his book *The Nude*, puts it thus: "Perhaps no religion ever again incorporated physical passion so . . . naturally that all who saw her felt that the instincts they shared with the beasts they also shared with the gods." [30]

In your light we see clearly but sensuously. You are not just the sometimes harsh shadowless light of midday but the rosy light of dawn and dusk, of the morning and evening star. Rosy-fingered dawn, Eros, is one of your aspects. The sun's connections with fertility, with life-creating warmth are brought into view through you. What we see in your light we see as feeling-toned. The memories and yearnings that things stir in us are part of what they are. Yours is a lyric consciousness—delicate, attentive, loving, detailed—very different from the consciousness of epic or philosophy. H.D.'s Helen (Helen is here again to be seen as an Aphroditic byform) articulates this personalizing consciousness:

> *The million personal things*
> *Things remembered, forgotten,*
>
> *remembered again, assembled*
> *and re-assembled in different order*
> *as thoughts and emotions,*

the sun clad the seasons changed,
and as the flower-leaves that drift
from a tree were the numberless
tender kisses, the soft caresses,'
given and received; none of these
came into the story,

it was epic, heroic.[31]

So long as we are tempted to dismiss such lyric consciousness as subjective, we are still outside your realm. We are confusing being conscious in relationship with being conscious about relationships as Apollo might encourage us to be—forever analyzing them, finding causes and analogues, undoing projections, learning to use them for our own growth. Friedrich, in his book *The Meaning of Aphrodite,* describes your mode of consciousness in terms of "subjectivity" because he wants us to see how your "work" is the creation of states of mind rather than, directly, of behaviors. (He describes beautifully how Sappho attributes her own intense feelings of love, passion, tenderness, infatuation, frustration, jealousy, loneliness to you.[32]) Yet I believe this is to ignore the degree to which all the gods and goddesses act in us as though from within, as inspirers of motives and feelings. What is distinctive about you is that you lead us to feel most ourselves when led by our feelings (rather than by our thoughts or perceptions or intuitions), and when intimately and emotionally involved with others.

In your realm, feeling is recognized as inherently valid—as a cosmic and awesome force. There is fearfulness and destruction in the passion you arouse; Ariadne and Medea betray their fathers and brothers, Helen abandons her husband, Myrrha entices her father into her bed, Pasiphae is filled with bestial lust for a bull. You are paired with Ares, the god of violent battle, more frequently than with any other consort. That union issues in strife *and* harmony; together you parent Deimos (Panic), Phobus (Fear), Eros, and Harmonia. Though Homer goes out of his way to describe your ineffectiveness at Troy, elsewhere you are often represented as yourself armed, as a goddess of

battle (like your eastern counterparts). As Aphrodite Ourania
you are also identified as a goddess who comes from the east,
from outside the Greek world, and one who pulls us outside
ourselves. Even though in Greece proper (except at Corinth)
your worship was as austere as that of any Olympian divinity
(and considerably less ecstatic than that of Artemis), the memory
of your original association with orgiastic rituals in your oriental
birthplace persists. Many passages in Euripides testify to his
view of you as a power causing oblivion to all duty and loss of all
restraint, and as a bringer of doom. Dionysos, the god who,
since Nietzsche, has come to epitomize the ecstatic, is your
great-grandson. In the *Phaedrus* Socrates associates you with the
highest form of "divine madness" and tells us such madness is
superior to "man-made sanity." The "madness" associated with
you is not unconsciousness but a mode of consciousness other
than the ego's "sanity."

What we first see of you, Aphrodite, is your golden-ness; you
appear as smile-loving, laughter-loving Aphrodite. Most of us
learn early that there is a dark side also—there is the terror of
being overwhelmed by our passion and sometimes guilt for
having lured another from what has been his or her life. There
is unrequited love and there is what feels like premature abandonment. (Syphilis and gonorrhea are not the only venereal
diseases.) Your dark side is admitted by the Greeks, but only
subliminally. As Kerenyi puts it, "The nocturnal connections of
Aphrodite are present in the classical tradition but deeply re-
served when they have to do not with the night of love but the
night of death." [33] Otto echoes him:

> we must again remind ourselves that to the breadth of this
> realm which is the world there belong also the horrible and
> the destructive. No power can cause such strife and confu-
> sion as can that whose office is the most luminous and
> blissful harmony; and it is only by these dark shadows that
> Aphrodite's magic brightness becomes a complete crea-
> tion. [34]

The inherent significance of your dark side is suggested by the
fact that the same act of dismemberment which gives rise to you

also generates the Erinyes: you emerge from the foam that swirls around the sea-tossed genitals, they form the blood that drips on earth as Kronos wields his sickle. You are spoken of as one of the Fates and are often associated with Nemesis. You are labeled the dark or black goddess, the goddess of graves, killer of man, the unholy. At Delphi you are known as Aphrodite on the Tomb.

What I have only recently been able to see, Aphrodite, though it has been there all along, is *your* sadness: the mourning Aphrodite. (What the gods do they suffer.) This aspect is most evident in the story of Adonis, the youth you loved, whose death brings tears streaming down your face. According to one legend you even fling yourself from the Leucadian rock in your grief. Perhaps we all have been too swayed by Frazer's amalgam of this story with that of Ishtar and Tammuz and his reduction of both to a vegetation myth. To Frazer, Adonis represents the dying and reappearing grain and thus becomes a symbol of human resurrection, but the story does not really go that way. The point is that Adonis really does die—and you are left to mourn. This is what distinguishes the Greek form of the myth—there are no eastern parallels to that second and true death, the death the boar inflicts. The myth is about death from the beginning—you put the infant Adonis into a coffin and give him into Persephone's keeping.[35] There is no protection from death—except in the realm of the dead.

I am coming to understand that among your most important teachings is the acceptance of transience, the recognition that love and passion are by their very nature evanescent. Divinity in Greece means immortality; what distinguishes humans from the gods is simply their mortality. Yet you, a goddess, embody the acceptance of transience as itself a kind of immortality. Adonis, your beloved, is identified with the anemone, "the enjoyment of (whose) flower is of brief duration; for it is so fragile its petals so lightly attached, that it quickly falls." [36] The "gardens of Adonis" on the roofs of Athens are planted with flowers which quickly bloom and die. Even your association with prostitutes can be connected to this theme: they are ladies of an hour.

The acceptance of the finitude of love does not, in your

realm, lessen its intensity; indeed, it may heighten it. In interpreting Zeus's impassioned response to Hera's appearance in your love-inspiring girdle, Kerenyi observes: "It is the paradox of this passion that without paying attention to those memories it believes itself to be the strongest ever in the present moment." [37] In the moment the love is everything, all-consuming.

In your realm, there is no holding back of love because it will not last forever, but also no denial of its impermanence. Eos, when consumed with love for Tithonus, persuades Zeus to grant him immortality but forgets to ask that he remain ageless as well; in time, of course, the beautiful youth becomes a shriveled old man. You, on the other hand, know full well that Anchises will age and die:

> But in fact
> a cruel old age will soon overtake you, the
> heartless kind that comes to men, killing,
> wearisome, the kind that even the gods hate.[38]

In your world there is no denying that the loss of a lover, the end of a love are painful. "Pain penetrates Me drop by drop," as Sappho cries.[39] The acceptance of transience in no way implies the mitigation of feeling. When one of her favorites turns to a male lover, Sappho acknowledges the hurt:

> Fortunate as the gods he seems to me, that man who sits
>   opposite you, and listens nearby to your sweet voice
> And your lovely laughter; that, I vow, has set my heart
>   within my breast a-flutter. For when I look at you a
>   moment, then I have no longer power to speak,
> But my tongue keeps silence, straightway a subtle flame has
>   stolen beneath my flesh, with my eyes I see nothing, my
>   ears are humming,
> A cold sweat covers me, and a trembling seizes me all over,
>   I am paler than grass, I seem to be not far short of death. . . .
> But all must be endured, since— [40]

In another poem she tells us:

I have had not one word from her
Frankly I wish I were dead.[41]

Though nostalgia and longing are important to you, what we most significantly learn from you is to choose the present, to choose love for itself not for what it brings. You teach the moment, this moment, not the last one or the next. You teach passivity transmuted into receptivity. You teach us to let go of the illusions of growth and development, while learning to recognize the inevitability of change, change which will sometimes be welcome but often painful. As Freud saw, the ancient identity between the goddess of love and the goddess of death implies that the hidden meaning of Paris's choice of you as the most beautiful of the goddesses is his acknowledgment of the necessity of dying. "Choice" is but a surface illusion; what you really teach is acceptance of the inevitable.[42] In Merwin's poem "The Judgment of Paris," Athene's offer of wisdom is qualified: "You will forget anyway"; and so is Hera's offer of pride and glory: "You will suffer anyway." Your words to Paris are "Take her, take Helen, you will lose her anyway." [43]

As the mourning Aphrodite, you are the teacher of the work of mourning. Inevitably only you can teach me how to separate from you. Inevitably, separation from you is a work of mourning. I had thought Artemis might effect this separation; in part, she does. I see now that only you can bring release from thralldom to you. I also recognize that indeed you never wanted such servitude, but had to leave me to discover that for myself. I do understand how Artemis contributes here, too. The stories are all interwoven. You are responsible for Hippolytus's death (a death incurred because he imagined he was immune to your powers). Euripides suggests that Artemis kills Adonis in revenge:

> *(Hippolytus)! You shall not be unavenged,*
> *Cypris shall find the angry shafts she hurled*
> *against you for your piety and innocence*
> *shall cost her dear.*
> *I'll wait until she loves a mortal next time,*

and with this hand—with these unerring arrows
I'll punish him.[44]

As I look more directly at you as the mourning Aphrodite, I
see more clearly your relation to Persephone, a relation at the
very core of the Adonis myth. In the past when I have reflected
on this tale, I always saw you, Aphrodite, as referring to other
women, beautiful women, golden, glowing women. I felt closer
to Persephone, who is introverted, in touch with loss, and still
in some way innocent and vulnerable. I remembered of the
Adonis story only that when he grew up and it was time for
Persephone to return him to you, she refused for she had come
to love the beautiful youth. Zeus (or, in some versions,
Calliope) was asked to judge between your claims. Often the
tale goes that the young man's time was equally divided between you and Persephone; but the version that always rang
more true to me was the one where each of you was given a
third of his time and he himself was allowed to choose how he
would spend the remaining third. And of course, he chose to be
with you, Aphrodite, whom I saw as the other.

But then I had a dream:

> That dream began with a vision I cannot imagine ever
> forgetting. One of my sons lay on the floor before me,
> dead, emptied of hope, emptied of life. I saw his beautiful,
> tanned, slim, golden-haired body lying on the floor, face
> down, among many scattered, meaningless but beautiful
> things, like the debris left after a party.
>
> "How could this have happened?" I asked.
>
> "If you want to know we will show you."
>
> And so I found myself back in a prior time. There were
> three presences. The proud and happy and oh! achingly
> beautiful youth, so happy in his own body and being and
> also in the cards he has been dealt in life. In some cosmic
> Tarot dealing he has been given what is obviously a win-
> ning hand, as he knows he deserves. I saw also another
> figure, a beautiful though mature woman. Her body was a
> little fleshy, there were lines on her face, but she was vi-
> brant with female power. There was nothing threatening in

her appearance; she was simply quietly confident, clearly in charge. She too held cards but betrayed nothing of how good they were. And, of course, the third presence was my own. I was watching as I'd been told I might. Though I also knew I was each of the others as one usually doesn't within the dream.

Then the laying down of cards began. They were all in some way life and destiny cards. My son always played his first, his wonderful success-bringing cards. Each time she matched it with a card just like his, only somehow a stronger version. He, undaunted ("What does it matter to lose a few?"), continued to lay down one magic card after another. And I already, after the third round or so, drew in my breath in fear, knowing that he was going to lose *every* time. He begins to realize what is happening only much later and still does not really take it in. After all, even to win only the last time would still be to win. He never doubts, never allows himself to doubt. As the game goes on my golden son becomes more and more, oh, breathtakingly beautiful. I see again his slender but well-defined body, the proud, slightly stirring phallus, the clear, untroubled, directly gazing blue, blue eyes. I see him standing there still not knowing what is happening. The last card is played, and hers wins. No triumph there, but no compassion either. It has simply happened as it was all along fated it would. The game is over and she is gone. In the beautifully appointed Grecian villa he is alone. And he is finished, still not comprehending and yet knowing: it is over.

Then I see again the dead body on the floor. O my son, O my son. And I know myself in him, and in the grieving powerless mother, and in the strange goddess of death.

The dream reminded me that the story goes on. Despite your caution, Aphrodite, Adonis goes out on a dangerous hunt and is gored by a boar. He dies and you grieve unconsolably.

In the dream I was Aphrodite, or so I felt it. Persephone played the cards. Perhaps you two are closer than I used to understand.

NOTES

1. *Sappho,* trans. Mary Barnard (Berkeley: University of California Press, 1958), p. 63.

2. W. S. Merwin, "To Dana for Her Birthday," *American Poetry Review,* November/December 1979, p. 3.

3. C. S. Lewis, *Till We Have Faces* (Grand Rapids, Michigan: Wm. B. Eerdmans Publishing, 1966).

4. *The Iliad of Homer* 14. 294–96, 314–16, 345–51, trans. Richmond Lattimore (Chicago: University of Chicago Press, 1951), pp. 302ff.

5. Carl Kerenyi, *Goddesses of Sun and Moon* (Irving, Tex.: Spring Publications, 1979), p. 55.

6. Lewis Richard Farnell, *The Cults of the Greek States,* vol. 2 (Chicago: Aegaean Press, 1971), p. 643.

7. *The Homeric Hymns,* trans. Charles Boer (Chicago: Swallow Press, 1970), p. 79.

8. H.D., *Selected Poems* (New York: Grove Press, 1957), pp. 23ff.

9. *Homeric Hymns,* p. 73.

10. *Iliad* 5. 427–30, p. 139.

11. Walter F. Otto, *The Homeric Gods* (Boston: Beacon Press, 1964), p. 101, quoting Morike.

12. Farnell, *Cults* 2:710f.

13. H.D., "Helen," in *Selected Poems,* pp. 251f.

14. Otto, *Homeric Gods,* p. 102.

15. Kerenyi, *Goddesses,* pp. 8, 53.

16. *Homeric Hymns,* pp. 83f.

17. *Iliad* 3. 399–405, 410, pp. 110f.

18. I love to read letters, too, and am easily moved by the kind of access they give to a soul's growth and to the importance of relationships. Yet not many have the gift of communicating the fullness of what is going on in their lives in this medium. The letters I value most are those which intermingle accounts of the mundane details of meals and trips, the excitement of reading a newly discovered or long familiar book, the delight of a good conversation, the things come across on a walk, or the puzzle of a dream. Such letters somehow express the writer's sense that the other is present though literally absent. Freud had a gift for such letters (I think especially of his correspondence with Lou Salome, a relationship that existed primarily in their letters), as did Kafka. Whereas Jung's letters, at least his published ones and especially those from the last decades of his life, have too public a quality and seem much lese personally revealing than does *Memories, Dreams, Reflections.*

19. *Homeric Hymns,* p. 77.

20. *Homeric Hymns,* p. 78.

21. Plutarch, quoted in Farnell, *Cults* 2:556.

22. Farnell, *Cults* 2:634.

23. Kerenyi, *Goddesses*, p. 59.

24. Otto, *Homeric Gods*, p. 161.

25. Kerenyi, *Goddesses*, p. 2.

26. Kerenyi, *Goddesses*, p. 58.

27. For a long time in Greece, in contrast to the more eastern representations, Aphrodite was pictured as fully draped; that a statue represented her was often indicated by the delicately graceful gesture with which a hand drew the drapery across the body. Praxiteles' fourth century Cnidean Aphrodite, recognized among all the statues of the world to be the embodiment of love and loveliness, may have been the first to represent her as nude: "When you stand before the Cnidean you greet her as the queen of gods and men, and Pallas and Hera themselves would admit that the judgement of Paris was true." The statue is lost but there is ancient testimony to the "radiant charm" of the face, to the "expression of yearning imparted by the slight drawing-up of the lower eyelid," to the lofty and sublime smile. This statue of Aphrodite as nude though at first seen as scandalous by the Greeks came to be regarded as the ideal form of her divinity. See Farnell, *Cults* 2:713ff.

28. J. J. Bachofen, *Myth, Religion and Mother Right* (Princeton, N.J.: Princeton University Press, 1967), p. 75.

29. Jane Ellen Harrison, *Prolegomena to the Study of Greek Religion* (New York: Meridian Books, 1957), p. 314. The sites of the temples dedicated to Aphrodite communicate this same sense of her as a mediator between earth and sky and sea. Her shrines are often found "on a lofty, wind-swept height, a promontory jutting out into the sea" where she "reaches out for the flaxen clouds" that she spins "into fertile rain for the earth." From such heights, like Parnes, Hymettus, Athoson Eryx, "earth and sky hold converse." Vincent Scully describes how different her sites at Troezen, Cnidus, Paphos are from those of Artemis: not remote and disquieting but "disturbing with the directness of explosive apparitions." They are located on strong masses that arise out of the sea, their force set off by the waters lapping below them. They represent "naked force, potent and intrusive, unexpected and irresistible." Aphrodite is also seen to mediate between sky and earth as morning dew and mist, cloud and fertilizing rain. In the *Odyssey* she is several times represented as protecting those she loves, such as Paris and Athene, by enveloping them in a mist and whisking them away from a potentially disastrous attack. See Elmer G. Suhr, *The Spinning Aphrodite* (New York: Helios Books, 1969), p. 62; and Vincent Scully, *The Earth, the Temple, and the Gods* (New Haven, Conn.: Yale University Press, 1979), p. 93.

30. Kenneth Clark, *The Nude* (New York: Pantheon, 1956), p. 63.

31. H.D., *Helen in Egypt* (New York: New Directions Publishing, 1961), p. 289. The reference to "the million personal things" reminds

me of Hans Schnier, Heinrich Böll's clown, for whom the simplest details of everyday life have been imbued forever with memories of the years he shared with his now departed lover, Marie. To see someone leave a tube of toothpaste uncapped, to watch someone butter a piece of toast will always evoke her presence. To try to isolate such activities from the memories associated with them constitutes (so Schnier believes) adultery. He recalls how often he and Marie had spoken together of their as yet unborn children, how they had even discussed how they would dress them:

> She was all for jaunty, light-colored raincoats, I preferred parkas, since it seemed to me that a child couldn't very well play in a puddle in a jaunty, light-colored raincoat, while a parka was ideal for playing in puddles. . . . Whether our children would actually be allowed to play in puddles was never completely clarified. Marie would just smile, be evasive and say: let's wait and see. If she was to have children with Zupfner she wouldn't be able to dress then in either parkas or jaunty, light-colored raincoats, she would have to let her children run around without coats, for we had gone thoroughly into the matter of coats of all kinds. We had also discussed long and short pants, underwear, socks, shoes—she would have to let her children run naked through the streets of Bonn if she didn't want to feel like a whore or a traitor (Heinrich Böll, *The Clown* [New York: McGraw-Hill, 1965]).

32. Paul Friedrich, *The Meaning of Aphrodite* (Chicago: University of Chicago Press, 1978), esp. chap. 5.

33. Kerenyi, *Goddesses,* p. 60.

34. Otto, *Homeric Gods,* p. 50.

35. Walter Burkert, *Structure and History in Greek Mythology and Ritual* (Berkeley: University of California Press, 1979), pp. 101, 110.

36. Ovi, *The Metamorphoses,* trans. Mary M. Innes (London: Penguin Books, 1955), p. 245.

37. Kerenyi, *Goddesses,* p. 55.

38. *Homeric Hymns,* p. 81.

39. *Sappho,* p. 61.

40. Denys Page, *Sappho and Alcaeus* (Oxford, England: Clarendon Press, 1965), pp. 19, 20.

41. *Sappho,* p. 42.

42. See Sigmund Freud, "The Theme of the Three Caskets," in *Character and Culture* (New York: Collier Books, 1963), pp. 75ff.

43. Discussed in Lillian Feder, *Ancient Myth in Modern Poetry* (Princeton, N.J.: Princeton University Press, 1971), pp. 415ff.

44. Euripides, *Hippolytus,* 1416–22, trans. David Grene, in *The Complete Greek Tragedies,1 vol. 3, Euripides,* ed. David Grene and Richmond Lattimore (Chicago: University of Chicago Press, 1959), p. 219.

·IX·

TO KEEP US IMAGINING:
The Child

Of childhoods I have so many
that I would get lost counting hem.
Arnoux[1]

s all the foregoing has sought to communicate, the goddesses are so "original" that a new world is born with each:

> Though [the gods] are present all the time, the mythologems which unfold in narrative form what is contained in the figures of the gods are always set in a *primordial* time. . . . Mythology tells of the origins or at least of what originally was.[2]

Mythology has to do with origins, *archai*, primary patterns, with worlds as they are coming into appearance and thus with epiphanies. Kerenyi suggests that the divine *child* in the god or goddess comes to the fore as part of the god's epiphany, its showing itself in its primal essence.[3] Thus the goddesses as appearing, as coming into being, will be manifest in their child form.

This recalls me once again to that dark cave in which I felt myself so palpably before *Her* but unable to discern her shape. A few days after I had had that dream, I found myself still occupied with it, still disappointed that I had not been able to see the goddess who was so evidently there. So, using what Jung calls active imagination, I reentered the underground cavern.

Statue of a Young Girl, a "Bear" of Artemis (from Brauron)
National Archaeological Museum, Athens, V. and N. Tombazi

Hoping this time to stay until She would come into view, I waited and waited in the darkness. Again I felt her presence all about me, but again could not see Her. Then I happened to look down at the earthen floor immediately before me. There, peacefully slumbering, lay an infant whom I somehow knew to be a girl child.

I can easily feel myself back in the cave, looking with astonished delight and recognition at this baby girl. To catch the goddess appearing is to catch her in her child form.

It seems obvious in retrospect that in the womblike cave divinity would appear in the form of a child—and obvious that at the end of all these reflections on the goddesses I would need to return to the child, as embodying an aspect of the goddesses which needs more explicit consideration than I have hitherto given it. To look at the goddesses as children—and as giving birth to children who are in some sense themselves—is subtly and yet essentially different from looking at them as mothers. We need to separate the mother-child mythologem, to see the child as a distinct archetype, related not only to mother but to nurse and grandmother, father and teacher, brother and sister—but, first of all, as simply: the child, the newly appearing one.

To look at the goddesses as they first appear, full of potentiality and yet already wholly themselves, is perhaps especially appropriate for us to whom the goddesses *are* new, just beginning to emerge into being. I know it is singularly appropriate for me for whom the child has been the form in which the divine has most self-evidently and spontaneously appeared in my imaginal life. That the divine *is* I have known more assuredly through these epiphanies than through any other experience. Certainly, the appearance of the child in that cave felt like a miracle. I say that I recognized her, as indeed I did, though I had not been sure I would ever see again this child who had first appeared in a dream years earlier.

The dream presented me with a beautiful baby daughter who lived in a room in our house which I only rarely entered (though in waking life this was the room that was most entirely my own). Yet whenever I would go to her she would be awake and well and utterly delighted to see me. I remember picking her up and holding her and then laying her down to change her diaper. She gazed up at me with a smile on her face and a look in her eye which clearly communicated, "We both know it is really I who take care of you."

I woke from that dream with a sense of joyous fulfillment I had never before known. I felt, she really *is* there and she does take care of me. I sense her room to be the numinous secret chamber I had first entered in my childhood dreams; her crib now occupying the center once occupied by a treasure chest or golden throne. When exactly the same dream recurred only a few months later, I began to wonder what it might mean. "I guess I'll know the third time," I told my husband. Eventually there was a third time, but this time the dream was different.

It began as before: although she was mostly left to take care of herself, whenever I came to my beautiful baby daughter she was vibrantly alive, blessedly content. But then one day as I came into her room and walked toward the crib, it seemed to be empty. Fearfully I approached more closely and still found no sign of the lovely child. Then in the farthest corner of the crib I saw a small shriveled bit of flesh, the size of a thumb, of a flaccid penis. I had neglected her too long, I knew. As tenderly, as carefully, as gently as I have ever done anything, I picked up the lifeless little thing, hoping that perhaps it was not quite dead after all. I carried it to the sink and let some lukewarm water run over it. Hoping... And then I awoke.

In the intervening years from time to time I had felt that somewhere this magic child was still alive, but I had not seen her again until she lay before me in the underground cave.

A few months earlier I had had a strange sense of in some way *being* that child, reborn. I was standing at the edge of the Pacific with seaweed swirling about my feet. As I moved in to the shore

I suddenly felt myself to be Aphrodite emerging for the first time and yet full-grown from the sea. I see now that, if the child shriveled up in the crib and the child in the cave are indeed one, she too is Aphrodite, born of the unattached phallus after its immersion in the water. Kerenyi's sense that the emerging child goddess first appears as Aphrodite seems confirmed in my own experience:

> The mythologem of the emergence of the child god out of the original condition of things is, in Greece, connected with two divinities, Eros and Aphrodite. . . . The image of the foam-born goddess puts the idea of genesis and time-less beginning as succinctly, as perfectly as only the language of mythology can. . . . The phallus is the child, and the child—Aphrodite—an external stimulus to further procreation. . . . From the high sea, stepping out of a mussel-shell, borne along by the wind and received by the gaily clad goddess of earth, Aphrodite Anadyomene arrives. . . . Botticelli's picture helps us, as modern men, to conjure up the vision of Anadyomene. And she must be conjured up if we want to understand the goddesses of the Greeks. She is the closest to the origins.[4]

Certainly, I knew from her first appearance that the dream child was a divine child. I do not know anymore whether I had already read Jung's essay "The Psychology of the Child Archetype" or Bachelard's "Reveries Toward Childhood," but all that they write of "child," signifying as yet unrealized potentialities of the self is congruent with my intuitive appreciation of the meaning of my dream child. I understand, too, why Jung affirms that images representing the archetype of the self and those embodying the archetype of the divine are functionally indistinguishable. The child was in some sense "me," yet she was undeniably a numinous sacred being.

The rediscovery of a child still alive in us, the recovery of the child's imaginal view of the world, may be regarded as the beginning of all *depth* psychology. When Freud realized, "I am Oedipus," he recognized his identity with the mythical child's exaggerated feeling of passionate love for his mother and parricidal jealousy of his father. The feeling-tone and the contents of those childhood emotions were still present in the adult man. Indeed, the childhood so important to depth psychology is never that of the actual child but that of the adult, composed as much of fantasy as of literal fact. Freud discovered this confusion of fact and fantasy when he found that the childhood seductions reported by his hysterical patients had never "really" happened. Bachelard says that our remembrances of childhood take place "at the frontier between history and legend."

> These images which arise from the depths of our childhood are not really memories. In order to evaluate all their vitality, a philosopher would have to be able to develop all the dialectics that are summed up too quickly in the two words "imagination" and "memory.". . . The soul and the mind do not have the same memory. . . . In order to force the past, when forgetfulness is hemming us in, poets engage us in reimagining the lost childhood. They teach us "the audacities of the memory." One poet [Robert Ganzo] tells us the past must be invented:

> *Invent. There is no lost feast*
> *At the bottom of memory.*[5]

Yet, as Bachelard sees, the relation between imagination and memory is dialectical. Our images of childhood are not unrelated to our memories of our own early years or to our experiences of our biological children. I know that the soul child is related to my own actual childhood. I experience her as pulling me to acknowledge that I am not only the responsible and consciously neglectful mother but also the child in the crib. Her happiness and her abandonment are my own. The dream child forces me to remember that when I was a child I was literally abandoned (by a father, not a mother)—a child's truth which the adult in me has always denied since it was Hitler's "fault," not my father's. The dream child also reminds me that the child who was myself was already back then in touch with the divine child, the imaginal child (as many children are). From the age of two at least until I went to school, the most important other in my life was a purely imaginary child (not a doll) whom I tended and nursed.

I have come to see the child's own relation to the archetype of the child as singularly important. Bachelard suggests:

> To understand our attachment to the world, it is necessary to add a childhood, our childhood, to each archetype. We cannot love water, fire, the tree without putting a love into them, a friendship which goes back to our childhood. We love them with childhood.[6]

This is clearly true for me. I still know the goddesses most intimately, most immediately, as I knew them as a child: Persephone, as a figure much younger than that represented at the beginning of the Homeric hymn, more like myelf at some preschool birthday with a wreath of spring flowers in my hair; Athene, as the intelligent and athletic girl, proudly encouraged in all her activities by her devoted father; Hera, as my own youthfully blooming mother. Yes, I love those goddesses with my childhood—and that early love enables me to love them with my adult womanhood as well, and to love even those aspects which the child did not know and might not have accepted.

Yet we need to add not only our own childhoods to each of these goddesses in order to understand them fully, we must also add their own. For her child form is not a stage that a goddess outgrows but a perennial aspect. Each goddess has a childhood that is uniquely her own and which shows her in the full perfection of her powers and outward form,[7] and each of these childhoods can be brought into relation to our own. For, as Bachelard so beautifully reminds us:

> When, all alone and dreaming on rather at length, we go far from the present to relive the times of the first life, several childhood faces come to meet us. We were several in the trial life (*la vie essayée*), in our primitive life. . . . Our whole childhood remains to be reimagined. . . . A potential childhood is within us; when we go looking for it in our reveries, we relive it even more in its possibilities than in

its reality. . . . What a lot of beings we have begun! What
a lot of lost springs which have, nevertheless, flowed!
Reverie toward our past then, reverie looking for childhood seems to bring back to life lives which have never
taken place, lives which have been imagined.[8]

Reveries looking for childhood return us not only to imaginings about our own past but also to our memories of our
children's births and early years. I know it was important to be
asked concerning the dream child in the crib, "Why couldn't that
be about your actual children?" I realized then that, of course,
one of the reasons the child has been such a primary image in
my dreams is that being pregnant, giving birth, nursing, wean-
ing, caring for young children has been so important in my
everyday waking life. Naturally this aspect of my daily existence
would provide the material cause of my dreams, would serve as
"residue." My concerns about my children, my delight in them,
my sense of fulfillment within the role of mother, my guilt
about my inadequacies—all would, of course, be reflected in my
dreams and used to express other anxieties and hopes. When I
was carrying my first child I experienced the fetus growing
within as my body's dream. The most perfect moment of my life
was that in which I first held that eldest son in my arms. It was
he who made me a mother:

> Little heart, little heart
> You have sung in me like the spiral
> You, who gave birth to this mother older-bud,
> comprehend, for how much longer? my mysteries.[9]

I know that looking honestly at the divine child must mean
confronting the archetypal dimensions of my relation to my
actual sons and daughters, just as coming to terms with Hera
involved, in part, a revaluaton of my relation to mother and
husband, a disentangling of the personal and archetypal, *and* a
recognition of how that is not fully possible. Athene had called
upon me to reexamine my relation to my father, Ariadne to a
lover, Artemis and Aphrodite to my sister and closest women
friends.

The relation between the archetypal image and the actual others present in our lives always goes both ways. That I had five children at all is clearly evidence of the power the child archetype held for me. They were literalization—and realization. They are expressions of both what is most healthy in me and most pathological, what was most whole in my marriage and most incomplete. I wanted sons and had four, wanted a daughter and had one. She was the gift child, the child of joy, perhaps as like as any human child could be to the divine child of the dreams. I believe that there is a sense in which all children need the love of someone for whom they are a miracle, as Emily was for the mother in Tillie Olsen's "I Stand Here Ironing":

> She was a beautiful baby. She blew shining bubbles of sound. She loved motion, loved light, loved color and music and textures. She would lie on the floor in her blue overalls patting the floor so hard in ecstasy her hands and feet would blur. She was a miracle to me, but when she was eight months old I had to leave her daytimes with the woman downstairs to whom she was no miracle at all, for I worked or looked for work and for Emily's father, who "could no longer endure" (he wrote in his good-bye note) "sharing want with us." [10]

Yet our actual children cannot be asked to carry the full weight of the archetype of the divine child any more than our mothers can carry that of the mother archetype. As Jung reminds us, the archetype has a cosmic transhuman aspect: "The mythological idea of the child is emphatically not a copy of the empirical child but a *symbol* clearly recognizable as such: it is a wonder-child, a divine child."[11] Kerenyi, too, recognizes the importance of not tying the archetype too closely to human childhood:

> In the image of the Primordial Child the world tells of its own childhood, and of everything that sunrise and the birth of a child mean for, and say about, the world. The childhood and orphan's fate of the child gods have not evolved from the stuff of human life, but from the stuff of

cosmic life. What appears to be biographical in mythology is, as it were, an anecdote that the world relates from its own biography.[12]

The archetype of the child has to do with the wonder of all beginnings and the wonder of all beginning again. We are led by it to imagine being in the world as on the first day of creation, seeing the world for the first time. The child embodies and encourages spontaneity and joy, imagination and celebration:

> "I am cherry alive," the little girl sang,
> "Each morning I am something new:
> I am apple, I am plum, I am just as excited
> As the boys who made the Hallowe'en bang:
> I am tree, I am cat, I am blossom too:
> When I like, if I like, I can be someone new,
> Someone very old, a witch in a zoo:
> I can be someone else whenever I think who,
> And I want to be everything sometimes too:
> And the peach has a pit and I know that too,
> and I put it in along with everything
> To make the grown-ups laugh whenever I sing:
> and I sing: It is true; It is untrue;
> I know, I know, the true is untrue,
> The peach has a pit, the pit has a peach:
> And both may be wrong when I sing my song,
> but I don't tell the grown-ups: because it is sad,
> And I want them to laugh just like I do
> Because they grew up and forgot what they knew
> And they are sure I will forget it some day too.
> They are wrong. They are wrong. When I sang my song,
>   I knew, I knew!
> I am red, I am gold, I am green, I am blue,
> I will always be me, I will always be new!"[13]

Otto Rank's *The Myth of the Birth of the Hero* was the first depth psychological interpretation of the mythologem of the divine child, though (as his title acknowledges) his attention is directed more to the birth and infancy of mythological heroes than of gods, and entirely to male figures. His careful analysis of fifteen myths and legends leads to this description of the typical pattern:

> The hero is the child of most distinguished parents, usually the son of a king. His origin is preceded by difficulties, such as continence, or prolonged barrenness, or secret intercourse of the parents due to external prohibition or obstacles. During or before the pregnancy, there is a prophecy, in the form of a dream or oracle, cautioning against his birth, and usually threatening danger to the father (or his representative). As a rule, he is surrendered to the water, in a box. He is then saved by animals, or by lowly people (shepherds), and is suckled by a female animal or by an humble woman. After he has grown up, he finds his distinguished parents, in a highly versatile fashion. He takes his revenge on his father, on the one hand, and is acknowledged, on the other. Finally he achieves rank and honors.[14]

Rank understands myth formation as deriving from the individual faculty of imagination, a faculty "found in its active and unchecked exuberance only in childhood." Thus he believes the myths about the male child may reflect the son's imaginal view of his world or (as he suggests later in his essay) perhaps myths are created by adults by means of "retrograde childhood fantasies, the hero being credited with the mythmaker's personal infantile history." Rank derives the myths from the necessity of the child's separation from the parents, his ambivalence toward them, and the tendency to overvalue the experiences of our earliest years. He understands the myths about a heroic childhood as being created mostly to compensate for the disillusions and hurts of the myth-maker's actual childhood and (even more) of his adult life. He focuses on the child's disappointment in his father's failure to be the great and powerful man he at first seemed and on the child's sense of being neglected. Thus the myth expresses the child's anger and represents an attempt at revenge and retaliation. The child projects his own desire to repudiate his father onto the noble father who, in the myth, is represented as abandoning him. At the same time, through the "family romance" of adoption, he announces that the insignificant father with whom he now lives cannot possibly be his "real" father. The myth-maker imagines a heroic child who is able to revolt successfully against the father. "The ego can only find its own heroism in the days of infancy," albeit that heroism too is illusory. Thus Rank sees the myths about the heroic child as deriving from the adult's sense of failure at not being a hero and from his longing to start anew, to be a child who is heroic and noble and successful. The adult elaborates a fantasy by which the child was already possessed; the child and adult share in this imaginal view of the child as hero.[15]

Rank's last pages imply a compassionate recognition of the pathology evident here, empathy for the deep wounds that these imaginings about childhood are intended to heal. However, Rank never moves beyond interpreting the myths as derivative of individual (though not idiosyncratic) personal history; he never tries to explore (as Jung does) how our personal experiencing is itself given shape by archetypal patterns. Jung's very different approach allows him to celebrate the archetype of the child because it enables us to imagine wholeness and happiness. His focus is on this imaginal capacity rather than on those hurts which impel us to turn to fantasy. Thus his "phenomenology of the child archetype" differs significantly from Rank's and yet many of the same motifs appear: *Miraculous birth:* Since the birth of the divine is "a psychic genesis, everything must happen nonempirically, e.g., by means of a virgin birth, or by miraculous conception, or by birth from unnatural organs." *Abandonment:* " 'Child' means something evolving toward independence. This it cannot do without detaching itself from its origins; abandonment is therefore a necessary condition, not just a concomitant symptom." *Invincibility:* "It is a striking paradox in all child myths that the 'child' is on the one hand delivered helpless into the power of terrible enemies and in continual danger of extinction, while on the other he possesses powers far exceeding those of ordinary humans. . . . [The child] is a personification of vital forces quite outside the limited range of our

conscious mind; of ways and possibilities of which our one-
sided conscious mind knows nothing; a wholeness which embraces the very depths of nature." *Hermaphroditism:* "The
majority of cosmogonic gods are of a bisexual nature. The her-
maphrodite means nothing less than a union of the strongest
and most striking opposites." *As Beginning and End:* "The 'child'
is all that is abandoned and exposed and at the same time di-
vinely powerful; the insignificant, dubious beginning, and the
triumphal end." [16]

Jung does relate the child archetype to individual psychology
but quite differently from Rank. For Jung the mytheme is not a
disguised representation of personal infancy, but an archetypal
pattern prefiguring the process by which an adult moves toward
individuated consciousness. At the beginning of this process the
patients typically identify themselves as abandoned, misunderstood, unjustly treated children. This is followed by a stage of
inflation which focuses on the patients' extraordinary powers
(accompanied by a shadow or negative inflation which accen-
tuates their heroic suffering). Only then does it become possible
to separate the conscious self from the unconscious images and
to shift the center of the personality from the ego to the self. The
emergence of the child archetype is thus here viewed as making
possible an authentic healing and not only a spurious one.

Jung, like Rank, is speaking though of the archetype of the
male child. Clearly the child archetype has profound meaning
for all of us, men and women alike; yet I believe the image of
the divine child inevitably figures differently in the lives of
women than in the lives of men. Hillman takes note of this
possibility (though he does not seem to know quite what to
make of it):

> The child is one of the faces—not stages—of the God, one
> of his ways of being. . . . Perhaps I speak now of men, and
> the image in which they are made since curiously we do not
> have comparable images of a Child Athene, a Child
> Aphrodite, a Child Hera or Demeter.[17]

Why is it that the childhoods of the goddesses are less accessible? What can we discover about those childhoods? How can

what we learn illuminate our experience of having been female children, of still carrying our female childhood within us, of having given birth to female children? How is our femaleness shaped by our finding ourselves essentially related to a female divine child? Or, rather, to several female divine children?

That the childhood of the goddesses is mostly obscured, lost, or denied in the classical literature is itself significant. They appear in their maiden form rather than in their child form and thus are marked by that adolescent consciousness which "puts a barrier to the childhood waiting to be relived."[18] To go in search of their childhoods is to go in search of their archaic history, before they were so clearly defined in relation to a particular life stage as they seem to be on Olympus. To go in search of their childhoods is to go in search of our own.

I have a sense that there may be more direct acceptance of the sadness and pain, the vulnerabilities and weaknesses, inherent in childhood in the mythological accounts of the child goddesses than in those devoted to the child gods or heroes—less denial, less fantasy. Yet the fantasy element seems evident in the myth of Persephone's childhood. Clearly, this representation of a primal dyad between mother and daughter, not intruded upon by a father or siblings, could fairly be called "a family romance"—as if those blissful first weeks at the breast could be prolonged forever. Zeus, the most royal and powerful father imaginable, never appears, so the mother never turns away from the child and is never disparaged. This is truly a divine childhood, and though Persephone outwardly becomes a maiden, she remains until her abduction this dreamy self-enclosed child.

But Demeter's own childhood is different, spent within her father's body along with the other four children he swallowed as soon as they were born. Robbed of a connection to her birth from birth, it is no wonder that she tries to create a fantasy bond with her daugher, no wonder that she overidentifies with her, seeks to give her the childhood she was herself denied. No wonder either that she is childish (not harmoniously childlike) in her raging grief when Persephone is taken from her. Because she had no real childhood of her own, she remains caught by the child archetype, sees it too sentimentally and is too easily overcome by its negative aspects.

Hera's childhood is essentially the same as Demeter's but as an adult she lives her unlived childhood differently. First, she, too, tries living through her children. But whereas Persephone was a more beautiful vibrant version of Demeter, Hera's daughters, Hebe and Eileithyia, are but pale shadows of their mother. Her sons (because reduced in her mind to being but pawns in her battles with Zeus) are each crippled, Hephaistos physically, Ares psychologically. She had sought to mother Zeus, to make him her well-sheltered son; she had asked him to mother her, wholly enclose her as her father had when she was young. When she discovers the inadequacy of all these modes of asking others to provide her with a childhood, she realizes she must herself go in search of that lost childhood. She returns to her motherland and reimagines the unlived childhood; only then, knowingly carrying her own childhood within her, is she ready for real relationship.

Artemis's childhood has some of the same elements as Persephone's. Zeus is again the absent father; experientially Artemis has only a female parent, one who is inordinately proud of her. But Artemis is robbed of her childhood by having a mother much more obviously childlike, dependent, and vulnerable than is Demeter. Her mother immediately needs help as she struggles painfully to give birth to Artemis's twin, Apollo, and then must be defended against all kinds of real and imaginary dangers. That fantasy of having to mother our mothers from the beginning will seem very familiar, very "real," to many women. Perhaps it functions as a kind of parallel to the male hero's having to reduce his original noble father to a poor and simple peasant. Both are in a sense true stories about the painful discovery that our mothers cannot really mother us, as the heroes' fathers could not really live up to the expectations aroused by the father archetype. The hero's eventually being able to overcome the father is nevertheless significantly different from the child goddess being able to support and care for her mother. Yet her childhood midwifery may lead Artemis to be too insistently self-sufficient in her adult form, and to be unwilling ever to renounce the solitude of the child. She remains tender toward children but easily becomes impatient with the childishly dependent adult. There is something eternally *young* in her way of being alone and distant; she too carries her childhood with her always.

At first glance Athene seems truly to have no childhood. She emerges full-grown out of the head of Zeus, dressed as a warrior, emitting a triumphant battle cry. She seems to begin life as the adolescent, closely identified with her father, with so-called masculine attributes like self-confidence and courage, intelligence and dispassion, and with the male world. She epitomizes the particular kind of strength that can come by denial of childhood, and of the mother bond. The denial is hers: she seems proud of having had no mother. Yet *we* feel something missing, feel that until we can connect her to her maternal origins there is something one-dimensional about her. Without her childhood she is incomplete. So we go in search of it and discover Metis, her intrepid, wise mother, whose potential progeny threatened Zeus, and we understand Athene differently. (And we recognize perhaps how our own denigration of our mothers, our too uncritical identification with our fathers, may echo Athene's.) Her version of her childhood, though it ignores or denies important aspects, is still a fantasy that deeply colors her life.

Kerenyi sees Aphrodite as the prototypical female embodiment of the child mythologem, but he reminds us that Botticelli's "Birth of Venus" represents not her birth but her arrival among us. Her *birth* is different: brutal and violent. As she steps out of the mussel shell, she is leaving it behind her as she leaves behind the whole of primitive mythology: the mutilation of Ouranos, the casting of his manhood into the sea, the whole terrible foregoing history, the titanic mythology of the world's beginnings. Her birth represents the "unity of that mythological moment when begetter and begotten were one in the womb of the water." [19] Aphrodite is motherless and fatherless, born of the depersonalized phallus immersed in the impersonal oceanic womb. She represents self-sufficiency which nevertheless is warm, receptive, open. Older than Zeus, coeval with the Titans, she symbolizes a more cosmic beginning than just individual human birth and childhood. She reminds us that the archetype of the child pertains not only to personal psychology—part of the divinity inherent in the archetype comes from its transpersonal, cosmic aspect.

Nevertheless, the human significance of each of these childhoods is plain. Perhaps we can love the goddesses in part because we feel they have shared our pain. To paraphrase Nietzsche: the goddesses justify human life by living it themselves, the only satisfactory theodicy ever invented. Each goddess implies a different way of viewing our own childhood—each whole, each very different, each true. Each also divine—in the sense of representing an eternally recurring pattern of childhood experience—in the sense, too, of making visible the numinosity present in those patterns.

The appreciation of the connection between our childhoods and those of the goddesses also serves as an initiation into the worlds constituted by them. We may never have heard their names (though I still feel blessed that I had) but these goddesses are present in the imaginal experience of our childhoods. My guess would be that we are likely as adults still to feel closest to the goddess whose infancy is most like the image of childhood we held when we were young.

Though the stories about the child goddesses are different from the stories about the gods or heroes, many of the motifs Jung named are present in them. Not all the births are miraculous, but all have something wondrous about them—Persephone and Artemis are almost fatherless; immediately after birth, Demeter and Hera are introjected into a male womb and then later reborn from it; Athene is born from her father's head, Aphrodite from Ouranos's severed genitals. All experience some mode of abandonment, some painful separation from their mothers, even Persephone—where the separation is the more traumatic for being so long delayed. The sadness of the child goddesses is provoked by the separation from the mother, not from the father, a separation which seems not to engender anger, perhaps because the mothers are not presented as rejecting their daughters purposefully. It is the intervention of the male order that effects the disunion—Zeus allows Hades to abduct Persephone and cannot seem to prevent Hera's jealous attacks against Artemis's mother; Zeus swallows Metis, Athene's mother, as his father had swallowed Demeter and Hera at birth and thus takes them from their mothers. Yet there are reunions too—Persephone returns to Demeter joyously though she will never again live only in her world; Hera returns to her Argive motherland; Artemis is always there for her mother and for all mothers in travail. The goddesses thus demonstrate a kind of invincibility. Their mothers are vulnerable but their fathers' power is also precarious. The fathers are not really viewed as "the enemy"; they are rather experienced as absent and ineffectual, or as afraid of feminine power and the alliance between mothers and sons.

(I am intrigued by how rarely these myths of the child include siblings, as though they reflect the fantasy or wish of being the only child. There is actually more of the sibling dimension present in the traditions about the male gods—as, for instance, in the Homeric hymn's account of the teasing rivalry between Hermes and Apollo or in the indication of Hermes' tender care for young Dionysos communicated by the lovely statue at Olympia. Where is the sisterhood? With the nymphs, I suppose—though that seems so anonymous and undifferentiated. Most of the tales, as we have already noted, are about the maiden goddess, not the child. Perhaps as maiden goddesses they represent not possibility as does the child, but self-contained, self-sufficient actuality. In that case, why another? Yet we who are not goddesses may miss the sisterhood nonetheless. Perhaps we shall have to create those sister bonds for them.)

In these childhood images I discern a wonderful promise that these goddesses can *be* goddesses, self-confident, beautiful, serenely powerful, each in her very individual ways, despite mothering and fathering that is flawed. (Yes, they each also have their dark side but in a way that is part of, not a diminution of, their divinity.) I think this is what Kerenyi means in a passage that puzzled me for a long time:

Divine maidens are so typical of Greek religion that it cannot be called either a "Father religion" or a "Mother religion," or yet a combination of both. It is as though the Olympian order had thrust the great Mother Goddesses of olden times into the background for the sole purpose of throwing the divine Korai [maidens] into sharper relief.[20]

The hermaphroditism Jung found to characterize the child archetype is present here, too, at least in a psychological sense (which it is more popular now to call androgyny). The myths suggest this by their emphasis on Aphrodite's birth from the phallus, Athene's from her father's brow, Artemis's twinship with Apollo, Demeter's single parenting, Hera's pull to a *hieros gamos*. The language of masculine and feminine attributes conjoined is there, even though it may not seem to use the best way of expressing the kind of human wholeness the goddesses embody.

Freud suggested that a child often serves as a self-image for women. Of course, the child carries this meaning for men as well; nevertheless, for women who can carry a child within themselves this meaning may have even more resonance. In any case, in mythology, too, one's children are viewed as images of the self. Fully to know the gods means to know them in and through their children. This is quite different from knowing them through the quality or style of their parenting (though that, too, provides a meaningful perspective). We receive a richer sense of the plurality of *their* childhoods, as we see them in relation to their several children.

Indeed, this may be another way in which their androgyny is made evident, for these goddesses have both female and male children. Even Demeter whom we tend to think of only in relation to Persephone was mother to Cryasor (or Areion), a magical steed whose father was Poseidon. The climax of the Eleusinean mystery was the cry, "Brimos is born," an announcement that Persephone had given birth to a son. (The most lovely relief inspired by those mysteries is that which represents the youth, Triptolemos, standing between the two goddesses, Demeter and Persephone.) The myths suggest that the full experience of giving birth means giving birth both to another like oneself (a daughter) and to a being who is other (a son). Aphrodite gives birth not only to sons—Phobos, Demos, Eros, Aeneas—but also to a daughter, Harmonia; Hera to Ares and Hephaistos, but also to Hebe and Eileithyia.

In the history of my own dreams of the divine child it has always felt self-evident upon awaking whether the child was a son or a daughter. It also seemed clear that the difference mattered, that it was even more important in imaginal life than in actuality to have both a son and a daughter. The difference feels clear even though I do not fully understand it and cannot adequately articulate it. *Perhaps* it has something to do with doing and being, or extroversion and introversion. When I try to test that out on the children of the goddesses or on my own dream children, I do not feel content with the formulation. Still, I *know* that my own well-being is tied up with my imaginal daughter and my imaginal son.

I have spoken already of the daughter, the child in the crib and then in the cave. She has appeared in later dreams as well—among them a particularly important one dreamt after the first evening spent with a lover who has since become my closest friend, but whom then I barely knew.

> In that dream this man and I were together in my house which now was *ours,* greeting and then bidding farewell to family members and intimate friends who were stopping by in some almost ritual procession. As he and I stood there, I was carrying on my hip, with her head nestled between chin and shoulder, my beautiful young daughter. She was simply *there,* quiet yet radiantly happy and healthy as always. It felt wonderful—but entirely natural—to have her there (for the first time) in the world of others. Then, just before I woke, as I felt her welcome weight on my hip, I realized that she still weighed exactly what she had weighed months before; I knew that it was time (though there was no sense of its being past time) for her to begin getting nourishment other than what my milk could provide.

I agree with so much in Hillman's essay "Abandoning the Child," including his insistence that:

> The child is one of the faces—not stages—of the God, one of his ways of being, of revealing his nature. There is no question of moral improvement, of increase, or of differentiation through developmental process in these child images. These gods do not leave the child behind in order to become mature.

But I hesitate when he goes on to say:

> The archetypal child personifies a component that is not meant to grow but to remain as it is as a child, at the threshold, intact, an image of certain fundamental realities that necessarily require the child metaphor and which cannot be presented in another manner.[21]

For I believe that the child does change and exhibit a mode of change for which growth is the best available name. Yet I, too, question the notion that growth equals health. Furthermore, I would want to affirm that there is always another childhood, another imaginal child. We don't outgrow the child in us, though a particular dream child may in some strange way grow up inside us.

I have had this experience particularly with my male dream child. He first appeared in the dream which initiated that attending to dreams so vital to me for the last twenty-five years. At that time I was pregnant with my third or fourth son—but it was clear that the child in the dream was not to be confused with any of my actual children, living or still unborn. I have spoken of this dream before, when writing of Persephone.

> It begins with my standing with the other young women of our tribe at the edge of a moonlit clearing watching our men go through the ritual of choosing a new chief. Then the young and handsome youth who has just been installed as chief comes to me and invites me to join him in a cere-

monial dance, thus signaling his choice of me to be his bride. Years pass. Our people are suffering the consequence of season after season of drought. We reluctantly realize that if the tribe is to survive it must go elsewhere in search of water and, of course, the chief must go with them. But I stay behind, confidently awaiting the birth of the son I carry in my womb, the future leader of our people. I stay as token of their expectation of returning to this land which is ineluctably *our* land.

Then, a few summers ago, I took a trip to New Mexico. I spent the morning at Acoma Pueblo, the sky city, now inhabited by only twenty-odd persons all year around, though many more appear at festival time. As the Indians displayed their pride in their skills and traditions, I could not help but wonder what it would be like to be part of a tribe whose existence as a people seemed on the edge of extinction. That evening in Santa Fe, I joined an old friend, a former colleague who grew up in New Mexico and has a deep sense of connection with the Indians who lie there. The night of our reunion I had a dream so powerful that, for the first time in many years, I got up in the middle of the night to write it down. The imperative to record the dream arose in large measure from my sense that somehow the dream had come to the wrong person, that it was not my dream at all but really belonged to my friend; I therefore owed it to him to remember every detail. Though not mine, it felt like a singularly important dream, one that could change one's life, a dream one would have to obey.

I knew the dream was not mine because the dreamer was clearly a young male. I do not mean that I had had a dream whose central figure was a male youth or that I was dreaming that I was a man—but rather that when I awoke it was absolutely clear to me that a young male had had the dream and that this dream was the continuation of a dream series to which he had been attending faithfully over a period of years. I will tell the dream in the first person for it was an I that experienced the dream, though that I seemed so clearly not to be me.

The message of the dream is clear: after many years of honest reluctance, I must now agree to be the tribe's keeper of symbols and the interpreter and renewer of those symbols. The I of the dream has but the smallest trace of Indian blood and has never lived as a member of the tribal community, yet for years I have devoted myself to being a loving student of my people's lore. Over and over again one of the few remaining members of our tribe has come to me and said, "You have been chosen to be the keeper of our symbols." Each time I have answered, "No, it cannot be I that is meant." Now they are back again. They have always respectfully accepted my refusal, but now they say, "It has to be you." They hand me a beautiful book made of heavy buff paper, containing page after page of beautifully painted symbols, flowing geometrics and stylized birds, plants and animals—always composed of the same four colors: turquoise, coral, black, white. These are the tribe's symbols which no one fully understands but which they all revere. I take the book from their hands and agree, yes, this time I must accept. There followed a ritual, a ceremonial exchange of blood between myself and a young man of my own age who was a full-blooded member of the tribe and had grown up living in its ancestral home. When the ritual was complete, he and I were truly one and I was now someone who really could take on the awesome responsibility that had been laid on me. I felt a calm certitude: "Yes, I can do it. Yes, it is time. Yes, it is intended."

When he woke the next morning, I shared the dream with my friend. He said, as perhaps one always does in such situations, "Yes, I see how it connects with me, but I also believe, Chris, that it is *your* dream." Because I still was not ready to accept that, I sent an account of the dream to a young friend, a poet very conscious of his debt to shamanic traditions. He responded, "Yes, Chris, the dream does have something to do with me and my work but, still, it *is* your dream." Then he spoke of having shared my letter with his wife who had said, "You know, that dream reminds me of another dream Chris told me years ago." Of course, she meant the dream about the young Indian bride. Only then, after she had made the connection, did I understand at last how the recent dream was mine after all. The dreamer was the young male child who had been in my dream womb almost twenty-five years earlier. It had never occurred to me that an inner child could grow up. It felt strange and wonderful and absolutely true, though, for that was what had happened. I also knew then that in some truly necessary way I did now need to take on the role of keeper of the symbols, a role which I may have begun to discharge through this book on the goddesses.

I was intrigued that this assignment should come to me and my young dream son at that time in my life when I would soon be entering upon the postmenopausal stage that in many cultures is the point of entry for women into a shamanic vocation. At this point a woman is believed to cease being *only* woman; she is no longer defined by her biological femaleness and may consciously and visibly adopt her own maleness. Thus the female shaman is androgynous, as in some sense my dream son and I together constitute an androgynous being. (Again: ideologically, I would prefer a different way of expressing such wholeness; experientially, this is the symbol that appeared.)

I began to understand that passing beyond literal childbearing might represent a deeper initiation into the archetype of the child. I also began to appreciate more than I had before Jung's reference to the connection of the child archetype with endings and death. I knew, of course, that birth (especially in Artemis's realm) is itself connected with the possibility of death and remembered Freud's rediscovery of the interchangeability of symbols for womb and tomb. By now I should have been well prepared to recognize that every archetype has its dark side.

When writing of my relation to Ariadne, I alluded to the child to which she gives birth in the underworld, the child born in death, who is thus clearly a psychic child, a soul child. I included there a somewhat veiled reference to the experience which taught me part of what such a birth into death can mean.

> A few years ago I discovered I was pregnant with a child I knew was not meant to be born, a child conceived on a strange occasion when I had felt my partner to be not the

dear friend who was actually present but Dionysos. I had told my friend of the god's presence; I did not tell him of the child's conception. Perhaps I did not speak because I dimly remembered a warning Eros gives Psyche as he is about to leave her: "Thou shall give birth to a child which will be a divine infant if thou dost keep silent, but a human being if thou dost reveal the secret." Then, in what felt like another visitation of the god, the child was spontaneously aborted.

I experienced that miscarriage not only as the death of the child and a ritual ending of my childbearing but, more importantly, as the birth of a death child, an underworld child, a soul child who in some sense replaces that young son who grew up. The death was in some way a birth into another phase of my life.

That the death of a child can, in some way, mean rebirth I had also experienced in a much earlier dream. The dream marked the end of a long period of deep despair (during which I had seemingly not dreamt at all) initiated by the departure of a lover.

> In the dream I found I was pregnant with a child fathered by the lover and understood this illegitimate conception as a sign that it was time to leave my husband. I realized I did not want to leave him to be with my lover but rather to be alone. Because I was not ready to bring up a child by myself, I knew I would have to end the pregnancy. I stuck a knitting needle up my vagina—and bled to death.

I woke feeling alive for the first time in months: I had dreamt again; something deep within was still living.

These experiences seem less strange when I find my interpretations anticipated by Hillman:

> The dead child is also the child belonging to death, alluding not only to the death of life but the life of death. . . . The child aborted then signifies life aborted, for the sake of Hades. The dead child may also be an image for the soul's child, performing the role of *psychopompos* which . . . leads the psyche to reflections about all that belongs to the child archetype but from a wholly psychic viewpoint.[22]

Then came last winter's discovery that I might have uterine cancer. During the week of waiting to learn whether that was indeed so, it seemed important to suspend belief and disbelief and live within the imaginal possibility. I found this mode of death (entirely different from any I had ever imagined as mine) deeply appropriate. It seemed a meaningful culmination of the long series of imaginal conceptions now to be carrying my death within my womb. I had a strangely beautiful sense of what it would mean to give birth to my death. I did not then know Anne Sexton's poem "Madonna":

> My mother died
> unrocked, unrocked.
> Weeks at her deathbed
> seeing her thrust herself against the metal bars,
> thrashing like a fish on the hook
> and me low at her high stage,
> letting the priestess dance alone,
> wanting to place my head in her lap
> or even take her in my arms somehow
> and fondle her twisted gray hair.
> But her rocking horse was pain
> with vomit steaming from her mouth.
> Her belly was big with another child,
> cancer's baby, big as a football.
> I could not soothe.
> With every hump and crack
> there was less Madonna
> until that strange labor took her.
> Then the room was bankrupt.
> That was the end of her paying.[23]

I know I would have rejected its sadness and anger as missing the point (for me, not necessarily for her mother).

The child's dark side is not confined to this association with death. The child, Freud's dream analyses discovered, was a child stripped of the romantic sentimentalization of the infant predominant in the conscious attitudes of his time. These dream children display primarily their sexuality, their wounds, their unsatisfied longings, and their fragmentation. Hillman reminds us that there is childishness, as well as childlikeness. The child means not only joyous spontaneity and creativity but vulnerability and dependence: the "cry that is never cured," the "things we never learn, cannot help," "the inaccessible places where we are always exposed and afraid."[24] The shadow child is one I know well: the child in me who is always crying, "When does it get to be my turn? Who will take care of me?" But who is almost never ready to voice that fear or need aloud. The child is not only "future springing from vulnerability itself" but "that which *never* grows,"[25] the past that stays past, being stuck.

That the child in us stays stuck, stays child, is, of course, not necessarily only a dark truth. Such an inner child can be alive and enlivening:

> I found myself before a man who summarized and clarified
> singularly, in a single look of his blue eyes, the idea of a
> maturity, invaded and somehow renewed by the freshness
> of a childhood which had not stopped growing within him
> without his knowing it.[26]

Though the childhoods growing within us are many and each is unique, I would be more ready to speak of *the* child than of *the* goddess. I could agree that child is more image than story, perhaps because that is the child's own view. There is much in this archetype that pulls us to the simplicities of fairy tale and its happy endings, to the pure anonymity of *the* child, *the* village, *the* sea—an anonymity to be filled in by each of us with our most precious memories and longings. As pure potentiality the child is always still to be conceived. At the end of these nine chapters, we become aware of all the images still waiting to come to appearance.

I am struck that Rank in his book on the birth trauma says that dreams of birth and childhood tend to occur at the end of an analysis—as though the child appears to keep us imagining. Bachelard speaks of childhood as "the archetype of simple happiness," as "an image within us, a center for images which attract happy images." "Childhood remains within us as a principle of deep life, of life always in harmony with the possibility of new beginnings. . . . The archetype is a reserve of enthusiasm which helps us believe in the world, love the world, create our world."

"When one dreams in depth one is never finished beginning." [27]

NOTES

1. Alexandre Arnoux, *Petits Poèmes* (Paris: Seghers, n.d.), p. 31, quoted in Gaston Bachelard, *The Poetics of Reverie,* trans. Daniel Russell (Boston: Beacon Press, 1971), p. 112.

2. C. G. Jung and C. Kerenyi, *Essays on a Science of Mythology* (Princeton, N.J.: Princeton University Press, 1969), p. 7.

3. Jung and Kerenyi, *Essays,* p. 52.

4. Jung and Kerenyi, *Essays,* pp. 55, 56, 103.

5. Gaston Bachelard, *The Poetics of Reverie,* pp. 101, 104, 110.

6. Bachelard, *Poetics,* p. 126.

7. James Hillman, "Abandoning the Child," in *Loose Ends* (Zurich: Spring Publications, 1975), p. 31.

8. Bachelard, *Poetics,* pp. 99, 100, 101, 112.

9. Robin Morgan, "The Child," in *Lady of the Beasts* (New York: Random House, 1976), cited in Adrienne Rich, *Of Woman Born* (New York: Bantam Books, 1977), p. 208.

10. Tillie Olsen, *Tell Me a Riddle* (New York: Dell Publishing, 1976), p. 10.

11. Jung and Kerenyi, *Essays,* p. 80.

12. Jung and Kerenyi, *Essays,* p. 45.

13. Delmore Schwartz, *Selected Poems* (New York: New Directions Publishing, 1967), p. 161.

14. Otto Rank, *The Myth of the Birth of the Hero* (New York: Vintage Books, 1959), p. 65.

15. Rank, *Myth,* passim but esp. pp. 66, 71, 75, 84.

16. Jung and Kerenyi, *Essays,* pp. 85, 87, 89, 92, 98. Kerenyi's description of the primary motifs associated with the primordial child closely parallels Jung's: The divine child is typically an orphan, threatened by extraordinary dangers often associated with his father; he is solitary and yet at home among the animals of the primeval wilderness; he is at once the orphan child and the cherished son of the gods—lowest and highest, weakest and strongest.

17. Hillman, *Loose Ends,* p. 31.

18. Bachelard, *Poetics*, p. 108. Kerenyi describes how in the classical literature (from which derives our most familiar traditions about the goddesses) the images of divine childhood are relegated to the margin of the new Zeus world, and the primordial child of mythology remains outside its borders. In this religion the youth (and maiden) is a more acceptable manifestation of divinity than the child (Jung and Kerenyi, *Essays,* pp. 65f.).

19. Jung and Kerenyi, *Essays,* pp. 102f.

20. Jung and Kerenyi, *Essays,* p. 106 (somewhat modified and reordered).

21. Hillman, *Loose Ends,* pp. 30, 31 reordered; emphasis eliminated.

22. Hillman, *Loose Ends,* p. 39.

23. Anne Sexton, *The Death Notebooks* (Boston: Houghton Mifflin, 1974), p. 14.

24. Hillman, *Loose Ends,* pp. 19, 20.

25. Ibid.

26. Franz Heliens describing Gorki, quoted in Bachelard, *Poetics,* p. 135.

27. Bachelard, *Poetics,* pp. 123, 124 (somewhat reordered), 114.

Index